MW01124360

Women and Judaism

Women and Judaism

Edited by
RABBI MALKA DRUCKER

For Marcia,
A model for us all !
With Love & Gratitude,
Malka Drucker

Women and Religion in the World
Cheryl A. Kirk-Duggan, Lillian Ashcraft-Eason
and Karen Jo Torjesen, Series Editors

PRAEGER

Westport, Connecticut
London

Library of Congress Cataloging-in-Publication Data

Women and Judaism / edited by Malka Drucker.
    p. cm.—(Women and religion in the world)
  Includes bibliographical references and index.
  ISBN 978-0-275-99154-8 (alk. paper)
  1. Women in Judaism. 2. Jewish women—Religious life.
3. Spiritual life—Judaism. I. Drucker, Malka.
  BM729.W6W657   2009
  296.082—dc22   2009004976

British Library Cataloguing in Publication Data is available.

Library of Congress Catalog Card Number: 2009004976
ISBN: 978-0-275-99154-8

First published in 2009

Praeger Publishers, 88 Post Road West, Westport, CT 06881
An imprint of Greenwood Publishing Group, Inc.
www.praeger.com

Printed in the United States of America

The paper used in this book complies with the
Permanent Paper Standard issued by the National
Information Standards Organization (Z39.48–1984).

10 9 8 7 6 5 4 3 2 1

For my granddaughters, Lesley Lilah and Sasha Chance,
my proud gifts to Israel and all the world.

Contents

Acknowledgments

It has been a great joy and privilege to gather these essays about Jewish women's spirituality. I wish my mother, Francine Epstein Chermak, of blessed memory could have seen this book. She introduced me to spirit and connected me with love to the Jewish people.

There are many to whom I owe a debt of gratitude. My community, HaMakom, patiently accepted my time away from them while I worked on the book. Our praying and learning together sustained me during the two years of its creation.

Thanks to Cheryl Kirk-Duggan, who asked me to edit this book. To the women who generously provided the book's wisdom, I have profound appreciation. I learned much from the articles and am pleased that you've added a profound new commentary to the evolving and exciting role that Jewish women are playing in Judaism. If mother Miriam could see us now!

Suzanne Staszak-Silva provided editorial assistance and support every step of the way. Cindy Freedman, my friend and well-organized assistant, assured me many times that the project was coming together and not to worry. There would have been no book without her. To all my teachers, women and men, who have shown me how past, present, and future live with us all the time, I offer great thanks and hope.

All books are personal, and the emotional guidance of my family is the unseen voice in this work. My life partner, Gay Block, brainstormed with me to find the subjects and writers most essential to the future of Judaism. My children, Ivan and Max, and their partners, Caroline and Betsy, and Solomon Ace, Lesley Lilah, and Sasha Chance, my grandchildren, are the ground beneath my feet and the vastness of the sky above. May I be worthy.

Introduction

Rabbi Malka Drucker

Traditional Jewish sources make clear that the Creator is non-corporeal and therefore without a sex, yet when we speak of being in the Image of God, women as well men struggle not to imagine maleness. The gender-specific language of Hebrew refers to God as male and therefore creates a picture of God. Furthermore, the predominant structure of ancient Middle Eastern culture was patriarchal, and Jews were part of that world. Men wrote the books, studied and canonized them, and apparently never considered how half the population might experience being almost invisible and silent.

The Talmud describes Torah as "black fire written upon white fire." The figure ground description of the script hints at two narratives. The black letters, seen in contrast to white, are the narrative we know. The white space surrounding and between the letters may be the other half of the story, the piece of wisdom that we are missing. The metaphor is apt in describing the relationship of women to men. The chapters in this book are keys to deciphering white fire, the often-ignored feminine in the Divine.

When Moses and the Israelites stood at the foot of Sinai, what did they get? Two tablets, the Five Books of Moses? Some believe that everything that would ever be known was revealed at that cosmic moment. The catch is that only a little bit is revealed in each generation. I hope the reader is as grateful and thrilled as I to be living in the generation that is revealing the unseen and unheard Torah of women. New readings expand upon what is whispered in the text. Women scholars of the Jewish Bible are not only offering a fresh way in which to understand Scripture, they are building the bridge between the tradition and contemporary women.

Midrash, which means in Hebrew "to investigate or explain," is a literature that attempts to wrestle new ideas from ancient text. This book, the first volume in the series Women and Religion in the World, is a modern midrash of Judaism through women's experience. The word *Israel* is the name that the mysterious stranger gives to Jacob after a nightly encounter. It means "one who wrestles with God." The past thirty-five years have produced remarkable holy wrestlings of women holding fast to the shadow of patriarchy until there is acknowledgment of Jewish women as equal partners with men.

The presence of women working to claim their place in Judaism is part of the great energy emerging in all movements, from Orthodoxy to Jewish renewal. It is the manifestation of this effort that the chapters in this book describe the many ways in which women are changing the face of Judaism. The effort to expand the meaning of Torah beyond male perspective, the creation of new rituals and the transformation of traditional rituals such as Bar Mitzvah to include Bat Mitzvah for girls, and the increasing presence of women spiritual leaders suggest that Judaism is moving toward an embrace of all its followers.

The writers in the collection give a dual picture of an ancient tradition that recognizes that its survival depends upon its ability to change. Judaism has been a traveling roadshow for over two thousand years; a story of a people in perpetual exile, and always struggling to overcome prejudice. Today the fear is that the population is declining. Simple demographics make clear that the gifts of women need to be embraced, developed, and included as part of the new canon.

The book contains five sections that reveal the many ways in which Jewish women are making a difference in Judaism. How women navigate themselves in the physical world, of which family is a major part, is the beginning of the exploration in Part I, "Family and Environment." Sandy Sasso describes the first Bat Mitzvah as a family affair, with Judith Kaplan Eisenstein being called to the Torah in New York, in 1922, by her father, Mordechai Kaplan, founder of Reconstructionism. Alice Shalvi compares the Binding of Isaac with two other cases where mothers are asked to surrender their sons. What would Sarah have done if God had asked her what he asked Abraham? Ellen Bernstein, one of the pioneers in Jewish ecology, describes how the holidays are connected to the natural cycles of the seasons, and to *adamah* (feminine), "earth" in Hebrew.

Part II, "Socioeconomics, Politics, and Authority," looks at women in the world of external power and shows how they have prevailed. The presence of women rabbis brings a new face to Judaism that shows God's representatives as both women and men. Children today who know only women as rabbis ask if men can be rabbis too. Rabbi Lynn Gottlieb, one of the first women to be ordained, describes her own journey and that of Regina Jonas, the first woman rabbi, who was murdered in Theresienstadt in 1942.

Perhaps the new authority of women will change the lonely, bleak world that Rabbi Judith Edelstein describes. As a chaplain at the Jewish Home for the Aged in New York, she brings us near seniors, of whom the great majority are women, and describes their yearning for spiritual connection. The isolation of the elderly, even in communal settings, exposes the fear of a society that values only the productivity and power of the fit.

Equally profound in bringing forth the Divine Feminine have been new readings of Scripture. Part III, "Body, Mind, and Spirit," introduces the challenges of keeping balance when you are part of a people who have survived on the edge of extinction from birth. Hara Person's chapter shows how biblical women's lives can guide and inspire us to live. The women she describes are heroic not only for feminine virtues such as patience and loyalty, but also for bold actions usually reserved for men. The brilliant deceptions of Rebecca, Rachel, and Leah; Tamar's holy *chutzpah* in seducing her father-in-law and making him take responsibility for mistreating her; and Miriam's prophecy are powerful role models for women to be active players in repairing a world in which the will to dominate prevails too often.

No event in recent history carries the power of the Holocaust for Jews. Through the voices of women survivors, social worker Pamela Treiber Opper allows us to enter the hell of the concentration camps and to witness the barest redemption of the surrogate families women created for themselves to sew, cook, give birth, and console.

Women spiritual leaders often demonstrate a different style of community that is inclusive and pluralistic. Sheila Peltz Weinberg candidly describes the choreography of keeping one's balance as a Reconstructionist rabbi and a student of the teachings of the Buddha.

Part IV, Sexuality, Power, and Vulnerability, shows us the ways in which the Bible hints at women's power and fragility. Debra Band, calligrapher and artist, gives a vivid picture of the frank sexuality of a well-born young woman's passion for her lover in "The Song of Songs." Joy Silver's interpretation of the Book of Ruth becomes a narrative of embracing the "Other," in particular the gay and lesbian community.

Like Ruth, Judith Willmore chose to become a Jew. In her chapter she shares her own and other contemporary women's journeys to join the Jewish people. The angst of leaving one's family as Sarah and Abraham did, the joy of finding one's authentic path, and what it means to become a Jewish woman are her story.

The final part, "Worldview and Religious Practice," reveals the newest rituals in Jewish life that are inclusive of women. Shelly Fredman illustrates how Jewish women's groups celebrate Judaism by creating new or resurrecting old expressions of spirit that empower women.

Rabbi Jo David takes the holiday traditionally associated with women, *Rosh Hodesh*, the celebration of the new moon, and shows how it is a time of renewal for both women and men. Another ritual traditionally connected to women, *mikvah*, the monthly immersion required for menstruating married women, gets a new interpretation from writer Leah Lax. She describes her first experience with mikvah as a Hassidic bride. In interviewing women around the United States, she describes new ways mikvah has meaning for anyone who understands how the ceremony uses water and prayer to mark transitions.

This volume carries an intention to do more than bring the reader new ideas to ponder. For Jewish women, it's a charge to claim and reclaim their rightful place in their tradition. For millennia, women have educated their children to be Jews, have offered their husbands their best ideas, and only recently have these efforts been written down. For non-Jewish sisters, we hope that it encourages you to bring change in your traditions as you learn of our effort to be counted as full members of an ancient spiritual community.

Finally, the women in the book are speaking to men, too. The Book of Proverbs, written by King Solomon, the wisest of men, says, "Do not forsake your mother's teachings" (Prov. 6:20). We need both the black fire and the white fire of Torah to bring a balance of feminine and masculine energy into our lives and into our world. May the words of this book and the meditations of the hearts and minds that composed them bring us closer.

PART I

Family and Environment

CHAPTER 1

Unwrapping the Gift

Rabbi Sandy Eisenberg Sasso

Over two thousand years ago, seventy men cloistered in separate rooms, tradition tells us, wrote the Greek Septuagint, the first translation of the Bible. On March 21, 1972, seventy women joined to speak out together, to honor and to celebrate with Judith Kaplan Eisenstein, the first woman to be referred to as a "Bat Mitzvah" fifty years earlier. Over two thousand years ago, seventy men wrote a translation out of their experience, a translation that influenced generations of those who read the Bible. We must dare imagine what the gathering of seventy women who seek to translate our sacred narratives out of their experience will mean for generations yet to come.

More than seventy years ago, Judith Kaplan, a young girl of twelve and a half, stood in front of her congregation, as no woman had done before, to recite the Torah blessings and read Torah as a Bat Mitzvah. There was no fanfare, no front-page articles—"no thunder sounded, no lightning struck." It's a wonder how all great revolutions begin with what at first sight seems only natural—like a black woman taking a seat at the front of the bus, like a Jewish woman, really still a child, standing in front of a congregation reading Torah. On second sight, it is an act of courage that becomes a gift unwrapped by future generations. What began that day with the determination of a young girl and the wisdom of her father, Rabbi Mordecai Kaplan, became a revolution in religious creativity. We are still unwrapping that gift.

From birth to death, the ritual life of the religious community has been renewed. From welcoming girls into the covenant, from menarche to menopause, through infertility and miscarriage, through marriage and divorce, new landscapes are being sculpted from the soil of tradition.

Mordecai Kaplan, a leading twentieth-century American Jewish philosopher, called upon his generation to "free religious ritual from its bondage and legalism."[1] He recognized the need to fearlessly evaluate traditional symbols, not "merely to conserve or reform" but to "construct or reconstruct." He sought both to preserve revered custom and tradition and at the same time to revitalize old forms and give affirmation to new spiritual yearnings. For Kaplan, "folkways" are the social practices by which a people externalize the reality of their collective being. The more alive a people, the more they abound in affirmative folkways.[2] Kaplan understood that we cannot simply remake the past in the image of our beliefs, but we can discover customs and voices, write new stories, and make them a part of our sacred doing and remembering. As he taught a new generation of Jews, "When we ... find ourselves without corroboration, or precedent in tradition for what we regard as true or just, we must seek to give effect to it ... to refuse to do so would be to turn our back on truth and justice."[3]

The need for historic continuity and contemporary transformation of ritual is highlighted in Robert Bellah's distinction between tradition and traditionalism. For Bellah, traditionalism is marked by authoritarian closure whereas tradition allows for "reappropriation of the past in light of the present."[4] In the last few decades women have reappropriated the past in light of the present and have evolved and reinvigorated rituals and traditions that have enriched the spiritual life of the Jewish people. As one young mother commented to me, after a ceremony for her new baby daughter, "Thank you for letting me speak. At the naming of my last child, I was silent. Now I feel included."

Rather than representing a break with tradition, new ritual and liturgical activity are the very essence of a living tradition. The authority to change or to reconstruct the prayer and ritual life of the community comes from tradition itself. It is the constant renewal of religious forms that keeps tradition vital and capable of giving meaning to each new generation of seekers.

Kaplan believed that "it is with ritual, not ideas, that religion begins."[5] And so it was with a ritual, a Bat Mitzvah, that the religious life of this century was renewed.

It is not easy to create or even reconstruct ritual. It is more than the weaving together of a few prayerful or poetic lines and symbolic acts. Rituals that last tug at the private heart and the communal soul. They resonate with not only the personal but also the transcendent. They help us make meaning of our private lives because they reach back to grasp that which is timeless, renewing tradition and traditionalizing the new. But Kaplan's challenge was to "look upon ourselves not merely as descendants but as ancestors of posterity, responsible for preserving and creating symbols and rituals for future generations."[6]

When my husband, Dennis, and I held open our daughter Debora's *tallit* (fringed shawl) for her to recite the appropriate blessing for the first time as she became a Bat Mitzvah (May 1992), we knew that what she did was neither ancient nor hallowed by generations of women who did the same. Her grandmothers and great-grandmothers did not wrap themselves in fringed garments. When I first put on a tallit as an adult, I did so as much as an act of defiance as of affirmation. For my daughter, it was different; that tallit belonged to her, it was her right and responsibility to wrap herself within it as much as any boy's. And yet, this was not all that I knew or felt. As I placed the tallit around my daughter's shoulders, I felt the flow of the generations reaching back to the beginning of our history as a people. And God's words to Abraham became my words: "Go forth and be a blessing." And God's words to Debora are heard anew, spoken from mother to daughter: "Awake, awake, Debora, and sing your song."

Our daughter was privileged to have as guests on the Shabbat of her Bat Mitzvah Dr. Ira and Judith Kaplan Eisenstein. When Judith spoke to Debora, she said, "Right now I am the oldest and you are the youngest Bat Mitzvah." A single moment held seventy years of history as a gracious and wise woman blessed a bright-eyed and promising daughter of Israel. At this one time filled with so many memories and so much hope, I heard ancestors' stories and grandparents' voices. All this embraced my daughter in an act that was both old and new.

Human stories are the narrative of life's cycle; ritual is the poetry that turns a personal transition into a holy pilgrimage. Our spiritual landscape has been filled with secret gardens, silences, and unrecorded journeys. With the first Bat Mitzvah began the speaking out of silence. While both men and women have engaged in this ritual process, it has been the unwritten narratives of women's lives, newly spoken, that have shaped the contours of our religious renewal. Women's questions have helped us to sanctify those unmarked passages of time, the spaces left empty by the generations.

In a religious culture that dictates ritual from awakening until preparing for sleep, can there be the symbolic acts and holy words that sanctify the moment of learning of a pregnancy? In a faith that celebrates escape from danger with a prayer, can there be a prayer for the healing of a battered woman or an abused child? In a tradition that counts hundreds of blessings, can there be one blessing upon the birth of a daughter? In a community that counsels an intricate and comforting ritual of mourning, can there be a ceremony to carry a family through the sorrow of a miscarriage or stillbirth?

Women have taught us that religious revelation comes not only vertically, from on high, but horizontally, from within. We have always looked

for spiritual truths atop some mountain, but we also have discovered that
we can find religious truths and God in the human encounter, in our places of gathering. In this spirit and in honor and memory of Judith Kaplan
Eisenstein, beloved teacher and friend, I offer a new pilgrimage prayer.

Must we always go up to some mountain
with Abraham, with Isaac to Moriah?
The air is so thin up there,
and it's hard to breathe.

Must we always go up to some mountain
with Moses to Sinai?
It's so far from the earth,
and what's below appears so small
You can forget it's real.

Must we always go up to some mountain
with Moses to Nebo?
Climbing—there's only one way
and loneliness.

Must we always go up to some mountain
with Elijah to Carmel?
The ascent is not hard.
It's the descending—
too easy to slip
with no one to catch your fall.

I'm weary of mountains
where we're always looking up
or looking down and sacrificing
so our neck hurts
and we need glasses.

Our feet upon the mountains
are blistered,
and our shoes are always wrong—
not enough "sole."

Can we sit with Sarah in a tent,
next to Deborah under a palm tree,
alongside Rebekkah by the well—
with Judith in the synagogue reading Torah,
to wash our feet,
to catch our breath
and our soul?

The religious imagination of the twentieth century has allowed us to catch our breath and our soul. Ritual is not simply handed down; it is shaped within community. It is not just acted out upon us, but we are the active participants in its drama. Barbara Myerhoff underscored the importance of our active relation to rituals as "constructed performances." "Instead of having rites performed on us, we do them to and for ourselves and immediately we are involved in a form of self-creation that is potentially community building."[7] Our generation has not only created new ritual; it has transformed the ways in which we enact it and in turn build community.

In the past decades, as legitimacy was given to ritual innovation within the religious community, all sorts of creations rushed in. We know that those creations are not final but are part of an ongoing process of humanity's sacred searching.

We have something to learn from the first Bat Mitzvah. It was a revolutionary, yet gentle step. Judith did not read directly from the Torah; she did not stand on the *bimah* (pulpit). The message was conveyed in a definitive yet not shocking fashion, in a courageous but not jarring way. This enabled the ritual to make its entry into community and to grow into posterity, to become a sacred expectation, a stage in the Jewish life cycle.

What will remain and what will fade of ritual innovation will be determined by time and the community that celebrates and commemorates life's passages and the marking of time and seasons. Bat Mitzvah in one form or another is a permanent feature of almost every synagogue.[8] A welcoming ceremony for girls is an expectation of almost all new parents. The revival and reconstruction of Tu B'Shevat Sedarim and Rosh Hodesh ceremonies are old forms invested with new meanings.[9] New voices have been added to Jewish liturgy and holy day celebrations.

The story is told that when Pablo Picasso presented his portrait of Gertrude Stein, a critical viewer commented, "But it doesn't look like Gertrude Stein." To which Picasso responded, "It will." We may say the same of new ritual. To the comment that it doesn't look like tradition, we may respond, "It will."

We are still on the journey. There is a continuing need for ritual transformation that is both evocative of the past and resonant with the present. There are dangers on both sides of the ritual spectrum. On the one end, there is the innovator who affirms that every breath can be ritualized, and on the other end is the traditionalist who believes all authoritative ritual has already been created and cannot be altered. We must navigate a course between a spiritual privatism which asserts that the holy can be completely custom-made and a religious fundamentalism which claims that custom was made once and for all. We are in need of ritual that honors both the individual and the communal, tradition and change, the repetitive certainty of established acts and words and the refreshing spontaneity of improvisation. We are in need of ritual that will give expression to our innermost longings and deepest fears and call us to transcend the personal. Ritual must be more than a sacred affirmation of who we are; it must also be a holy challenge to what and who we may become in solidarity with a community of holy travelers.

Ritual not only sanctifies our moments of passage but also obligates our being. The power of the covenantal birth ritual is in its ability to call forth joy at new life, but also to evoke awe of the responsibility we have to raise the child to Torah, *huppah* (wedding canopy), and good deeds. The power of Bat Mitzvah is not simply the celebration of emerging adolescence and the beginning of a parental letting go; it is also the handing on of values, and of stories, tears, and laughter, from one generation to the next in the hope that the ancient chain will continue through this newly responsible child. Good ritual is not a massage to our vulnerable selves, not private therapy. Ritual works, when it does, because it connects us to something beyond ourselves and places us in a community and tradition to which we are accountable and for which we are responsible.

How easy it is after more than seventy years, after increased opportunities for women and a resurgence of ritual creativity, to forget how extraordinary and how difficult and how lonely it was to take those first steps. How important it is for us to remember, to retell those early stories and to honor the struggle, and not to take all that we have received for granted. In a time of increasing fundamentalism that seeks to co-opt religious language and constrict the spiritual landscape, we must say the following:

We create ceremonies, we tell stories, we make and enliven rituals in the tradition of Sarah and Abraham, who celebrated Isaac's weaning; in the tradition of our ancestors, who taught a new generation not to sit in darkness but to light Sabbath candles; in the tradition of the rabbis, who told the Hannukah story of the cruze of oil and began a new custom that lasted for generations.[10] In their name, in the name of all those who went before them, and in the name of all those generations yet to come, we light candles, we preserve, and we create. We marvel at how much remains the same in our cycles of time, what ancient words still move us, how different we are, what silences must still be broken. What really matters is not just that we are descendants, but that we are ancestors who bequeath our spiritual quest to the next generation.

We accept this awe-filled responsibility with a deep sense of humility. After all, who are we, tied as we are to our own time and place, to fashion the sacred words and create the holy drama to carry us through the passages of our years? We accept this responsibility with a strong sense of duty. After all, who are we, bearers of the image of God, not to pour our souls into the crucible of time, to affix our name to the holy narrative of our people?

One Shabbat over seventy years ago, a young girl read the sacred words of our tradition and became a Bat Mitzvah. There was no thunder and there was no lightning (or perhaps there was), just a sacred affirmation of her belonging to a holy people. Who could have known then what would come of this one seemingly simple symbolic act? Thank you, Judith, for your first step, and for the steady hand and wise heart with which you guided us.

NOTES

1. Mordecai Kaplan, *The Future of the American Jew* (New York: Reconstructionist Press, 1967), 210.

2. Mordecai Kaplan, *Judaism as a Civilization* (New York: Jewish Reconstructionist Foundation, 1957), 431–33.

3. Mordecai Kaplan, *Questions Jews Ask* (New York: Reconstructionist Press, 1956), 435–37.

4. Robert Bellah et al., *Habits of the Heart* (Berkeley: University of California Press, 1985), 155.

5. Mordecai Kaplan, "Religion as the Symbolization of the Values of Holiness," in *Symbols and Values: An Initial Study,* ed. Lyman Bruser and Louis Finkelstein (New York: Reconstructionist Press, 1954), 189.

6. Kaplan, *The Future of the American Jew,* 210.

7. Barbara Myerhoff, "Rites of Passage: Process and Paradox," in *Celebration Studies in Festivity and Ritual,* ed. Victor Turner (Washington, DC: Smithsonian Institution Press, 1982).

8. Bat Mitzvah has become an expectation of all Jewish girls between the ages of twelve and thirteen. Orthodox Judaism limits ritual participation and does not allow a woman to read Torah. Often the girls who do choose to become B'not Mitzvah in an Orthodox congregation offer a commentary on the meaning of the Shabbat Torah or Haftarah (prophetic) reading.

All Reconstructionist, Reform, and most Conservative synagogues welcome the full and equal participation of girls as B'not Mitzvah. The girls chant Torah and Haftarah and lead in major parts of the liturgy. Whereas practice differs from congregation to congregation (some Conservative synagogues only permit girls to read the Haftarah or restrict their participation to Friday evening), most Jewish girls entering adolescence in the United States become B'not Mitzvah, and many put on a tallit for the first time on this occasion.

9. A special meal modeled after a sixteenth-century Sephardic tradition that celebrates the Jewish new year of the trees and the renewal of nature.

10. The legend of the lights is not told in the Book of Maccabees, which first chronicles the Hannukah events, but appears centuries later in rabbinic literature as the basis for a new ritual.

CHAPTER 2

The Ecological Message of the Holy Days

Ellen Bernstein

Many years ago, before I was actively involved in Jewish life, I asked my friend Jeffrey Dekro, a pretty serious guy, what was compelling to him about Judaism, and he answered simply, "It's fun." I couldn't believe my ears. Judaism, fun? Meaningful, yes; transformative, maybe; but fun? I realized that he was talking about the holidays, but I had never had any fun on a Jewish holiday before; I had known them as solemn, mournful, or boring occasions. Still, I thought he might be on to something, and I began to explore for myself.

One reason the holidays were no fun for me was because I simply could not relate to the historical events they commemorated. What was the liberation from Egypt, the receiving of the Ten Commandments, the Maccabean victory, to me? Mine was the attitude of the *rasha* (the wicked child of the Passover seder), the one who sees oneself as an outsider and holds back in judgment. However, as my attitude toward Judaism evolved from condescension to curiosity and I began to dig beneath the surface, I realized that the holidays were not, as I had once thought, isolated moments that fell randomly throughout the year, simply memorializing Jewish historical triumphs.

The festivals marked the seasons—the joy of rain at its proper time, the ingathering of an abundant harvest, and the birthing of the lambs— long before they were associated with historical significance. The holidays were bound to each other and to the world in a grand seasonal tapestry.

And while we are not connected to nature in the way our ancestors were, and few of us depend on the agricultural cycle for our livelihood, I understood that the holidays were indeed *holy days* that could capture the moods of the different seasons and connect us to nature and our souls.

Over time I became completely convinced that Jewish holidays were not just celebrations of the special historical events of a distant past; the natural dimensions of the holidays—the seasons, the weather, the produce of the land—were equally important. The holidays were like a double helix: the two strands of history *and* nature are bound up together to create a rich, complex, and wise tradition. For someone who went to the woods—not the synagogue—for spiritual sustenance, this was a powerful recognition. It meant that I might be able to find a home in Judaism.

I also recognized that these two dimensions of the holidays, history and nature, were symbolic of the two parts of ourselves: male and female. By this I mean that each person is a blend of male and female energies or characters. Just as our society tends to value male energies over female energies, so our society puts more stock in history than it does in nature. Male energies are associated with linear movement, reaching forward, striving ahead, progress: everything that supports the "hunt." Female energies are associated with cyclical movement, relationship, community: everything that supports the home. He—the sun; she—the moon; he—heaven; she—earth; he—time; she—place. It bears noting that in Hebrew (where all words carry a gender), most place-names, including names of countries and cities and the words for land and city and stone, are all feminine.

One can see the confluence of the male type with history and the female type with nature or place. Ecology—the study of nature (literally the study of the house), is all about the natural processes of the earth, which can be characterized as feminine: interdependence, relationships, and cycles.

This chapter, then, seeks to explore the often-overlooked natural dimensions of many of the Jewish holidays. In so doing I hope to model a way for others to celebrate, question, and create meaningful holidays that integrate nature and thereby the feminine.

Exploring the natural meanings of the holy days can deepen and ground our experience of them. In Hebrew the word *zeman*, "time," is connected to the word for "invitation." Festivals are invitations to capture the seasonal moments and celebrate them. In Jewish tradition, the holy days can act as a compass to orient us to who we are and where we're going in our personal and spiritual lives at periodic intervals throughout the year; they provide a way for us to tune into our souls and the soul of the world.

The Jewish year, Rosh Hashanah, begins in the fall as the days are growing shorter. Nature is turning inward from the flowery exuberance of spring and summer to the seeded containment of autumn and winter. All the world is in a state of change. Rabbi David Zeller, *z'l* (deceased) called Rosh Hashanah (literally head/*rosh* of the year/*shana*) "Change Head" day, because *shana* also means "to change." The autumn welcomes the change, blows off our dead leaves, and invites us to go inside to change our minds: to return to our true being in preparation for the next round of life. The renewal in nature invites the renewal of our souls.

The primary theme of the Rosh Hashanah liturgy is kingship. Sadly, many feminists find the image of the king—male and hierarchical—to be offensive. But kingship is intimately linked to creation. The king is first and foremost master of the universe, the One who wrests creation into being, who overcame the watery chaos in the beginning—a male energy, to be sure, yet absolutely necessary in the grand round of life. Though male (energetically speaking), God's kingship is not invulnerable. Chaos/evil lurks behind every door, waiting to upset the king and undo the order of creation. The evil that threatens to topple creation is no satanic force; it resides within each of us: our mindlessness and our obliviousness to the consequences of our acts.

Today the metaphor of God as supreme king, struggling to keep the watery chaos at bay, is particularly poignant as we reflect on the chaotic waters and weather associated with climate change and all the destruction, pain, and suffering that our ecosystems and peoples around the earth must endure because of our vanity.

On Rosh Hashanah, the day the rabbis called *harat olam*, or "birthday of creation," we are given the opportunity to re-enthrone the king and give creation a chance to re-establish herself. Because, metaphorically speaking, only when the king sits securely on the throne will order and peace reign and the glory of God fill the earth.

Another symbol of the Rosh Hashanah liturgy that embodies nature herself is the *shofar*. I love the spiraling horn and its piercing cry: the ram is calling us, waking us to life. Perhaps it is the ram of that archetypal sacrifice, come back to connect us with holiness, beckoning us to live each moment.

While the ram calls us to awaken to our own lives, the ram is also calling us to wake up to nature. Putting our lips to the horn and listening to its call, we have an intimate experience of our primal connection to the world of nature. The ram's horn provides an entryway, a path back to our most primitive, earthy roots.

Every year on the balmy Indian summer days of Rosh Hashanah, I like to have friends over for a festive lunch in our backyard. Eating outdoors on the Jewish holidays is such a simple way to connect to them, and yet, for most of my life, holiday meals were formal, stiff affairs in stuffy dining rooms. It's a lot easier to experience God's company in the fresh air, where I can actually feel like I am breathing God's breath, and it's much easier to experience the natural or agricultural dimensions of the holidays outdoors, where I can tune into the flavor of the season I am commemorating. I might have become enamored of Judaism at an early age had my family simply celebrated the holidays on the porch or in the backyard.

Of all the holidays, Yom Kippur is the one I associate least with nature. Perhaps it's because it is a holiday of intentional deprivation—no food, no sex, no attention to the body, no enjoyment of the world. A day without color; a day for death; a day for the inner work of self-reflection and forgiveness that is necessary in order to return to life with a whole heart, ready to begin again.

Sukkot, following quick on the heels of the New Year, is the eight-day harvest fest and the beginning of the rainy season, a time to gather in the fruits and vegetables of the year's labors. Many Jews build flimsy little huts called *sukkah* to commemorate the sheds the ancient Israelites built to store their harvest (some say these huts commemorate the journey in wilderness).

With its festive decorations—like twinkly lights and miniature pumpkins—and its unassuming posture, the sukkah has always found its way into my heart. It's a *mitzvah*, or "good deed," to make the sukkah beautiful, and in Mt. Airy, where I lived for twenty years, we enjoyed a friendly sukkah decorating competition. My friend Anna, who fancies herself a Jewish Martha Stewart, is always concocting new Sukkot recipes using green beans, squash, potatoes, and fresh herbs from her garden, and she's forever decorating her sukkah with makeshift window dressings of cheery fabrics she finds hidden away in the back of a closet. One year I grew a garden full of gourds just to have exotic decorations for my sukkah. Now I cultivate many late-blooming flowers: cleome, Mexican sunflower, zinnias, goldenrod, boltonia, and asters. I collect seed pods—the best are blackberry lilies—grasses, and spent yarrow and make lavish bouquets to hang upside down from the rafters of my sukkah.

In my neighborhood on the Saturday afternoon of Sukkot, you'll see hundreds of people enjoying the annual sukkah walk, strolling, biking, and pushing carriages up and down the streets, admiring the simple beauty of each sukkah, delighting in the bounty (we all cook up a storm; my standard is sweet potato soup) and the pleasure of the company. On Sukkot, you're actually commanded to be joyful. I love this idea. It's as if we've forgotten how to be happy and must be taught. True joy comes by inviting all your friends, as well as your long-departed ancestors and a few strangers, to squeeze into your open-air hut for a big picnic or a sleepover, rain or shine.

At the end of Sukkot comes Simchat Torah, and with it one of the most beautiful prayers in all of Jewish liturgy: the prayer for rain. This prayer eloquently expresses all the patriarchs', and ultimately our own, utter dependence on God for rain and water and food and life. And this is cause for celebration. In my community everyone, old and young alike, join in wild singing and dancing (a little schnapps helps). On Simchat Torah, more than at any other time in the calendar, I have a fleeting glimpse of God's presence in the world. I get a little giddy seeing that my community's renewal is inextricably tied to the renewal of the land, food, and rains. We are indeed one.

As the day length reaches its shortest, we celebrate Hannukah. The historical dimensions of this holiday have never really resonated with me. I can't get excited about the Maccabees, and I find myself irritated with the Christmasization of Hannukah.

My favorite part of Hannukah is simply the oil: the oil for the lights and the oil for the latkes. Hannukah falls on the darkest day of the year, and the light of the candles acts as a beacon and the hot greasy latkes provide comfort food during the cold, nasty days of winter. On a more ecological level the festival lights and the latkes are an expression of our gratitude for oil and the energy it provides for all our most basic needs, from seeing to cooking to eating.

In the heart of winter comes Tu B'Shevat, the Jewish new year of the trees. Tu B'Shevat has particular significance for me because it was the first holiday I ever embraced as my own; it provided me an entry into Judaism.

I first grasped the possibilities of Tu B'Shevat when I recognized that holidays could be interpreted in creative and ecologic ways; ritual celebrations are not so different from any other art form. The success of the ritual depends, in part, on what the artist brings to the piece. Artist and teacher Chris Wells taught me how to capture the imagination of an entire community to move it toward an ecological vision and practice by utilizing pageantry and parades to create memorable and moving holiday occasions.

Having participated in the festivals of many native cultures in South America, Chris decided that the earth needed its own holy day. He created All Species Day as a way to give expression to the earth's creatures and to engage his community in the conservation of habitat and the protection of species.

For Chris, the preparation for All Species Day was just as important as the day itself. Chris and his partners began working with schools and community groups in the fall of the year to generate interest in the many varied species and habitats of the world. They used the arts, stories, and music to help engage the students. Participating individuals and groups

chose species or habitats or ecosystems, learned all they could about their
chosen creatures, and developed costumes and floats to represent them.
Then, come spring, the residents of Santa Fe, old and young alike, donned
their homemade, environmentally friendly creature costumes, and gathered
together on foot, in carriages, on stilts, in wheelbarrows, on roller blades,
on bicycle, or on horseback to proudly march in the All Species Parade.

Chris taught me about the power of holiday festivals to pull a community together and transmit a serious ecological message. Holiday celebrations, when conceived and executed sensitively, have the unique ability to
change people's attitudes and behaviors because they engage people in a
full-bodied—not just a mental—experience. Participants are so subtly
changed that often they do not realize that anything is happening to them.
Contrast this with the standard top-down moral religious education that
often yields a negative reaction.

Chris's All Species work inspired me to rethink Tu B'Shevat. For most
of the twentieth century, Tu B'Shevat was a neglected relic of a holiday,
recast by the Jewish National Fund, the charitable organization specializ-
ing in the development of Israeli land, as a tree-planting day for children.
But it is, in fact, the perfect environmental holy day with deep ecological
roots, a time for all of us to celebrate nature and our connection to her.

Established in rabbinic times as a day to pay taxes on the fruit trees,
Tu B'Shevat was invigorated by the kabbalists, the mystics of Safed, in the
1600s. They created a seder, a ritual following a particular order, to celebrate the day. You can imagine a Tu B'Shevat seder as a four-course ritual
meal organized around the kabbalistic four worlds of *Atzilut* (spirit), *Briyah*
(thought), *Yetzirah* (emotion), and *Assiyah* (doing). Each meal consisted of
biblical and mystical readings about nature, garnished with fruits, wines,
and blessings. The more fruit you taste and the more wine you drink, the
more blessings you're required to say, the more the earth is healed.

I was eager to develop a Tu B'Shevat ritual that could evoke the mystical experience of soul and nature envisioned by the kabbalists and, at the
same time, could lift Tu B'Shevat out of obscurity and give it the visibility
it deserves. I believed that Tu B'Shevat had the potential for more pageantry and poetry than most people give it credit for.

I wanted to create, in eco-philosopher David Abram's words, a spell of
the sensuous. Because a sense of place is such a subtle but vital aspect of
ecological (and, I might add, religious) education, I chose to set my first
seder in one of Philadelphia's boathouses on the banks of the Schuylkill
River. In this seder, the kabbalistic four worlds translate naturally into the
elements of earth, water, air, and fire, and they set the stage for the ritual
drama. Artists in the community decorated the space and created a virtual
Garden of Eden, a garden of earthly and heavenly delights. The two

hundred guests at the seder chose to represent creatures from the worlds of earth, water, air, or fire and dressed accordingly. Integrating pageantry, art, and theater, along with religious insights and ecological understandings, we created a beautiful and evocative new ritual.

People entered the space, silently admired each other and the paradisial setting, and took their places on the floor. World-by-world, we read from the Haggadah, ate fruit and drank wine, listened to musical offerings composed by local musicians, and sang. And world-by-world, we sat in silence, contemplated our place in nature, and expressed our gratitude for all the diverse fruits we have been given.

Our *brachot* (blessings) were all the more meaningful on Tu B'Shevat. According to the kabbalists, the point of the seder is to repair the world. Repair of the world begins with repair of our minds. On Tu B'Shevat we are asked to overcome the fundamental flaw of our consciousness (which began when Adam ate the apple): our belief that we are the masters of creation and that the earth belongs to us. "The earth belongs to God," sang the psalmist. We are all part of one interwoven system, and we all belong to God. The seder provides the context for us to recognize how utterly we depend on God the Creator for all the fruits of creation. Through our blessings and our humility we give back in gratitude to God the Maker of all and so participate in the process of repair.

Next in the cyclical round is Purim, which, like Hannukah, holds less of an ecological connection than do the biblical holidays. But all peoples need a topsy-turvy holiday to relieve them of cabin fever at the end of winter and lift their energy in raucous communal celebration. In this way Purim is a close cousin of Mardi Gras and Carnival, and I always revel in the release that Purim brings.

Passover, or *Pesach,* heralds the end of the winter rains, the beginning of spring; it is the time of freedom and renewal. My most memorable Passover was a backpacking trip in the Grand Canyon with a group of science teachers about thirty years ago. While all my companions were busy analyzing the geologic layers of the Grand Canyon, I was imagining my ancestors journeying through the wilderness. I wanted to live the experience of liberation on my trek in this desert.

It was not hard to convince my new friends that celebrating Passover in the desert could be great fun. I instructed them in the symbols of the holiday and sent them out to hunt down appropriate artifacts for a seder plate. They returned laden with various skeletal remains licked clean by wolves to serve as shank bone(s), the remnants of a bird's egg, a variety of greens for *karpas* (hors d'oeuvre), sage for bitter herbs, and Indian paintbrush and other wildflowers for a festive centerpiece. I had brought a few pieces of *matzoh* (unleavened bread wafers) and some apples and nuts for *haroset*. As the sun set, we gathered together for a homemade vegetable feast cooked over a little camp stove. We found a beautiful spot where the red canyon wall formed an overhang to protect us from any possible rain, and there, cradled in the most awesome river canyon with the full moon rising overhead, we sat and talked the night away, asking and answering questions, eating, and telling stories of our own liberation.

These days my Passover seders generally take place indoors; but this year with Pesach falling late in the season during a warm spell, we decided to set up the seder table on our deck, where we could actually witness the re-greening of the earth as we celebrated the renewal of spring and our freedom.

At the seder we don't just talk about our freedom, we eat it—by eating all the ritual symbols. And because each element of the seder plate is also a reminder of the season of Aviv, it is as if we're eating the springtime herself.

The first course of our seder is no measly strand of parsley dipped in salt water. Rather, it is a deep green karpas salad of arugula, watercress, and cilantro (and whatever other lettuces are available) dressed in vinegar. I love the complex bitter yet fresh taste of these humble greens; this is as close as it gets to ingesting the earth's dark, rich soil. In addition to setting the stage for an earthy holiday, a real karpas salad right at the beginning of the seder promises that your guests will be happy, not hungry, and more eager to participate whole-heartedly in the seder.

The other primary symbols of the Passover—the matzoh and the Pascal lamb—also bring to life a sense of spring and a feeling for the land. Matzoh is the bread of our affliction and the bread of our liberation. It consists of wheat flour and water—nothing added to preserve, sweeten, or enhance its flavor. It is the most basic of all food: the grain of the earth, the staff of life. Similarly, the shank bone not only memorializes the lamb of the Isreaelite sacrifice but also reminds us of our connection and debt to the animal world. The ancient Israelite economy was a mixed agricultural and pastoral one. Shepherding was as much a part of Israel's life and identity as was farming. The matzoh and shank bone symbolize the two primary dimensions of Israelite life: farming and herding.

The early rabbis said the real meaning of the Passover lies in the telling of a story of transformation from degradation to dignity, from slavery to liberation. This is not just the story of the ancient Israelites who threw off their Egyptian oppressors; it is also the story of each of us, and we relive the story again and again in our own lifetimes. On a more cosmic level this is the story of the transformation from chaos and destruction to re-creation. Over and over the Bible recounts stories of an orderly world (creation) that is undone by the forces of evil, only to be recreated anew.

The plagues of the seder symbolize the undoing of creation; the Red Sea incident in which the Egyptians are swallowed up symbolizes utter chaos and destruction, and the receiving of the Ten Commandments and the law on the other side of the Red Sea is symbolic of a new creation. This cosmic story resonates more than the particular Israelite one; it's gratifying to know there are multiple ways to understand our texts and customs.

While Passover is in itself a holy day, it also marks the beginning of the *omer*, the forty-nine-day period between Passover and Shavuot when the Israelites watched apprehensively, waiting for their spring wheat to sprout and grow. Too much rain in spring could ruin the tender shoots of wheat; no grain meant no bread in the coming year. The Israelites tentatively counted off each day, acknowledging this period of uncertainty.

In medieval times, the mystics who lived in cities did not grow their own wheat, yet they still took the omer seriously, counting the days between Passover and Shavuot. They were on the lookout for hidden energies, subtle nuances of each day, by which they could transform themselves spiritually. Just as the Israelites purified their hearts, even if unconsciously, on the vigorous trek through the empty wilderness, so the kabbalists purified themselves by invoking the energies of each day of the omer in preparation for a culminating revelation on Shavuot. They developed a mystical calendar to tap into the subtle qualities of the days.

Shavuot marks the end of the omer and, with it, the ripening of the wheat and God's revelation of the Torah to the people. Passover and Shavuot are the two bookends of the omer period—the first celebrated with matzoh, flat un-yeasted bread that commemorates the escape from Egypt; the second celebrated with two whole-wheat loaves that commemorate the receiving of the Torah at Mount Sinai. In both cases, wheat is central.

Shavuot is not only the holiday of wheat; it is also the holiday of milk. Milk is symbolic of the suckling lambs born in Aviv. It is reminiscent of the land of "milk and honey" and the "milk beneath the beloved's tongue" in "The Song of Songs." Milk from a mother's breast keeps her babies alive, and milk is the complete food that can keep us alive—just like Torah. In its high regard for milk, Shavuot is surely the most feminine of all the holy days.

Whereas Sukkot is celebrated with the fresh fruits of the harvest, Hannukah with the oil of the latkes, Tu B'Shevat with dried fruits and nuts, and Pesach with unleavened bread and bitter herbs, Shavuot is celebrated with wheat and milk. Thus each holiday is marked with the food of its particular season. It's not just what we think and how we behave, but also what we eat that makes us Jews.

God gave the Torah on top of a mountain, and so it seems only fitting for Jewish communities to commemorate Shavuot by hiking to the top of a peak for a vision, although I've never met a community that honored Shavuot this way. Instead, most Jews are busying themselves studying text all night long and eating copious amounts of cheesecake and ice cream. But praying with our feet is as important as praying with our minds—and our guts—and the view from the mountain provides a God's eye perspective that could give us the sense of connectedness and wholeness that many of us long for. We Jews would be pleased and invigorated to find how our tradition expands when we abandon the buildings we hold so dear and take to the mountains.

The last of the holidays of the Jewish year is Tishah-b'Av. Although a minor holiday, it holds deep ecological significance for me. Falling in mid-summer, invariably during a heatwave or drought, Tishah-b'Av marks the driest time of year. My garden is parched and so am I. These are the dog days of summer. I don't have to look at the calendar to know Tishah-b'Av has arrived.

Tishah-b'Av remembers the destruction of the ancient temples at Jerusalem (in 586 BCE and 70 CE), symbolizing the breakdown of Judaism's center and the drying up of the wellspring of life. It is a time of profound grief and loss, of haunting mournful laments. I am always more acutely aware of our environmental vulnerability this time of year. I surrender to the sadness of this time—the grief I feel every day about global warming and my own inability to do enough. I mourn the loss of species, the instability of weather, the destruction of habitat; I mourn what the earth and her peoples and creatures must endure; I worry about climate catastrophes yet to come. But I am eternally grateful to Judaism to have a place and a time and a community in which to grieve all the losses that I feel. Over time, Tishah-b'Av has become one of my most beloved holidays.

In the communities in which I have lived, Tishah-b'Av is a simple and beautiful ceremony. We come together at the synagogue as the sun is lowering in the horizon. We light candles and walk in a silent processional into the sanctuary, where we sit on the floor in thick darkness illuminated only by the flickering of candlelight. Then out of the night come the haunting verses of the lament of Eicha. I lay bare my own heart and my tears flow like a river, and I find comfort in this sanctuary-turned-womb.

I pray that in the cycle of life we will overcome our harmful, self-indulgent ways, and that we, and the land, will have the opportunity to begin again. Rosh Hashanah is just around the bend and with it the promise of life-giving rains and a new year.

Sadly, most Jewish communities—out of convenience and habit—observe the holidays indoors, in artificial light and air-conditioned halls, seated in orderly rows in straight-backed chairs, cut off from the moods, smells, and flavors of the particular time of year. In such a setting, the observance of the holidays invariably becomes more of a mental exercise—a remembrance of time past, rather than a celebration of time present. When the holidays are cut off from their natural context, they may seem less relevant to many of us. Outside their natural context, the prayers lose their meaning and flavor—they are like an empty shell. It is no wonder that Jewish leaders are perplexed as to why modern synagogues, by and large, aren't able to capture the imagination of the masses of Jews.

The festival days were designed to orient us to the nuances of time and the cycles of nature. When we celebrate the holidays true to their seasons, they are saturated with meaning and a sense of the feminine, and they are irresistible to child and adult alike.

CHAPTER 3

Sacrificing the Son

Alice Shalvi

braham, the first monotheist, is generally considered a prototype of religious faith and obedience to God's will. These qualities, first displayed in his unquestioning response to the original command to "go forth" from his native land to an unknown destination, reach their climax in the "binding" of his beloved and long-awaited son and heir, Isaac.

This episode has generated a multitude of problems of all kinds—theological, psychological, ethical, and so on. On the most basic human level, one inevitably wonders how any human being—and especially so moral a person as Abraham has been shown to be—could respond so unquestioningly to so horrendous a command. This, after all, is the man who bargained with God about the number of uncorrupt citizens of Sodom and Gomorrah that would suffice to spare these cities from destruction. Yet here there is neither questioning nor bargaining. (Earlier, when Sarah asked Abraham to cast out Hagar and his firstborn, Ishmael, the request did irk him, and it was only God's reinforcement of the request that led him to "heed her voice.")

Precisely because of the major role that Sarah plays in the entire family story of the profound longing for a child, the extensive period of barrenness, the joyous birth and its festive celebration, her absence in this crucial paradigmatic episode demands an explanation that is not to be found in the biblical text. Does she know about God's command? If so, is she as acquiescent as Abraham, or is there an initial conflict, as in the case of Ishmael? If she does not at first know, does she ever find out? And

if she does, what is her response then? Is it significant that the next time
her name is mentioned, it is in the dry reference to her death?

Numerous *midrashim* (interpretations) have been composed in the
attempt to "fill in the white space around the black letters" of this enig-
matic episode in the saga of the first biblical family.

Some indication of rabbinical responses both to Abraham's apparently
unquestioning obedience in the Isaac episode and to Sarah's role may be
found in the non-Pentateuchal Haftorah (prophetic) readings that accompany readings from the Torah on Sabbaths and festivals. The "Binding of
Isaac" story is read twice in the course of the year: initially on the second
day of New Year (Rosh Hashanah), one of the holiest days in the Jewish
calendar, and again in the course of the regular readings, which in the
space of a calendar year cover the entire Pentateuch. It is surely significant
that on both occasions the Haftorah selection presents an episode that
relates to a *mother* who "loses" her son.

The first of these stories is that of Hannah, which we read on Rosh
Hashanah. The Book of Samuel opens with the description of a devout
family—Elkanah and his two wives, Hannah (which means "graciousness"
or "favor") and Peninnah (pearl). While Peninnah has borne both sons and
daughters (no number is specified), Hannah is barren. Like Hagar in the
earlier story, Peninnah taunts Hannah and makes her life miserable. But
Hannah is her husband's favorite, and he displays his preference by giving
her a larger portion of the sacrificial offering. This situation apparently
continues "year after year." Hannah is inconsolable, despite her husband's
evident love and concern: "Am I not more [devoted] to you than ten sons?"
he asks, with a notable degree of pathos.

Finally, the grief-stricken Hannah takes action, turning in prayer
directly to God, "weeping all the while." Her prayer is in the form of a
vow, entering into a *quid pro quo* bargain with the Almighty, while also
stressing her subservience to him. (Note the threefold repetition of her
self-description as God's "handmaiden" [verse 11].) If God remembers her
and grants her a son, she will in time return him to God, dedicating him
to a life of priesthood.

When Hannah's prayer is answered, she appropriately names her son
Shmuel (Samuel), "I asked God for him." (The name can also be read as a
contraction for "God has heard.") Now the time has come for Hannah to
fulfill her part of the bargain, but she clearly finds it hard to surrender the
son she so longed and prayed for. The next time Elkanah and all his
household go up to offer the annual sacrifice, she stays at home, giving as
explanation that she is waiting until the child is weaned, since once he
appears before the Lord he must remain there for good. Elkanah accedes
to her wishes, and so Hannah stays at home, nursing her son "until she

weaned him." While the period of time is not specified, we may conjecture that it is a matter of several years, until the boy could be independent of his mother. When Hannah finally feels she can no longer delay keeping her promise, she takes materials for a sacrifice and goes to the house of the Lord in Shilo. The pithy text stresses the boy's youth: "and the boy was a boy" (v. 24). Yet one more delay—for the sacrifice of the bullock she has brought as a token of thanksgiving (a possible substitute for the son, like the ram for Isaac?)—and then comes the inevitable moment of separation. She brings the boy to Eli, the High Priest, identifies herself as the woman whose form of praying he had mistaken for drunkenness, and presents the boy to him. The words and repetitions here, particularly notable in the Hebrew text, dramatically convey how, even at this late stage, she is playing for time, indicating how much the child means to her ("For this child I prayed"), as well as the mingling of reluctance and readiness with which she keeps the bargain she struck with God. The Hebrew text has a wonderful (and unfortunately untranslatable) wordplay with the root שעל, which is the root not only of the verb "to ask" but also of the verbs "to borrow" and "to lend." Since God has given her what she *asked* him for, she is *lending* that gift to God for life. The word "lending" implies that she considers herself as still retaining a hold on her son, though he will no longer be part of her household. We feel how hard it is for Hannah to give up what she so longed for, and yet how indebted to God she feels for having granted her prayers.

Chapter II opens with Hannah's second prayer, a soaring, poetic expression of religious faith in God's rule and providence, which expresses not only Hannah's personal exultation over her rival Peninnah but also a general affirmation of God's unique greatness. In both content and tone, this prayer resembles other great songs of praise—that of Moses (and Miriam) after the crossing of the Red Sea (Exod. 15) and that of Deborah after the defeat of Sisera's army (Judg. 5). This similarity surely affects Hannah's status in our eyes; it is no wonder that the rabbis listed her among the seven women prophets of Israel.

Hannah's prayer over, Elkanah returns home, while Samuel stays with Eli. And where is Hannah? This is not specified. (Nor is what happened to Isaac after the aborted sacrifice.) Perhaps in body she returns with Elkanah while in spirit she stays with her son?

Such an interpretation can be supported by the later (and last) reference to her (2:18–21). The child Samuel ministers before Eli, "being a child girded with a linen ephod." His mother makes him a little coat (note the tenderness implied in the adjective) and brings a new one with her every year when she comes with Elkanah to offer the annual sacrifice. The Hebrew verb used for her bringing of the garment is identical with that used for bringing the sacrifice, indicating that for Hannah both "offerings" are equally important expressions of her dedication—to her son, as well as to God, of whom she had "asked" him. Although Hannah bears five more children, her firstborn, Samuel, clearly remains the apple of her eye. She has found a way other than taking her child's life by which to express her faith and obedience; though absent, "taken" by God, her son is still alive. Might Sarah, unlike Abraham, have made a bargain with God, to "lend" him her son, rather than take his life?

When we next publicly read the story of the "Binding of Isaac," it is followed by an episode taken from the Book of Kings (2:8–37)—one of the many legends associated with the prophet Elisha. Like all legends, it is typified by a lack of rationalization of events, presenting them in neither emotional nor psychological depth, and always dealing with wondrous or mysterious events that are enveloped in a veil of incomprehensibility. Dramatic and presented largely in dialogue form, the story of Elisha and the Shunamite can readily be divided into four distinct "acts," the first of which (which we can title "The Prophet") itself comprises both a kind of prologue and the prophecy that is the mainspring of the drama (8–16).

The prologue presents the major protagonists, Elisha and the unnamed woman who, recognizing that he is "a holy man of God," not only entertains him to a meal every time he passes through Shunam but also realizes that since he pays regular visits to the place, he may also need comfortable overnight accommodation. In typically female detail, she enumerates the necessary items: a small, enclosed upper chamber (that is, privacy), a bed, a table, a chair, and a lampstand.

One day Elisha realizes that he should repay this gracious hospitality in some appropriate manner and offers to speak to the authorities on her behalf. When she rejects this offer as unnecessary because she is sufficiently respected in her community ("I live among my own people"), it is his more perceptive servant Gehazi who points out that "she has no son, and her husband is old." Thus prompted, Elisha prophesies to her, "At this season next year, you will be embracing a son." Hers is a somewhat incredulous and humble response (perhaps comparable also to Sarah's laughter of skepticism and disbelief): "Please, my lord, man of God, do not delude your maidservant" (the same self-deprecating word as Hannah uses about herself).

Act II, "The Death of the Child" (17–24), tells of the promised birth but at once goes on to depict most graphically the manner of the child's sudden death. While out with his father in the field, the boy cries to his father, "Oh, my head, my head!" The father bids a servant carry the boy to his mother, who holds him on her lap until noon, when he dies. Without further ado, she lays him on *Elisha's* bed, closes the door, and bids her husband provide her with a servant and a she-ass so that she can hurry to the man of God and back. Puzzled, the woman's husband asks for the reason, since this is neither a new moon nor a Sabbath, two occasions on which such a visit was apparently customary. Her curt reply is "Shalom!" (here meaning "It's all right" or "Goodbye"), and she hastens away.

Act III, "The Demand," takes place on Mount Carmel, at Elisha's abode. Recognizing the Shunamite woman from afar, Elisha again sends his servant Gehazi, this time to inquire after her husband and child. The Shunamite, with the same curtness we've already witnessed, dismisses Gehazi and presses on to Elisha, prostrating herself before him and clasping his feet—an audaciously physical act that apparently appalls Gehazi, who tries to push her away. Elisha, however, recognizes both her "bitter distress" and the fact that it has not been revealed to him by God. Thus reassured, the Shunamite reproaches Elisha: "Did I ask my Lord for a son? Didn't I say: 'Don't mislead me?'" Typically, as we've now learned, Elisha again sends Gehazi as a proxy: he is to take Elisha's staff and hasten to place it on the boy's face. But the boy's mother is not prepared to accept a proxy and insists, "As the Lord lives and as you live, I will not leave you"—so vehement a protest that Elisha feels compelled to obey.

Act IV, "The Miracle" (31–37). Prior to the arrival of Elisha, Gehazi has already attempted to resuscitate the child by using Elisha's staff, as instructed, but to no avail. Isolating himself with the boy, Elisha first prays and then, placing himself over the child, "put[s] his mouth on his mouth, his eyes on his eyes, and his hands on his hands." This is an act of ultimate identification with the victim, and it is successful: the boy comes back to life. When the Shunamite woman returns at Elisha's call (again conveyed by Gehazi!), she once more falls at Elisha's feet, but this time in grateful acknowledgment of his powers. She bows low to the ground, then she picks up her son and leaves. Not a word is spoken; no song of praise is sung.

What we have here is a mother's more extreme response to loss of her son. The Shunamite simply refuses to accept being deprived of the child that God (through his prophet) had promised her. It is as if she were saying, "Sorry, but you just can't take away what you gave me! Although I lacked a son, I did not ask for one. It was you, through your prophet, who recognized my desires. Unasked, you fulfilled them. You cannot go back on your word. I WILL NOT LET YOU!" Of the three parents, she is the most extreme and defiant.

Both Hannah and the Shunamite are devout and God-fearing women, comparable in their respective ways to Abraham himself. Yet, unlike him, neither of them readily surrenders the child God has granted her. Hannah maintains a touching relationship with Samuel despite the physical separation that results from the fulfillment of her vow; the Shunamite compels God to return the son he has taken from her.

From their response, we may perhaps deduce how Sarah would have responded had her faith, rather than that of her husband, been tested by a demand to sacrifice her child. Mothers do not willingly give up their sons, even when God demands such a sacrifice. Implicit in these stories is Judaism's awareness (and that of the Jewish God) that a mother's love is essentially different from that of a father.

PART II

Socioeconomics, Politics, and Authority

CHAPTER **4**

Woman Rabbi in Spiritual Leadership

Rabbi Lynn Gottlieb

A "woman" rabbi has her own stories to tell. Why shouldn't she? Once people recover from the initial shock of encountering a "woman" rabbi, the term "rabbi" kicks in and stimulates certain preordained responses in the psyche of all Jews. If I happen to be the first rabbi they've seen since their Bar Mitzvah, I turn into a confessional booth. Jews expect rabbis to listen.

Rabbi, do you know why I quit being kosher and started eating pork during World War II? Rabbi, do you want to know how much I hated my Hebrew school teacher? Rabbi, I have been practicing Buddhism for thirty years, but I celebrate Hannukah; am I still Jewish? Rabbi, what do you think of circumcision? Rabbi, where was God during the Holocaust? Rabbi, does a bug in the salad really make it *traif* (unfit to eat or use according to Jewish dietary law)? Rabbi, have you heard the joke about the priest and the rabbi? And, rabbi, what do you call the husband of a woman rabbi?

Confusion over proper descriptive terminology for a "woman" rabbi and the spouse of a woman rabbi uncovers the anxiety and slight displacement people may feel when interacting with women in roles traditionally held by men, or gays and lesbians in roles traditionally held by straight people, or people of color in roles traditionally held by those defined as racially white. Over the last three decades, most women rabbis have settled on the masculine term "rabbi" to describe themselves. There seems to be a consensus against using a term that differs from the one used to describe male rabbis, regardless of the incorrectness of the grammar. We have struggled for acceptance of women in this role and do not want to diminish our position by having a separate title that may encourage some in our community to see us as less than equal. I find a good deal of irony in our use of the masculine form of identification so that we can maintain a sense of our equality.

How many generations will pass before what to call us is no longer an issue? One gauge is the attitude people possess toward women in spiritual leadership. When women who defy conventional norms regarding "appropriate" gender behavior become targets of negative speech, even if they assert leadership in a feminine way, such as educator of young children, then prejudice is still present. Pushy, bossy, hysterical, overbearing, naïve, and a host of other epithets may accrue to women who assert knowledge and authority.

Hannah Rochel Werbermacher (1805–1892) lived her life as a Hasidic *rebbe*, or rabbi. Her story sheds light on what it was like for one of the first women in Jewish history to assume the rabbinic role. By telling her story, perhaps we can measure how far we have come and how far we still have to go to achieve gender parity. Her story is highly defined by her contemporaries' reaction to her gender. Hannah Rochel Werbermacher of Ludomir, in Ukraine, was treated as rebbe by thousands of regular Jews of all stripes who consistently showed up to receive her teachings and blessings for sixty years. She attained this position, in part, because of the expanded status of women in Hasidic circles (Zolty, p. 247). Women were welcomed at the courts of rebbes and *tzaddikim* (righteous people), and many achieved leadership status in ways that exceeded their sisters in the non-Hasidic religious world. There has always existed a cadre of exceptional women throughout the Jewish world who became scholars because they were daughters of scholarly men who married scholarly husbands. On the other hand, they were not given permission to overtake the spiritual authority of men. Hannah Rochel fits this portrait, and yet she took her role beyond the boundaries acceptable for women in her day. As a result, the Maid (Virgin) of Ludomir, as she came to be known, endured a very strange episode.

My accidental place in history brought awareness of her story to my attention. We intersected as sites around which the question of the nature of women in spiritual leadership was tested and explored. We both had access to amazing male teachers who encouraged us and devoted our studies to the inner pathways of Judaism. Neither of us remained in a marriage to men for very long. The following narrative is a storyteller's account of a real experience that illuminates women rabbis in spiritual leadership in the

1980s. For a more historical account of Hannah Rochel's life, other Jewish women scholars, and "proto" rabbis, consult Shoshana Pantel Zolty's book *And All Your Children Shall Be Learned: Women and the Study of Torah in Jewish Law and History.*

Since my arrival at the first—since the Holocaust—Yiddish Theatre and Music Festival in Amsterdam in November 1985, I have been a continuous topic of conversation. This occasion provides the first opportunity for many of the European *klezmorim* (wedding musicians) and actors to meet a woman rabbi. Each day starts with eight o'clock coffee in the dining area of our modest hotel, progresses into dozens of workshops and performances, and culminates with midnight forays into Amsterdam's night life for Indonesian food, music, and beer. Even though none of us goes to sleep before two A.M., we can't resist getting up early to enjoy the first opportunity for compelling camaraderie over continental breakfast—an in-gathering of Jews getting their schmooze on. I'm sitting a table away from Elsie.

"So nu, what do you call the husband of a rabbi?"

All within earshot turn their heads toward Elsie's question. A lively Talmudic bout of *pilpul* (a contentious style of argumentation about the detailed meaning of Talmud) ensues among thirty or so groggy but creatively dressed Yiddish klezmorim, cantors, actors, dancers, scholars, and dramaturges from Vilnius to London, New York to Tel Aviv. What Jew can hear a question like that and not jump in?

"Ha, the husband of a rabbi is something new under the sun. Ecclesiastes is wrong!" insists the atheist from Russia who already possesses a reputation for disputing the accuracy of the Bible as often as possible. Yiddish, English, French, Dutch, Hebrew, Russian, and Polish opinions fly around the room but don't alight on the question of whether women rabbis have a right to exist. That issue seems to be settled for the moment. Here I sit drinking coffee in the flesh. Most Jews inaugurate their relationship with me with a test to my scholarship or examination of my credentials. At the moment, my fellow artists are still fixated on my physical characteristics. One of the Vilnius crowd, the production manager, inquires whether my waist-long hair is for religious purposes. An elder violin player jokingly offers me money to cut it off so he can wear it as a beard. Another wonders why I haven't donated my hair to cancer victims, how long it took to grow, and if it I have *payot,* or side locks.

"The husband of a rabbi is called *rebbetzer,*" I announce, making up a term there on the spot to change the subject, so unleashing a flurry of counter opinions. One of the dancers from France prefers *rabbiner,* without the "tz" sound, but a musician from Amsterdam corrects him. "Rabbiner applies only to the female gender case." A musician from California inserts his ardent belief that the husband of a rabbi should not be given a title "so he can just be himself without all the expectations." He sounds like many wives of male rabbis I know from the States who also refuse to play the role. No one in the breakfast crowd considers the possibility of lesbian or gay rebbetzin/rebbetzers, so I educate my comrades about their existence and throw another length of cloth over the discussion of gender-appropriate language.

"Have you ever heard of the Maid of Ludomir? She refused to marry altogether." Finished with her tea, Elsie introduces the story of the first woman rebbe, Hannah Rochel Werbermacher. She lights a cigarette that dangles between maroon nails on fingers bedecked with thick gold rings. A henna-colored and highly coifed hairdo sits atop her brightly painted face. She radiates the gutsiness of an accomplished life in spite of spending the war in Auschwitz.

Elsie takes a puny puff from her cigarette and spits it back into the air; the entire room turns in her direction. We are ready for a story. The version I am about to tell you is an elaboration of the tale I remember hearing over breakfast. Memory itself is an art form, a creative act that reformulates the past and places it in a narrative framework that may have nothing to do with what actually happened. In this case, the event happened, but I have since researched Hannah Rochel's story and thought about its meaning. I identify with Hannah Rochel's struggle, which, for me, is an indicator of the long way we have come, as well as the distance that still lies before us on the road to gender equality.

"Hannah Rochel, what an amazing story!" Elsie edits her own narrative as she goes. The Virgin Maid suffered a lot over her decision to act like a rebbe. And who would have expected her to become one? Hannah grew up as a normal Jewish girl, the only daughter of an otherwise childless but wealthy couple living in Ukraine. Her father, a follower of Rabbi Mordecai Twerski of Chernobyl, gives her a good Jewish education and allows her to study Torah with him, as he has no sons.

When Hannah is 14, her mother dies. In a state of grief, Hannah runs to the cemetery, throws herself into her mother's open grave, and remains there overnight, weeping and praying. When her distraught father finds her in the morning lying in the open pit, Hannah Rochel is in a coma. For weeks the young girl lingers on the border of life and death. When she awakes, Hannah Rochel announces she has a new soul, the soul of an *admor,* a Hasidic rebbe. She breaks off her engagement to the love of her life, starts wearing *tzitzit* and *tefillin* (prayer shawl and phylacteries) as did Michal, the daughter of Saul, and performs *mitzvot* (commandments) like a man. She doesn't stop there. Hannah Rochel builds herself a house, where she teaches disciples Torah behind a curtain, receives *kvitlech* (prayer requests), and presides weekly over the third meal of the Sabbath, where she spins stories, sings *niggunim* (wordless melodies), and distributes *shirayim* (leftovers) from her plate to her Hasidim who consider her crumbs a blessing. Hannah Rochel used to say, "Sometimes, when your heart is so pained that it feels as if it must burst, let it burst!" That's because so many of her disciples were from the impoverished class of *Yidden* (Jews).

Hannah Rochel's popularity grew and multiplied year by year. An uproar of biblical proportions was brewing among the rabbinic establishment. At first they considered her a minor aberration. But now, thousands of yidden journey to Ludomir to learn at her holy table. What does this mean? When Shabbtai Tzvi, may his memory be forgotten, wanted to force the coming of the Messiah, he started calling women up to bless the Torah (*aliyahs*). God forbid, and look what came of that! Was the same madness infecting hopeless Jews with impossible dreams?

One night the chief rebbe of Chernobyl dreams that heaven is also in an uproar. A woman rebbe? Angels, prophets, and patriarchs cluster around the Holy Throne clamoring for an explanation. What could this mean? Has the Messiah come? If so, why is the golden bird still in her nest? Satan, the ironically witted prosecuting attorney, seizes the opportunity and whispers into the ear of the chief Hasidic rabbi: Bring charges against her. She is wearing the clothes of a woman yet pretending to be a man. Does this not violate the Torah? The chief rabbi awakes the next morning with a headache. He orders his disciples to bring the Maid of Ludomir to his court, where he intends to arrange a trial. Enough nonsense. Such irresponsible behavior could start a precedent! Women everywhere will refuse to obey the orders of their husbands. Soon the daughters of Israel will roam freely in the streets. No one will discern the difference between men and women. The world will return to original chaos. The Jewish world will go to ruin! "Bring her now!"

But what will the *bet din* (court) charge her with? Impersonating a rabbi? She is not serving as a judge or showing her face in public. She teaches behind a curtain in her own *shul* (school) to preserve her modesty, and there are no laws preventing a woman from teaching. The chief rabbi himself believes that women should learn that which applies to them! He knows that the sages remained silent on the matter of Michal, daughter of Saul, wearing *tallit* (a fringed shawl) and tefillin, thus implicitly granting her approval. It is too late to render Hannah's vow null and void? How, then, should he proceed? No one in the heavenly chamber knows what to do either. The Judge of Judges is not available for comment.

On the appointed day, Hannah Rochel, the Maid of Ludomir, walks down the main street of Chernobyl to Reb Mordecai's shul followed by her disciples and half the population of Ukraine. Onlookers crowded around the door of the shul divide into factions. Hannah Rochel's disciples regard the holy virgin as a miracle, a sign from The Holy One that the Shechinah herself is with them. A rabbi's soul in a woman's body! Perhaps this is the first footstep of the Messiah! Others compare this phenomenon to the curse of the false Messiah Shabbtai Tzvi. An entire generation fooled by a charlatan who called women to the Torah!

The majority of villagers, however, take a more practical approach. If the Messiah decides to show up that day to make a point, well and good. People have to eat. Housewives set up stalls along the main street and sell roasted almonds, raisins, bread, and hot tea. Farmers with goats, chickens, and cows hawk milk and eggs; water carriers, woodcutters, and rag sellers sing out their songs, innkeepers haul barrels of beer out of the cellar, fiddlers play for food. Such a commotion! And on a Tuesday when, normally, the only excitement is waking up and eating borscht.

Elsie pauses and everyone breathes out. She exchanges tea for coffee and fills her plate with an overweight cheese blintze that drips over the side of the plate. "What a great scene! What theater!" She can't resist commenting on her own story.

As people shove and push their way into the shul in anticipation of hearing Hannah Rochel defend herself, Reb Mordecai is struck with the realization that he cannot allow her to open her mouth in public. If he permits Hannah Rochel to speak before the whole community, he is unintentionally opening the door to the possibility that she may convince people that she actually possesses the soul of a rebbe, and then even more people will become her disciples.

He tries a different tack. "Hannah Rochel, dear orphan, bereft of your mother at such a young age, you have our sincere sympathy. It is known that the evil urge can enter a human soul during times of great grief. I have determined through prayer and fasting and on the advice of heaven, that at the moment of your mother's death, another entity did indeed enter your body. However, this spirit did not come from the pure soul of a deceased admor. By the authority of heaven, I pronounce this spirit a *dybbuk* [wandering soul]. And not just any dybbuk, but the perverse dybbuk of Moshe Wassermann, a known heretic who cut off his beard when he moved to Warsaw!" The crowd gasps and the rebbe seizes the moment to turn the crowd against her. Because the rebbe accusing her is her beloved father's personal rebbe, she is momentarily stunned by his remark.

"And so Hannah Rochel, dear orphan, the best way to banish the dybbuk from your body is to get married! That is the only way to banish this evil spirit from your body and soul." He lowers his voice to a whisper. The crowd leans forward. "A male dybbuk will not tolerate the presence of another man inside you, Hannah Rochel, and that is the only way to banish this spirit from your body and return you to a normal state." The rebbe believes that once she has sex with a man, the male dybbuk will leave her body. "The holy act of consummating your marriage will 'restore' the natural balance of creation. Do not think of this as any form of punishment for what has previously taken place, dear sister. That is the last thing on my mind. After all, your father was my friend and disciple. I am acting out of deep concern for your welfare and your future. Hannah Rochel, you must submit to marriage to rid yourself of this evil dybbuk and assume your rightful place as a Mother in Israel."

Before Hannah opens her mouth to defend herself, the entire community yells out its agreement. Marriage seems like a good solution to a very strange occurrence. Besides, marriage is normal for a woman, as opposed to telling people you're a rebbe. Who does she think she is? The holy sages in their great wisdom teach us that although Deborah and Hulda were prophets, it was held against them. At least they appeared at times in Jewish history when they were needed. At this time, reason the Jews of Chernobyl, no such crisis exists. Life goes on as usual around here. There is no need for a girl rebbe. There are already plenty of male rabbis, are there not? The assembled congregation does not give her the opportunity to speak one word, and she is forced to leave without having uttered a sound.

The rebbe has already picked out a husband for the aging virgin, and the marriage date is set one week hence. Hannah Rochel returns to her room behind the curtain and refuses to talk to anyone. Her disciples also retreat for fear of being accused as heretics, Sabbateans, or worse, perverts. Constant pressure to marry from her father's own teacher Reb Mordecai and the abandonment of her disciples cause Hannah Rochel to doubt. Perhaps, she thinks, they are correct. "Perhaps I am possessed by a dybbuk."

When the day arrives to execute the nuptial agreement, Hannah Rochel awakens in the darkness. Doubts plague her mind and she feels like she's being forced to eat wormwood. As the sun makes visible the day, elder women enter her house to escort her to the *mikvah* (ritual bath) and prepare her for marriage. Inside the humble wooden bathhouse, bald women with rough hands remove her scarf, take off her clothes, shave off her long hair, cut her nails, and inspect her body. Hannah Rochel's jet black hair falls to the ground like broken stalks of wheat. Naked and ashamed, Hannah prays as she descends the steps of the mikvah and dips her body into the cold water. "Answer me, she screams, answer me!" The elder women ignore her cry and mumble instructions about wifely duties, when to be touched and when to avoid touching, all the while wondering if they will see the dybbuk leave her body.

Slowly, the women dress the matron bride and veil her face. Reb Mordecai himself greets her at the door of the bathhouse to accompany her like a father to the *chuppah* (bridal canopy). Hannah Rochel follows Reb Mordecai out the door, touches the silver *mezuzah*, and walks silently down the main street of town packed with curious onlookers. The holy virgin endures smirks and stares until she passes through the synagogue door and is led to a small chamber, where the chosen groom lifts her veil. She stares into a weary bearded face and recognizes the aged widow with five children who has been assigned the deflowering task. He winces slightly and then manages a kindly smile. Yes, this is my bride, he announces. They sign papers. In silence she walks down the aisle to her groom under the chuppah, circles him seven times, and receives the ring, all the while her lips moving in a silent prayer. After the festivities the newlyweds are ushered into a private room with a bed, but as the hours pass it becomes known to the entire community that Hannah Rochel refuses to consummate the marriage. Reb Mordecai dispatches one of the elder women to instruct the shy bride about sex, but all she finds in the marital suite is a desolate bridegroom sitting on the edge of the marital bed weeping into his hands. Hannah Rochel has vanished.

The town spreads out looking for her, but she is nowhere to be found. With the cleverness of Rivkeh, Hannah speaks softly to the groom, strokes his hand, and asks for his permission to go and prepare herself for the holy act. He gives the first and last permission to his wife in his short-lived marriage to descend the stairs and take another mikvah in private. Hannah Rochel takes the back stairs, travels on the path behind the shul to her house, where she gathers up her most precious books, packs her mother's candlesticks, her tallit and tefillin, hitches her own wagon, and rides out of town in a southerly direction. After several months of worry and wondering, the Jews of Chernobyl receive word that the Maid of Ludomir is living in the holy city of Jerusalem teaching Torah on Rosh Hodesh by the grave of Rachel and has accumulated a large following.

One day in the month of Elul on her way to Rachel's Tomb, Hannah Rochel meets a kabbalist on the road who sees in her the embodiment of the Shechinah. He convinces her that together they can pray in perfect harmony, unite the Kadosh Baruch Hu to the Shechinah, and thus bring the Messiah. She promises to join the mysterious stranger on three days before Rosh Hashanah at a certain cave in the hills of Jerusalem to fast and pray until they both feel the pangs of the Messiah. On the agreed-upon day, Hannah Rochel sets out to bring the suffering of exile to an end. On the way, however, one of her disciples begs her to help him with a personal problem, and she is delayed. When she arrives at the cave, the stranger is not there. Hannah Rochel enters, lights a penny candle, finds a place in the darkness, and begins to pray for the redemption of the world; but the stranger never appears, and she realizes the moment has passed.

As she sits and meditates on these things, a realization wells up inside her. She can bring comfort and peace to Jerusalem even without the Messiah, just as she has done her entire life. Like Yohanan Ben Zakai, she will continue planting seeds, inspire them to grow, water them with hope and vision, and tend them to fruition. Hannah Rochel has already witnessed several generations of her students grow to become people of compassion and grace. She is grateful for the gift of spirit that has blessed and healed so many lives. Hannah Rochel rises from her place and returns to the grave of her namesake, Mother Rachel, to spend the rest of her days teaching her disciplines that creating peace in our own hearts, and in the life of our community, is the greatest principle of the Torah. Blessed by a spiritual life, Hannah Rochel lives well into her eighties. She is buried in the land that gave rise to so many prophets. "Perhaps," remarks Elsie, "her prayers and teachings were successful, and the time of the Messiah is upon us, for look, there is something new under the sun, a woman rabbi sits among us and women are now equal to men."

The tiny crowd of Jews eating breakfast in Amsterdam nod their heads. A young Jewish woman from Germany adds, "After the Holocaust how can we afford not to have women rabbis? We live in a time when every Jew counts, every Jew is needed. It will take all of us, men and women, boys and girls, to restore us to our rightful place and banish the ghosts of genocide that wander the land. If a woman knows Torah, let her teach!" I have just been given the 614th commandment. If a woman knows Torah, let her teach.

* * *

Within several decades of Hannah Rochel's death, another Jewish woman would rise up with the passion to be a rabbi. In 1935, the same year Nuremberg's racist laws were imposed upon the Jewish community of Germany, Regina Jonas initiated her rabbinic career. Ordination was conferred upon her by the liberal rabbi Max Dinnemann in the city of Offenbach. Regina was thirty-two years old. No one accused Rabbiner Regina Jonas of being possessed by a dybbuk. Nonetheless, she too was bombarded with the question of what to call her. People referred to her as Mrs. Rabbi (even though she was not married) as well as Miss Rabbi. German Jews could also not decide whether to use the masculine or feminine form of the word: in her case *rabbiner* or *rabbinerin*. In spite of the confusion over what to call her and where to allow her to serve, she was destined to shepherd her people through one of the greatest tragedies of Jewish history. Unfortunately, Rabbiner Regina Jonas became a rabbi during the period in which Germany murdered two-thirds of the Jews of Europe, approximately six million people. Despite the violence of the times, Rabbiner Jonas struggled to secure the right of women to enter the rabbinic profession for the first time in thirty-five hundred years of Jewish history. She authored the first rabbinic treatise titled "Can Women Serve as Rabbis according to Halakhic Sources?" the subject of the thesis that was accepted as the final requirement for ordination. For her it was not a theoretical question. By working as an ordained rabbi from December 25, 1935, to her death on December 12, 1944, she answered the question in the affirmative, thus paving the way for those of us who came after her.

Even though she was never assigned a formal congregation, Regina's professional life encompassed a wide range of activities, including spiritual counseling; cultural innovation; ceremonial leadership; scholarly research and writing; religious education; chaplaincy service at hospitals, old age homes, and a school of the deaf; spiritual resistance to Nazism; and the promotion of Jewish women in leadership. Regina Jonas helped define the scope of activity for women in spiritual leadership within the Jewish community. She challenged the notion of woman's sphere and the social convention that woman's value lay in her "natural" reproductive and domestic function as mother and wife, for neither of these aspects played a major role in her life. She devoted herself almost entirely to her profession.

Rabbiner Regina Jonas rejected the idea that women's place was limited to the private realm and subject to the control of men, a view popular in Aryanism of the period. The Nazi regime promoted motherhood and housework as spiritually elevated and, at the same time, the only sanctioned role for women. In the case of Nazism this biological concept of womanhood existed within the project of their genocidal racism. Germany engaged in eugenics (the so-called hereditary improvement of human beings through selective breeding), a psuedo-science that was put into practice by forced sterilization of non-Aryan populations as well as Aryans considered unfit or unworthy of producing life. Individuals categorized as mentally ill, alcoholic, or impoverished and the so-called morally deficient, such as prostitutes, were either sterilized or murdered. It was in this climate that Regina overcame childhood poverty and struggled for the right to be a woman rabbi for the sake of educating and uplifting the Jewish people. Rabbiner Regina Jonas's life is a shining example of the creativity, tenacity, courage, and intellectual capacity of a Jewish woman committed to spiritual leadership. She pioneered the dismantling of millennial barriers to women's equal participation in Jewish life while her people were being slaughtered by the millions.

Yet, the record of Regina Jonas's life was buried for a half century. Famous male Jewish sages and intellectuals such as Leo Baeck and Victor Frankel, who knew her, admired her, and even ordained her, did not record one detail of Regina's life in any of their writings or mention her in their oral presentations. The next generation of women rabbis arose fifty years after her death without the benefit of being nurtured by her courageous struggle or by her considerable scholarship in behalf of women and, indeed, the whole Jewish community. When the Berlin Wall fell and the archives of East Germany were opened, many researchers took up the task of uncovering what had previously been hidden. Regina's papers were discovered in 1991 in a small archive in East Germany by a Christian theologian named Dr. Katerina Von Kellenbach, a researcher and lecturer at St. Mary's College in Maryland. In an amazing turn of history, Dr. Von Kellenbach, whose uncle was tried for crimes against the Polish Jewish population of Pinsk, devoted her scholarly research to challenging the new wave of anti-Jewish expression emerging in German Protestant feminism and to uncovering the way in which the Christian doctrine of forgiveness was used to avoid dealing with Germany's Nazi past. On this occasion, Dr. Von Kellenbach was researching the Protestant and Jewish establishments' attitudes toward women seeking ordination in Germany during the period before World War II when she uncovered an envelope in which all of Regina's papers were stored. Jonas's romantic interest, one Rabbi Joseph Nordin, had placed her papers there three days before he was deported to Theresienstadt.

Regina Jonas's historical obscurity reflects the challenge those of us who first entered rabbinic life faced—no knowledge of those who came before us. The records of women's achievements and activities have been deleted from our collective knowledge base, sometimes within a single lifetime. The Jewish historical and spiritual narrative has been constructed without placing women in the house of memory. When women do surface on the page, it is often as a sidebar or supplement to the stories and interests of men. Male leaders are given credit for events and creative acts that were, in fact, initiated by women. Whether it is the invention of agriculture or the impetus for the exodus from Egypt and other liberation struggles, women's contributions are often co-opted, used against them, dismissed, disparaged, made invisible, or narrowed in scope. Erasing women's historical imprint stems from the still powerful impulse to assign primary status to men. The millennium-long rendering of economic, social, political, and religious advantage based on male-gender privilege known as "sexism" adds tremendous weight to our struggle for liberation. The system of male-gender privilege is maintained through physical and emotional violence, legal coercion, denial of access to public space, and the value given to the past over the present, a past heavily endowed with male privilege.

As we uncover the shards of forgotten stories, our hearts rejoice at this newfound treasure. Yet, to the next generation of woman rabbis, the loss of Regina Jonas's contribution meant that those of us who entered the profession early on had no role models. If only we had been privy to Regina Jonas's rabbinic thesis, which foreshadowed all the discussions that occurred during the first decade of my own professional life, 1973 to 1984, when arguments for and against women rabbis were flying over the tops of many traditional fences. In her thesis Regina Jonas carefully reviewed all the relevant materials in a way that demonstrated in her mind that no serious *halakhic* reasons—that is, reasons pertaining to scriptural law—existed preventing women from studying and teaching Torah. Although she emphasized the role of *zniut* (modesty regarding the role of women), doing so did not stop her from declaring that the many tasks that rabbis must undertake are permitted, including being an expert in written and oral Torah, an accomplished teacher of both children and adults, a preacher in the synagogue and at Jewish life-cycle ceremonies, a decision maker (*posek*) in Jewish legal matters, an overseer of marriage and divorce (with kosher witnesses present), a pastoral counselor and spiritual guide, a mediator of conflicts, an advocate for communal welfare including youth, and an exemplar of Jewish living.

In the case of Regina Jonas, it has been mostly women scholars and researchers who have brought attention to her life and work. In fact, the majority of works that concern women are still researched and written by women. Women are still more invested than are men in bringing to light and analyzing female production in all fields. This is true of women in spiritual leadership who feel it is incumbent upon us to continue to lift up women's lives as we transmit our tradition to our children and unknown female and male descendants. There is always the chance that our efforts, like the efforts of so many others, will be forgotten by history unless we mainstream women's lives into the way all academic, artistic, religious, and social disciplines are passed on to the next generation.

The lack of historical consciousness around female contribution was a major concern of the first generation of women rabbis and scholars. We realized that much of the history of Jewish women was either invisible or framed in social messages that, in some cases, we found damaging to the project of our own liberation. Jewish tradition exists in a religious system in which women's voices are scarce. Only three women are mentioned by name in the Talmud in comparison to hundreds of male names and the stories that go with them. Women are disadvantaged in their efforts to dismantle Jewish male privilege because they do not enjoy the long chain of memory and tradition that has been established in relationship to the wisdom of men. The influence of Jewish women scholars in the project of restoration is significant. From Ellen Umansky's important work documenting one of the first "unofficial" women rabbis, that is, Lilly Montagu, to the more recent listing of one hundred Jewish women leaders from 600 BCE to 1900 CE by Emily Taitz, Sondra Henry, and Cheryl Tallan, women who are interested in Jewish women's contributions to Jewish life past and present continue to sort through the memory boxes of our tradition to uncover the treasurers that lie within. In addition, we can count on the record of significant sages in Jewish tradition who supported women's education and honored the women from whom they learned. Yet, we continue to perpetuate female absence. Women are still catalogued as a supplemental or separate topic in most presentations of Jewish learning. Our bodies may be present in the room, our names may be a paragraph or even a chapter in a book, but what we collectively teach has not yet fully redressed the structural situation of our missing piece. Part of our role as rabbis is the task of integrating women's history into mainstream accounts, a task that remains largely unfinished in every field of Jewish study. Obviously, researching the lives of women is also not the only interest of women who engage in Jewish scholarship and spiritual leadership. Our field of interest is as broad and wide as the men with whom we share our tradition.

At the same time women rabbis recover what is lost and prune and transform sexist elements of our tradition, we are also deeply invested in preserving Jewish traditions that have been a source of nourishment and beauty in our lives. Navigating the currents of preservation and transformation is both challenging and inspiring. Which aspects of Jewish collective wisdom shall we maintain and which shall we lay aside? Although sorting through the past in order to adequately respond to the needs of the present is not a new position for Jewish leadership, it is the first time that women are so intimately involved with the task. Regina's life demonstrates the tension inherent in the work of innovators who assume a culturally conservative role in order to gain access to the communities they wish to influence.

Strategies used by cultural innovators to justify and claim the rightness of their efforts are diverse. Convincing her community that women could assume a role traditionally held by men, Regina distinguishes between what she dismisses as idiosyncratic prejudices of certain rabbis whom she calls "the minority" and the stronger, broader opinions reflected by "the majority," which values women and their wisdom as it appears in the texts of Torah, Talmud, Midrash, and Halakha. Regina claims the anti-woman minority are quoted by the text to highlight the more pro-woman, rational view of the majority, and she supports her thesis with such stories as the Beruria cycle. She claims, as do most innovators, that the seeds of innovation are already present within the very tradition they critique. In the contemporary period, the work of Tikva Frymer-Kensky, Judith Hauptman, and Judith Antonelli illustrate this approach. In their case, they promote the value of Jewish tradition by saying Jews have always behaved better toward women than have surrounding cultures in any given time because at the core of Jewish tradition, we embrace the principle of liberation theology, which holds an essentially positive view of womanhood. Stories of the midwives, Deborah, Miriam, Hannah, Ruth, and the five daughters of Zelophad are used to prove this point, in addition to the progressive nature of halakhic law toward women. Other scholars are less inhibited about revealing the second-class position that Jewish women hold in Jewish society by detailing the ways in which women's lives are circumscribed by law, custom, and social standing. Their approach is to articulate sexism clearly without apology in order to advance women's rights. Judith Baskin, Judith Plaskow, and Aviva Cantor are examples of this approach. The tension between apologetics and dismantling sexism remains an active force in the lives of women in spiritual leadership.

The recovery of Regina's lifework, along with a proper positioning of her importance in the legacy of Jewish wisdom traditions, is a first step in a more accurate picture of women's part in shaping Jewish history. After her death almost fifty years passed until the next woman was ordained a rabbi in Israel. My own story is part of the next wave. Although I did not know that Regina Jonas existed in the world, her struggle to become a rabbi paved the way for me and many others. To honor Regina I have created a historical *midrash* (interpretation) based on her own words: her last sermon given to the Jews of Terezin on the eve of their deportation to Auschwitz. May their memories be a blessing.

These are the generations of Regina Jonas. Rabbiner Jonas lived forty years. She begot many disciples, although at first they did not recognize her, for she lived as one of the thirty-six hidden ones who walk with Shechinah and willingly offer their hearts to those in need. For that reason, the world continues to exist.

The eve of their deportation to Auschwitz, Regina faces a massive crowd of concentration camp Jews clamoring to hear the singular voice so many people find odd, even dangerous. Every Jew in Germany, from the culturally assimilated to the extravagantly pious, spews forth contested opinions, contemptuous dismissals, and abrupt denials as to whether Frauline Rabbiner Regina Jonas's only goal is to show herself off to men, whether her argument that women can be rabbis is a cold cup of coffee, whether her ordination is genuine, and even whether she may decide what kind of clothes she should wear, let alone what they should call her. Among the *Juden* (Jews) of Berlin, Regina's green velvet dress with puffy sleeves and the removable extension generates more commentary than twenty tractates of Talmud. Among the Juden of Terezin there is more acceptance of her activities, since there is a shortage of rabbis and she is a recognized *seelsorger*—one who ministers spiritual salve to wounded souls.

Regina is momentarily distracted by a frayed thread hanging from the inner band of her black hat, and rather than curl it around her finger and pluck it off, she tucks it behind her ear. She likes her rabbinic hat and has managed to keep it on her head during the past two years of living in Theresienstadt. Each night, Regina removes the head covering she wore to her ordination and places it by the crown of her head on the third level of the bunk bed where she sleeps. In the hour before dawn, she rises from the wooden platform, puts her hat in her pocket, slowly descends to the ground floor, does her business outside, washes her hands with the dampened kerchief tied to her wrist, and dons her rabbinic hat with the same prayerful devotion as men who wrap tefillin. She prays that God give her the same strength bestowed upon Esther and Deborah, who served their people in perilous times. Every day Regina wears her hat when visiting the elderly, teaching Torah to children, lecturing in the evening. On the days a transport arrives, Regina assumes her role as seelsorger, caregiver to the soul. She stands next to the camp's most important dignitary, Paul Eppstein, head of the *Judenrat* (Jewish Council), who wears a dark-wool ankle-length dress coat, a snappy paisley silk scarf, and a hat as he offers the official welcome. He is fond of saying, "Here in Theresienstadt we implement ideas, find the good in the bad, lay the groundwork for a new life for all of us," failing to mention he is the one who decides whose name shall be placed on the Daily Order, the list of those chosen for liquidation. Germans appoint Jews for that task; and while they are in Theresienstadt, Jews compete for access to those with the authority to decide their sorry fate. Eppstein places his hands behind his back and, with the erect posture of officialdom and a crisp nod of his head, wishes new arrivals, "Good morning" or "Good afternoon, welcome to the city of Terezin." He refuses to call Terezin a prison or the inmates prisoners, preferring the word "pioneer," believing as he does that Theresienstadt will be given to Jews after the war as a self-ruling enclave in the midst of Europe.

Regina is not so sure. In any case, it is she who takes the new arrivals' trembling hands in her own, helps them carry their meager possessions from Eppstein's island of stoic optimism to the overcrowded, vermin-infested city of starvation known as The Fortress. Some *Yidden* (variation of "Jews") think they are coming to a spa, have even paid high prices for the tickets to get here, and so expect to sleep in a private room. Instead, the flesh of one hundred ninety corpses burns in the crematorium daily to make room for more of the recently damned. Regina greets endless waves of tormented souls traumatized by dislocation, death of family members, vermin infestation, extreme filth, starvation, typhus, and horrific stress, such as the stress of seeing hundreds of Bialystok orphaned children herded screaming and crying into a cattle car bound for Auschwitz while you could do nothing. Nothing. She has taken on the burden of lifting up their souls, kindling a tiny spark of hope, sharing a small measure of their overwhelming grief.

Even a suburb in hell is better than the devil's own house. In spite of the fact that Terezin is a concentration camp, some Jews thought being deported here had its advantages. It wasn't Auschwitz. The masters of propaganda already sold the world on their beneficence regarding the prominent Jews of Germany. "Terezin: Germany's model ghetto" was a veritable showcase of famous Yidden, an entire sardine-can full of brilliant cultural entrepreneurs, diplomats, scientists, lawyers, rabbis, psychologists, sociologists, doctors, intellectuals, artists, conductors, a few Zionists, and the world's first woman rabbi in history. The indomitable Jews of Terezin lend credence to the stereotype of Jewish brilliance by producing classical orchestras, jazz ensembles, chamber groups, puppet shows, theater productions, art exhibits, magazines, and evening lectures, all held in secret rooms and assembly halls after long days of forced labor spraying protective covering on Nazi uniforms, stacking covers, and riveting, and all this on a starvation diet.

Outsiders like the Red Cross think the Jews of Terezin live in houses with red flowers. For insiders, reality does not suffer much illusion. Flowers or no flowers, when dawn stains the grey stones of Terezin, they pick up the dead.

Tonight Regina faces her community as she has dozens of times throughout her career, to give a talk about life and religion. Only tonight is different. The final decree has been delivered by Eppstein, and there is little chance for escape. She will not leave her mother, and so her fate is sealed. Trains await on tracks unbroken, guns are pointed at innocents as the world sleeps. But they are awake. Tonight, the committee that is in charge of lectures, concerts, and community events has assigned her the task of bolstering their spirits before they embark. Like Hannah, who watched her seven sons die before her eyes, Regina too must witness the death of those whose spirits she has tended with utmost care and love. She too must find the inner strength to bear an unspeakable sorrow and lift up the spark of hope hidden within. Like the Shechinah who watched the destruction of the Temple in Jerusalem and accompanied the people into the desolation of exile, she too must go with her people on their final journey, their last days.

The tremor in the crowd is palpable. She dabs her upper lip with the handkerchief tied around her wrist and struggles not to dissolve into tears. Thoughts of her murdered brother Abraham and her beloved Joseph wash over her. Joseph was always pleading with her, "Reynele, don't cry so much. You're like Leah. Your beautiful lashes will fall off from the amount of tears that pour from your eyes."

Regina takes advantage of the commotion her mere presence can stir up among Jews. She plans to lure them away from their crushing depression by introducing the topic of women's equality. She knows that a good argument is a faithful device for engaging Jews and hopes they can be led from there into a message of hope. Regina's faithfulness resides in her belief in the power of good residing in Jewish religion to overcome evil, even if they do not. She believes the eternal Jewish remnant will rise from the ashes of destruction to reconstitute Jewish life in the next generation.

The first woman rabbi parts her lips for her last public speech, although she imagines she will be comforting Jews in the cattle car, during the process of selection, and in the gas chamber even unto her very last breath:

My beloved friends. Let us not shed tears tonight, even though our hearts break. Instead, let us conduct ourselves as did our Talmudic sister Beruria, the brilliant wife of Rabbi Meir, who kept the death of her sons hidden from her husband during the Sabbath by telling him they were away. When the sun set, three stars appeared and the ritual of Havdalah performed, Meir wondered when his two boys would return home. Beruria responded by posing a rabbinic question to her husband, a question he would find familiar, a question that would allow him to be slightly irritated, since he loved to be challenged by his wife's razor-sharp mind, and this question he would find too simple. "Meir," said Beruria, "What if a person were loaned two precious jewels, and then after many years, the Master requested their return. Should the borrower give them back or, since he had grown to love them, keep them in his house?" Meir was indeed surprised by the simplicity of Beruria's question. "Why, you must return the jewels, of course, since they were only a loan. The job of the one who receives a loan is to use it wisely and then return it to the lender." Beruria touched the shoulder of her husband and said: "So it is with us. The Master came for his possessions in our keeping. Our two precious jewels have been taken back to the Master's house; our sons have been returned. Blessed is the one who gives and blessed is the one who takes away."

My friends, so it is with us. We are returning to the Master's House. In these times of fog and fire, we must have faith that our lives have not been lived in vain, that we are here for a purpose, the same purpose that has been our guiding light since the day we stood at Sinai, received our precious Torah, and pledged ourselves and our children to struggle for goodness and peace in the world. Even though we find ourselves abandoned without hope, let us comfort each other with words and deeds. Even though we struggle to survive in conditions of extreme cruelty the world cannot yet imagine, we remain determined to do good to others wherever we go. Sometimes, as we know, struggles lead us into darkness instead of light. And sometimes our struggles are not successful despite our best effort. But that is no reason to lose faith in our ancient calling to be a gentle people above all else. Spiritual leadership is given to those who are loyal to the struggle for goodness regardless of social rank or perceived national superiority.

Tonight, as I stand before you for the last time, I pray that we may be remembered, not for how we died, but for how we lived, as it is written in Torah of the death of righteous matriarch Sarah of blessed memory, she "lived one hundred and twenty-seven years."

And so tonight, I have decided to share with you one last time my opinion and the opinion of Jewish tradition regarding the issue so recently resolved among the people of Israel—can a woman serve as a rabbi? To this question, there is only one answer, and that answer is a resounding yes.

We have much to laud on account of the progress of women's rights in the Jewish community. May our achievements and our efforts to open the doors of equality for women in every area of life not have been in vain.

I acknowledge that my life has taken me on a road few could predict, given that I am the very first of my kind. So many of you have asked me again and again and in a hundred different ways why I didn't leave Germany before it was too late. I could have become rich and famous as the first woman rabbi in America, where they might put up with such an outlandish novelty as myself.

My friends, first let me assure you that it has meant more to me to have stayed in Germany than to leave you behind for my own personal fame and comfort. Besides, I could not leave my dear mother! To be with you here is the path I have chosen. As Ruth said to Naomi, "Do not ask me to leave you, for whither you go, I shall go, and wherever you lodge, I will lodge; your people shall be my people, your God my God; where you die, I shall die, and there I will be buried." Perhaps that is why God called me forth as a woman rabbi at this time, to walk with those I love in a time of abandonment and exile.

Most of you know I grew up in the horse barn district in Berlin among the very least of us, economically speaking. Scheunenviertel was a district of sex workers, gangs, and police raids flourishing in the midst of impoverished neighborhoods of pious Jews, most of us coming to Germany seeking shelter from pogroms and the harsh law of the Russian czar. We lived in crowded conditions, several families sharing a toilet located in the hallway or backyard. Seems like luxury now.

My family was Orthodox, but my father believed that women could and should study Torah. He did not abide the opinion of Rabbi Eliezer, who believed teaching women Torah was like teaching them to sin, or other sages who considered teaching women the Oral Torah was akin to teaching them frivolities. My father thought Eliezar's minority opinion was mentioned only to emphasize the correct position: that women can be

learned, and that there is no barrier to teaching them other than the prejudices of the time. I was naturally drawn to Torah study because of my father, Olov Hashalom, who, even after a long day of work, would light a
candle and study in the evening. As a very young child, I would sit at his
feet and listen. Soon, however, I began to ask questions, yes, more questions than even my brother Abraham used to ask! My father never pro-
tested or turned me away. Rather, he encouraged me just as the daughter
of Rabban Gamliel must have been encouraged when she boldly challenged Caesar himself to prove that women are just as precious in the eyes
of God as men. God has placed abilities and callings in our hearts without
regard to gender. Thus each of us has the duty, whether man or woman,
to realize those gifts God has given.

I wasn't the first woman to study Torah with her father. Otherwise, how
do you explain Rashi's daughters, or Beruria and Yalta, to name a famous few?
The great and learned Beruria cannot have possessed such enormous knowledge through simple listening or meager self-education. She was instructed like
the men and proved her superior reasoning time and time again.

Many women could have reached similar heights of knowledge had
they not clung overwhelmingly to the basic principle *"Ayn ishah ela leyofi,"*
a woman is only for beauty. Natural beauty is there with or without
makeup and fraudulent beautifiers. If a woman's spirit is exercised through
learning, her horizons are extended, her essence refined. To objectify ourselves as adornments to attract and satisfy men is to rob ourselves of more
spiritually motivated satisfaction and accomplishment.

Here in Theresienstadt women proved themselves worthy of great cultural accomplishments without the benefits of adornment. There is no longer any reason to hold us back.

Women have studied and learned because of our Scripture and its holy
regulations and the spirit of freedom that speaks through the texts. It must be
this spirit that speaks in favor of woman and that has an illuminating effect
on this question. It is the spirit of freedom that speaks through the text, that
enlivens the text, that gives meaning to the whole. It must be this spirit of liberation—the same spirit of liberation that caused our ancestors to rise up
against their unjust servitude—that speaks in favor of woman and on this
question of women rabbis and all women in leadership positions. Aside from
prejudice and unfamiliarity, there is almost nothing halakhically opposed to
the woman taking on the rabbinical role. I have also heard the slander heaped
upon me for the sole reason of my womanhood. These are the same prejudices we find burdening the pages of the oral tradition, because prejudice
against women has a long history. If I wanted to prove something, it was on
behalf of all women, that we are capable of great accomplishment if only we
place the effort in our own hands.

I hope a time will come for all of us in which there will be no more questions on the subject of "women": for as long as there are questions, something is wrong. But if I must say what drove me as a woman to become a rabbi, two elements come to mind: My belief in the godly calling to live a compassionate life and my love for people. God has placed abilities and callings in our hearts without regard to gender. Thus each of us has the duty, whether man or woman, to realize those gifts God has given. If you look at things this way, you will see woman and man for what they are: human beings. For me, it was never about being the first. I wish I had been the hundred-thousandth!

Perhaps it is the role of women to be the custodians and upholders of compassion and justice, of all that is good and right, of love and kindness. Where women enter, hate and enmity must fall silent. This is what it means to create and maintain religious culture and to point the way to faith through rituals and rites.

Our Jewish people are sent from God into history as a "blessed" people. Wherever we step in life, in every situation, we are asked to bestow blessing, grant goodness, and faithfulness. This is the way of humility before God's selflessness, whose devotional love for his creatures maintains the world. To establish these pillars of the world was and is Israel's task. Men and women, women and men, have undertaken this work with the same Jewish faithfulness. This ideal has served us well in Theresienstadt. Tonight, like Beruria, we affirm our role as God's servants and as such prepare ourselves to move from earthly to heavenly spheres. May all our work, which we have tried to perform as God's servants, be a blessing for Israel's future and humanity. So may the young women rabbis of the future, and all the Jewish generations to come, honor our memory by promoting Jewish life and spirit that is dedicated to blessings and peace. This is how I would like us to be remembered and how our memory shall be established in the generations to come.

My beloved friends, as we kindle this tiny flame in the great darkness that has befallen us, we remember other days and seasons of great suffering that were eventually overcome by the enduring presence of the One Who Loves Us. Our fires will be rekindled, our flame will burn strong again, our people will rise up, and with the strength of spirit that has endured the most difficult of times, we shall again transform this harsh decree into a blessing for future generations. *"Z'khor Adonai mah haya lanu,"* remember, O Lord, what has befallen us. *"Hashevanu Adonai elecha v'nashuva, Hadesh Yamenu k'kedem,"* restore us to fullness of days.

The following day the Jews of Theresienstadt were herded onto cattle cars bound for Auschwitz, where they perished. May their lives and memories be a blessing.

***

Women in spiritual leadership face the forces of violence within our community as well as those that target our communities as objects of violence. As one of the first "women" rabbis, I found myself the recipient of shocking stories in an area I had not considered before. A few years into my work as I began to travel the country, women and young girls pulled me aside, asked for a moment of my time, and told me their stories of abuse. "Do I have to forgive my father, husband, brother, uncle, brother's friend, teacher, doctor, camp counselor, rabbi, the stranger who molested me?" Hearing stories about violence against women caused me to readjust my feminist thinking. Not only unequal access, but the very physical, emotional, and spiritual safety of women arose in my mind as one of the clearest signs that we had not yet achieved the goals of feminism. The link between violence against women and the oppression of women is one of the oldest stories in the world.

> *Adam tells Lilith:*
> *"You will lie below me and I will lie on top of you,*
> *for I am superior*
> *to you."*
> *Lilith refuses.*
> *"I shall not lie beneath you,*
> *but only on top*
> *for we are equal*
> *to each other*
> *in as much as we are both*
> *earth."*
>
> *Alphabet of Ben Sirach*

From the mouth of Judith Plaskow, Carol Christ, and other feminists, women across North America have interpreted Lilith's refusal to be on the bottom as a revolutionary act in behalf of women's autonomy. Lilith's refusal to be on the bottom symbolized a new spirit of independence among Jewish women. We came together in circles throughout North America and began sharing our understanding of Jewish life and culture, text and tradition, history and our story, the untold stories of women. In hundreds of gatherings I heard women identify flesh-and-blood versions of the Adam who refuses to relinquish his assertion of dominance and threatens implicit or explicit use of force to cause harm in order to keep things going his way.

The tale of Lilith's scorn for Adam elevates her to the status of Satan's wife as ruler of demons, killer of newborns, and seducer of men in the stories of Jewish people. My generation read Lilith in a new light. We recited

the story of Lilith to expose derogatory messages about female power embedded in sacred texts and replace them with existing or fictional narratives that value female self-assertion. In contrast to the story of Eve, Lilith
chooses to leave the garden, which, as it turns out, was not such a safe
place for a woman to be. Instead of reading Lilith as a warning tale to
good girls about the dangers of big-mouth women who offend God and tradition by disobeying their fathers and husbands, Lilith became a midrashic
affirmation of female choice. Notions of female modesty, submissiveness,
and domestic industriousness as the pinnacle of women's spiritual aspiration were giving way to more proactive forms of female self-expression.

The assertiveness of Lilith was a profound discovery for another reason.
The women's health movement uncovered direct links between the occurrence of domestic violence and sexual abuse and the negative attitudes,
behaviors, and beliefs about women found in society. In other words, in the
Jewish community and in society in general, attitudes, beliefs, and behaviors about women in relationship to power are responsible for creating a climate in which one out of four Jewish women experiences domestic violence
in her lifetime. In any other circumstance, one-quarter of any population
undergoing this level of disease would be termed an epidemic. Rowdy, self-
assertive, wildly irreverent, playful, and sexually active female behavior is a
potent antidote to acceptance of a submissive stance on the part of women
facing violence. We have to break the silence, speak our truth, and make
the changes that create a safe and secure environments for women and children at home and in the community.

Shalom Bayit, signifying "peace at home," cannot mean that women
and children who experience abuse at home must suffer in silence. Rather,
a meaningful response would include communitywide education, establishing network relationships with all those involved in domestic violence
prevention and intervention, including health-care institutions, social service agencies, rabbinic seminaries, Jewish sisterhoods and brotherhoods,
Jewish educators, women's centers, law enforcement, and young women's
and men's organizations, in order to cast a meaningful safety net.

Many people question whether abuse is even an issue in the Jewish
community. Fortunately, numerous health-care professionals and women's
groups have been gathering statistical information for decades. Emotional,
verbal, economic, sexual, and physical abuse impact approximately 15 to
25 percent of Jewish women in their lifetime. Ninety-five percent of
domestic violence is male toward female. Domestic abuse occurs in same-
gender relationships as well, and toward the elderly (mostly women). The
setting of domestic violence within the Jewish community happens across
denominational, class, age, and ethnic lines. It is a phenomenon that
knows no boundaries.

The 95 percent of male abusers who attempt to control the thoughts and behaviors of their partners also need support to make healthy choices in their lives. In the past, society created the expectation that to be good girls, young women must please others, be objects of beauty, and not show anger. Young women are vulnerable to violence in the context of dating. Jewish Women's International reports that more than one in four teenage girls endures verbal abuse in a relationship, 13 percent have been in a relationship where they have been physically hurt or hit, and nearly 80 percent of girls who have been physically abused in their intimate relationships continue to date their abuser. Students who report physical dating violence are more likely to engage in sexual intercourse, episodes of heavy drinking, physical fighting, and attempted suicide. More than half of young women who are raped (68 percent) know their rapist either as a boyfriend, friend, or casual acquaintance. Living in a female body, or in a body that is not heterosexual, remains an issue for women who are lesbian or transgendered. Our bodies are not safe from violence that originates in attitudes about sexuality and gender.

Rabbis in spiritual leadership are responsible for the ongoing reflection and examination of our cultural, spiritual, and social assumptions from the perspective of gender privilege. What stories, rituals, laws, and social structures in our tradition prop up attitudes and beliefs that permit violence against women? In order to prevent violence against women and children, the entire community must be involved in an ongoing basis. Every social and religious institution in the Jewish community should be held accountable for proper training of clergy, educators, rabbinic students, and cantors who, because of their role, are the recipients of pleas for help. When 100 percent of ordained rabbis have been professionally trained in domestic violence and sexual abuse prevention and intervention, we will have crossed an important threshold in furthering safe families and communities.

Fortunately, women and men in spiritual leadership have made tremendous strides in the past decade. Thousands of individuals have participated in Jewish Women's International, an organization that launched a massive domestic violence prevention campaign in 2001 and is committed to providing the support women need to leave and heal from abusive relationships within the Jewish community. There is a growing awareness that every synagogue throughout the Jewish world must become a true sanctuary for those who seek safe environments for themselves, their children, elder relatives, and friends.

The willingness to confront domestic violence and sexual abuse is challenged by the profound sense of betrayal and pain on the part of those who are attached to rebbes, teachers, and spiritual guides who molested, raped, or seduced women in the context of their rabbinic role. But the victims will not be silent. I believe the role of a "woman" in spiritual leadership is to support the victims in their recovery and to make sure the synagogue is a safe place.

We have not yet arrived at a commonly agreed-upon set of procedures for handling domestic and sexual abuse in our communities. One hopes such procedures will emerge within the next few decades.

Can we count on the support of our brothers? According to Rita Simon and Pamela Nadell, when we women rabbis compare ourselves with men who graduated rabbinic seminaries the same year that we did, we see ourselves as less formal, more relational and approachable, more concerned with empowering others rather than wielding power, more willing to accept differences within our communities, less hierarchical, and more willing to change tradition to accommodate the personal needs of our congregants. When women choose forms of communal egalitarianism that permit each person to contribute his or her own resource, whether it is traditional knowledge or some other field of knowledge, they are implementing a strategy for ending male gender privilege. Lifting up voices that have previously been marginalized is part of women's project for change. The same study, however, found that male rabbis seem to think that gender does not play a role in determining how they perform their duties and that there is no essential difference between the way men and women structure their rabbinate. Male rabbis tend to be dismissive of women's experience of difference and sometimes indifferent to their concerns. This seems to indicate that men are not as invested in maintaining an atmosphere of egalitarianism, which is crucial for dismantling oppression based on male gender privilege. It reminds me of the opinion of some white people that the age of racism and white privilege is over, or that anti-Semitism has been eradicated. We need our brothers to take note, follow our direction on this issue, and institute change in partnership with their sisters.

***

The pattern of violence against women intersects with other forms of structural violence that impacts the Jewish community. Anti-Semitism, racism, homophobia, classism, adultism, and sexism are systems of thought and behavior that enable some people to enjoy economic, social, religious, and civil privileges while denying others those same privileges on the basis of identity. Objectification, categorization, dehumanization, and legal discrimination all are stepping stones on the road to collective oppression that can lead to genocide. Jewish women are carriers of at least two targeted identities: Jew and woman. We may also be in other targeted classes such as lesbian, bisexual, or transgendered. We may be Jewish women of color. With survivors of the European genocide of six million Ashkenazi and Sephardic Jews still living among us, women rabbis are well aware of the necessity to be in pursuit of peacemaking within our own community and with the non-Jewish world.

My own pathways in spiritual leadership have consistently led me to establish relationships with individuals and communities with whom Jewish people are in conflict as well as with those who seek to establish a relationship with us. I also continue to place myself in the presence of those who speak of their experience of torture and war. Survivors of Hiroshima, the killing fields of Cambodia, Northern Ireland, Israel, Palestine, apartheid South Africa, Colombia, Lebanon, Vietnam, Guatemala, Salvador, Sudan, and Bosnia and, of course, survivors of the Holocaust. I am also aware of the high rate of suicide among gay youth; the violence that impacts youth all over the world, including on the streets of south-central Los Angeles; those who survived the genocide against Native Americans; and the U.S. prison system. I cannot forget. A woman in spiritual leadership cannot remain silent. Our silence could be understood as tacit consent. To save a single life is to save the whole world. In order to save life, however, we have to organize, give witness, plant the seeds of reconciliation in every generation, and continue to educate ourselves so that we consistently choose methods of repair and restoration that promote long-lasting well-being of those who have been historically targeted for discrimination.

In the past several generations a revolution in the use of strategic nonviolence in behalf of positive social change has emerged in history as one of the greatest hopes of humanity in transforming conflict and avoiding the use of harmful force. Scores of successful nonviolent campaigns have been waged in behalf of ending conflict across the globe. Nonviolence took on religious proportions in my life in my early teens and early twenties through exposure to the civil rights movement, the women's movement, the Vietnam War, the Fellowship of Reconciliation, and two rabbis, Everett Gendler and Michael Robinson, both devotees of the practice of nonviolence from within the calling of Jewish faith; both walked with Martin Luther King Jr. I have thus been a student of strategic nonviolence for four decades.

Several years ago I felt the need to formalize my practice of Jewish nonviolence by creating a new movement in Jewish life based on nonviolence: Shomeret Shalom. *Shomer* means "spiritual stewardship." Jewish tradition contains the term *shomer* (keep) the Sabbath, *shomer* (keep) kosher, and *shomer adamah* (earth stewardship). I choose to live the Torah of a Shomer Shalom, one who practices strategic nonviolence in the service of peace as a primary obligation from which all other religious obligations flow. In the context of looking at women rabbis in spiritual leadership, nonviolence is a natural choice for the half of humanity that has traditionally not used harmful force to make social changes. Seventy-four percent of violence is male on male, and one-fourth of all women worldwide experience male violence in the context of their homes. Clearly, we have a spiritual problem on our hands as women. Forming networks with men who are committed to nonviolence gives women a better chance to prevent violence because the practice of nonviolence as a spiritual and social methodology for healing the world is grounded in measurable outcomes. People who experience violence on a daily basis need real results, not ideological pronouncements. Nonviolence offers us a history of concrete achievements.

My life has been an experiment to create community that is grounded in good outcomes for women on the theory that good outcomes for women mean good outcomes for the entire community. Peacemaking is not an intuitive response but an acquired skill, one that needs cultivation in each generation, beginning at home. Tracking the pathways of nonviolence in Jewish tradition has helped me uncover layers of Jewish women's history and the presence of contemporary heroines committed to peace in our own time. As Jewish tradition teaches us through the stories of Abraham and Sarah, who kept an open tent for guests on the road, peacemaking often begins with a simple act of hospitality, a welcome smile, an extended hand, a willingness to be present and share the bounty of one's household. Creating a welcome place is the core of my spiritual work as a "woman" rabbi. The prophetic spirit begins with the demand that all people be equally welcome in the community as long as they leave violence at the door.

CHAPTER 5

Circles of Healing in the Time of Old Age

Rabbi Judith Edelstein

Cast me not off in the time of old age; when my strength fails, forsake me not.

(Ps. 71:9)

Western society has not dealt kindly with its elders. The demands of modern life have eroded the traditional support systems for caring for the elderly, and we have not developed adequate replacements. We lack sufficient services for the aged seriously ill, especially those facing special challenges near the end of their lives, the vast majority of whom are women. In addition to reasonably priced and adequate medical care our elders require spiritual renewal.

Immigrants from other countries are shocked to see children in the United States place their parents in long-term nursing facilities rather than care for them in their own homes. Ironically, as these groups assimilate, they too admit their parents to institutions. Concomitantly, second- and third-generation elderly Americans, fiercely independent and extremely respectful of privacy, do not want to live with their children, fearing that they will be an intrusive burden to them.

How best to safeguard those who are elderly and too sick to sustain themselves is a complex problem that has no simple solutions. The cost of medical care in the United States and the fact that the baby-boomer generation will be retiring soon—with some already requiring geriatric medical attention—indicate that we are rapidly heading toward a severe crisis in geriatric medical care. In addition to the obvious material necessities of shelter, food, and health care, the elderly have unique spiritual questions and yearnings that are too often treated as an afterthought or neglected entirely.

In our youth we are filled with hope for what we will accomplish in life, and for who we will become as we mature. No sooner do we become aware of our gifts and expectation to conquer the world than we encounter reality. Time, hardship, and experience tend to diminish our sense of uniqueness. Our sense of individuality can erode further as our life becomes increasingly routinized and the search for meaning is supplanted by absorption with health matters and surviving the day. We must find a way to synthesize our dreams with our reality to retain a sense of uniqueness. Martin Buber (1994) writes:

> Every person born into this world represents something new, something that never existed before, something original and unique. "Every single man is a new thing in the world and is called upon to fulfill his particularity ... that this is not done, is the reason why the coming of the Messiah is delayed." Every man's foremost task is the actualization of his unique, unprecedented and never-recurring potentialities, and not the repetition of something that another ... has already achieved.[1]

The elderly, in particular, are at great risk of losing their sense of individuality and uniqueness. Many of those who are institutionalized have essentially given up, believing that they cannot alter what occurred in the past nor change themselves at this late stage of their life. Their days seem unending and unvarying, despite "reality orientation boards" posted on the wall at the nursing stations, indicating the day and date, the weather, and the next holiday. Time is meaningless. Thus, in addition to feeling useless to others, the aged institutionalized feel helpless to affect their present and future destinies, as well as their relationships to their families and to God.

BACKGROUND

The Jewish Home and Hospital Life Care System (hereafter referred to as JHH or The Home) is the largest long-term-care institution for the elderly in the New York metropolitan area, with three nursing homes (fifteen hundred beds) that provide long-term and sub-acute care as well as a full range of senior adult programs. The vast majority of its clients are indigent women, which means that JHH relies upon fundraising and reimbursement from insurance companies as well as the government to survive.

Facing constant threats of reduced funding and impacted by steadily diminishing resources, staff and clients experience recurrent stress. Residents who are particularly frail, lonely, and otherwise vulnerable feel acute loss when staff, for example, the CNA (certified nurse's assistant), who toilets, bathes, dresses, and feeds them, is laid off. Furthermore, the future appears quite bleak for baby boomers because if present fiscal realities persist, facilities will not be able to maintain a level of acceptable service—even in the near future.

As the chaplain responsible for the spiritual life of all JHH constituencies, including residents, acute care patients, family, friends, and staff, I encounter the daily concerns of those who live there, for example, waking up only to wait interminably for an attendant (who may or may not speak English) to take care of her basic needs: going to the bathroom, diaper changing, washing, dressing, and eating. Few are happy about relying upon others for these basic daily needs, let alone having to wait for what feels like eternity to have them met, and often express their frustration to the staff. Some residents share that they would just as soon be dead and wish each day were their last. For the nursing staff to face them on a daily basis is difficult and leads to emotional burnout, which in turns has additional deleterious effects on the residents, increasing their sense of isolation.

While long-term care facilities usually employ a psychiatrist, her job is limited to medicating; similarly, social workers are inundated with paperwork, and, despite their best intentions, rarely have time to counsel. Everyone's caseload is burgeoning and is larger than any individual can handle well. It is apparent that the chasm of loneliness, confusion, and fear in the client's life cannot be filled by the steadily shrinking staff. To further complicate matters, residents of nursing homes generally suffer from the limitations that are imposed by advanced age. As one observer put it:

> By the time people enter into nursing homes and care communities, they have generally experienced some loss of function, be it impairment or disability or generalized aging. This can include reduced vision and hearing, limited mobility, short term memory loss, dementia and the entire range of physical and mental challenges known to humanity.[2]

THE CLIENTS

Seventy-five percent of the admissions to long-term care at JHH are women. They comprise a broad cross-section of backgrounds and needs and bring with them the legacies of their lives—their unresolved personal emotional issues, a social network (or not), the remnants of their personal, spiritual, and emotional resources, and material possessions. Although a small portion of residents go home once their health has stabilized, the vast majority reside at JHH until they die. During the average two-year span of living at JHH, they experience diminished control over their own lives. Some never even get to see the world outside again.

A large number have family and friends who provide emotional support through regular visits, phone calls, and hired companions to spend a few hours a day with the resident. Children who admit their parents to The Home tend to feel guilty at being unable to care for their parents at home. They are simultaneously grateful for and repulsed and frustrated by the environment, and they are overwhelmed by the myriad medical and end-of-life decisions that confront them. They may also experience financial pressure while helplessly observing their parents' deterioration.

Optimally, parents and children will have the opportunity to resolve long-standing conflicts at this time. Borowitz (1999) describes how, when roles are reversed and children become their parents' caregivers, this can lead to an enriched relationship.[3] However, quite a few of these children, even those who live near the facility, sever ties with their parents. Following their mothers' admissions, power-of-attorney in hand, these children never step foot in the facility or call again.

Other residents, never married or partnered, rely upon aged siblings, friends, and/or distant relatives: nieces and nephews or cousins whom they rarely see. These individuals maintain contact through the telephone. There are also the extremely aged, substantially over one hundred years old, who are the sole survivors of their families and friends, living longer than anyone in their circle. Finally there are the few remaining Holocaust survivors who, more often than not, are alone in the world.

For the women who have no contacts outside the facility, the institution is their last home, and the residents, staff, and volunteers become their "family." Within this quite a few adjust well, grateful for the safety, the medical attention, the regular nutritious meals, and the clean environment.

Overlaying this patchwork exists a ubiquitous sadness, fear, and isolation with occasional sparks of joy, for the women's emotional burdens weigh as heavily upon them as their physical incapacities. The reality is that they gave up their homes and independence to move the entirety of their lives into a private, double- or four-bed room, their possessions reduced only to what fits into three drawers, a night table, and a four-foot-wide closet. The overwhelming majority live in non-private rooms, sleep within six feet of a stranger who may not speak the same language, may not speak at all, and may be demented or imminently dying. In these rooms the beds are separated by a thin opaque curtain. If the bed is near the door and the woman is confined to it, she may never get to look outside the window again. Privacy becomes a memory as these women are forced to adjust to roommates, staff, and other strangers walking into their room at any hour of the day or night.

It is no wonder that so many individuals retreat into their pasts to retain a connection to reality. Their memories are far more comforting than their present, which consists of TV, bingo, institutional food, and the frightening, alien world around them reverberating of sickness and death. "There is a lot of evidence that the elderly feel isolated, even in the midst of communal life. Chronic pain, limited functioning, the losses of mobility, freedom, family and friends, and ensuing depression can make it difficult for aging people to reach out and connect yet again with other people."[4]

Thus, these women, some of whom were pillars of society, are forced to give up lives they led as adults for fifty or more years and are thrust abruptly into an environment where they are in close proximity with others from diverse economic, social, cultural, and educational backgrounds, not to mention the extremely ill and the severely demented. At worst, to them their circumstances are an anathema that they never overcome; at best, they adjust over time, adapt, and manage still to experience pleasure. I am struck by the irony in the Jewish tradition that writes, "Gray hair is a crown of glory" (Prov. 16:31), when I hear: "How could this have happened to me? I want to go home. When will I go home? This is not where I live; I live at home. I feel like a prisoner. I have no friends here! I'd rather die than live here for the rest of my life." This litany expresses patients' deep anxiety and despair about their present and future. Bartell (2004) describes the "spiritual suffering" they endure:

> When one can no longer trust those nearby, spiritual suffering is experienced. When beauty is absent from one's life, one suffers spiritually. When one's hope is gone, spiritual suffering can be acute. Much as physical pain signals an injury to the physical body, spiritual suffering can be seen as an indication that one or more spiritual needs are threatened or going unmet. While physical suffering can include a threat to one's mobility, spiritual suffering includes threats to one's belief and purpose in life. It is often experienced as "spiritual dissonance," where the dissonance lies between one's faith and critical events in one's life. Spiritual suffering is found clearly in those difficult times "when individuals are unable to find sources of meaning, hope, love, peace, comfort, strength and connection in life."[5]

For those who were active members of a religious community or who included religious ritual in their daily lives before admission to The Home, continuity of worship and a relationship with the chaplain can significantly help their adjustment. This call to fellowship is relevant to Jews and non-Jews alike, as these women take some responsibility for themselves, especially because there are so few areas in which they have control over their lives.

Nevertheless, according to Hamlen, while many value religion, their intention to participate in religious practice can recede as a result of physical or mental impairment.[6] Involvement in spiritual practice may be too complex a task for them. Even those who are regular worship attendees at JHH stop coming to services when their health declines, despite the fact that they are brought to and from services.

Some forget what the service is about but may become very aroused when a prayer is sung to them in another context. Others wind up going to religious services of a different religion because they have lost sense of time but associate the room where services are held as a worship space. Thus, regular synagogue-goers absent on Shabbat may appear at Sunday services. Some, unknown to the minister as Jews, also take communion on Sunday. Similarly, about 15 percent of attendees at Jewish services are non-Jews. Many sleep during worship; others do not have the ability to hold onto the prayer booklets; quite a few can no longer read, despite the large type. Most cannot hear well despite their hearing aids. Then there are the shouters, who regularly interrupt, and the "mover-abouters," who wheel themselves in and out of the room during the service. The variations are infinite. In spite of the multiple impediments, these souls yearn to connect with tradition and God. "The cognitive impairment, memory, and functional loss that accompany [it] create special challenges."[7] When we add those afflicted with mental illness to the mix, the picture is daunting and brings to mind this parable:

There was once a man who was very stupid. When he got up in the morning it was so hard for him to find his clothes that at night he almost hesitated to go to bed for thinking of the trouble he would have on waking. One evening he finally made a great effort, took paper and pencil and as he undressed noted down exactly where he put everything he had on. The next morning, very well pleased with himself, he took the slip of paper in his hand and read: "cap"—there it was, he set it on his head; "pants"—there they lay, he got into them; and so it went until he was fully dressed. "That's all very well, but now where am I myself?" he asked in great consternation. "Where in the world am I?" He looked and looked, but it was a vain search; he could not find himself. And that is how it is with us, said the rabbi.[8]

THE CHALLENGE

In modern times, medicine's goal is to eradicate disease so that humans can live longer lives than ever. Judaism has a vast and deep belief in the power of physicians and science. Borowitz (2002) cogently identifies a paradox in Jewish thinking regarding the extraordinary esteem for physicians, their power and knowledge, in contrast to our faith in God as a healer. He points out that "the classical Jewish theology of medicine is dialectical. God sends illness ... yet God also commands doctors, and by extension all of us, to cure those ailments ... there is not just one but two effective sources of energy in the universe, God and people."[9]

In describing this dichotomy, Borowitz reveals the deep-seated ambivalence many Jews have toward praying to God for health. Their faith is more reliant upon the medical staff, especially the doctors, who heal them. The vast majority of Jews make far more visits to their doctors than to their rabbis. Countless jokes about the proud Jewish mother whose son is a doctor attest to the primacy of medicine over religion in contemporary Jewish culture. Medicine has supplanted religion, and death is an illness to be warded off for as long as possible, so long as one is able to obtain the proper treatment. Although Jewish sources view death as part of a natural process that occurs to all living beings, many Jews nevertheless view sickness and its concomitant suffering as undeserved punishment for sins they did not commit. A common refrain is: "Why is God punishing me like this? I haven't done anything to deserve it."

And while most of us take adequate bodily functioning for granted, we ignore physicians' admonitions to pursue healthy lifestyles. Belief in therapeutic interventions has largely eradicated the self-discipline required in both a proper diet and regular prayer. Yet when Jewish women are admitted to The Home, many are shocked that they are sick because they have been under a doctor's care, taken medication, had surgery, and so on. It is impossible for them to accept the reality that their bodies will not endure interminably. Furthermore, they may avoid associating with other patients out of denial of their own condition or from embarrassment. This tendency toward social isolation may only intensify their depression, ultimately creating further problems of isolation and low morale for them, as well as for the staff who are not trained to deal with emotional and spiritual issues.

Thus along with physical breakdown, they suffer from morale decline, for often they have lost whatever modicum of faith they had. What will maintain them as their bodies and souls evanesce?

As we age and gradually (or suddenly) lose important parts of our physical selves and the core of our former identity—health, beauty, intellectual and physical prowess, ability to accomplish, treasured possessions, to name but a few—we are simultaneously given the opportunity to expand our souls. Yet it is a struggle for women to view themselves in a mirror as an "old lady" because our society puts such emphasis on youth and sex appeal. Men struggle less with aging, for gray-haired men may be perceived as debonair, whereas gray-haired women flock to dye their hair. In an effort to come to terms with this process of physical change, I envision the ever-widening gap between our youthful, healthy bodies and our older, weaker ones as an invitation from God to fill this new space with an expansion of the divine presence. The greater the expanse, the more capacity for the sacred. God's purposeful design enables us to make room for and get closer to the Holy One, to ease our passage from focusing on "doing" to concentrating instead on "being," from individuals who have based our identities upon productivity and ownership, to souls who are abandoning the material world to merge with God.

Once I grasped the situation, I resolved both to find a way to establish relationships with the women to try to support them through what is likely the most difficult period in their lives. Believing that physical and spiritual health are intertwined, I concluded that the spiritual support I offered would abet the healing process, preparing them for the next stage. Martin Buber captures my sentiments: "What is meant by unification of the soul would be thoroughly misunderstood if 'soul' were taken to mean anything but the whole man, body and spirit together. The soul is not really united unless all body energies are united.... A man who thus becomes a unity of body and spirit—he is the man whose work is all of a piece."[10]

I surmised that a number of the women who had not included religious practice in their lives when they were healthy might be receptive to some kind of informal religious gathering at The Home, for

> religion and spirituality play vital roles in the lives of people across the lifespan, especially in times of crisis. A recent study suggests that the increased use of religious/spiritual coping strategies is directly related to the severity of illness ... [and] studies have found that higher use of religion/spirituality as a coping mechanism is related to lower levels of the negative affective symptoms ... associated with stress and illness among hospitalized patients. Religious beliefs offer the additional benefit of hope, particularly for people with serious illness. Faith invites the suffering person to search for meaning and perspective through a source greater than one's self and, in doing so, gain a sense of control over feelings of vulnerability.[11]

How could I help succor these aching souls? "A person is obligated to show great care for orphans and widows because their spirits are very low and their feelings are depressed. This applies even if they are wealthy."[12] I came to recognize that it was imperative for me to create a forum in which the women could find fulfillment for their spiritual needs. "The chaplain occupies the unique and important position as one who companions the patient in his or her wholeness as a human person. Providing space for the patient to 'be,' the chaplain facilitates the possibility of growth and integration as illness threatens to annihilate the person's sense of self."[13]

Hamlen articulated my concern when she posed the question, "How will we meet the spiritual and religious needs of this aging institutionalized population?"[14] I concluded that a number of patients and residents (and perhaps staff, too) would benefit from some kind of contemplative prayer time outside the regularly scheduled weekend religious services.

PRAYER

"Refuat ha nefesh oorefuat ha guf," Heal the body and heal the soul.
From the Misheberach, Jewish prayer for those who are seriously ill

Prayer is one of the most efficacious ways to alter a person's mental state and to stimulate comfort and hope. In 1 Samuel 12–20, the despairing Hannah continued to trust in God and devoted herself to prayer long after others would have given up. Her prayers were not scripted but came from the depths of her heart. Perhaps the spontaneity and the intensity of her prayers healed and strengthened Hannah, enabling her to conceive, or her story may simply be an allegory to illustrate the transformative potential of prayer.

The pertinence of prayer in healing has become a hot topic over the last several years; the subject even made the cover of *Newsweek*. Studies have attempted to prove that when someone prays for another in need of healing, the sick have a higher recovery rate. According to O'Connor and others (2002):

> Spirituality is receiving considerable attention in the medical literature. Much research has been devoted to exploring spirituality and religion's impact on health. One perspective that has drawn some of the evidence maintains that spirituality and religion can be a positive determinant of health.... Some argue that family physicians ought to pray with and for patients if both ... are agreeable.[15]

The Jewish *misheberach* (blessing) for health, above, is a prime example of this belief. In a communal setting a blessing is recited as part of the prayer service, and congregants have the opportunity to offer names of people who are in need of a "complete healing."

In his chapter "Prayer," Michael Fishbane (1987) talks about prayer's centrality to Jewish spiritual life, citing early rabbinic sources, including the Talmud, which he notes refers to prayer as "'more precious than

sacrifices' [Babylonian Talmud, *Berachot* 32a; Kuzari 5:5]."[16] Fishbane
continues, "Judaism does not consider prayer to be either a casual or su-
perfluous adjunct, but rather the nurturant wellspring of its entire active
life and an inherent component of it."[17] Over time, prayers and the act of
praying became fixed and formalized within Jewish daily life, providing little opportunity for individual expression. Landes (1998) talks about the
individual call to God and its institutionalization in Jewish liturgy:

> *Halakhic* (Jewish legal) texts require us to recite the prayer for healing
> on a daily basis (Babylonia Talmud, *Megillah* 17b and *Avodah Zarah* 8a).
> The prayer for health in the Amidah, "Heal us and we will be healed,"
> also offers us the opportunity to include the names of others who are ill.
> The briefest prayer for healing occurs in Numbers 12:13, where Moses
> pleads with God to cure his sister Miriam from leprosy. "Heal her now,
> God, please." While prayer may not cure the sick, it helps them to cope
> better with their adversities, for it provides us with language with which
> to approach God. "The *Zohar* (Exodus 20a, the primary document for
> Jewish mysticism) heaps lavish praise on the spontaneous prayer that
> arises directly from the human heart." ... Rabbi Berachiah said: "When
> people pray and weep and cry so intensely that they are unable to find
> words to express their sorrow, theirs is the perfect prayer, for it is in
> their heart, and this will never return to them empty."[18]

On other occasions, we require concrete language to connect us with
our feelings. That is when we need to see the words before us, for we are
blinded by emotion. This is when fixed liturgy works best. Prayer, whether
spontaneous—wordless and silent torrents from our heart—or annunciated
aloud from a prayer book surrounded by community, is a vehicle to express
our deepest feeling to the Other (God), for "a man's prayer is not heard
until he places his very life into his uplifted hands. . . . A man's prayer is
not heard until he makes his heart [soft] like flesh."[19]

SOLUTION

I sought a means to create an environment in which the women were able
to support one another emotionally while sharing common concerns. Combining this idea with the efficacy of prayer, the thought occurred to me to
create a daily afternoon prayer time for residents, open to staff as well,
fashioned after the Jewish *mincha* (afternoon prayer service).

My goals were to

- Promote spiritual connection with a Higher Power
- Create an atmosphere of acceptance and hope through, prayer, blessing,
  and song

- Bring patients out from the isolation of their rooms to socialize with one another
- Provide them with the opportunity to describe personal situations and to elicit feelings about problems with which they were grappling
- Validate their feelings through mutual affirmation

For, as Buber writes:

Where is the dwelling of God? "... God dwells wherever man lets him in." This is the ultimate purpose: to let God in. But we can let him in only where we really stand, where we live, where we live a true life. If we maintain holy intercourse with the little world entrusted to us, if we help the holy spiritual substance to accomplish itself in that section of Creation in which we are living, then we are establishing, in this our place, a dwelling for the Divine Presence.[20]

One of the therapeutic recreation (TR) leaders identified a group of women on a unit where she was assigned to participate in the first service. I spent several days creating a prayer book that included selections from and reflected the Jewish afternoon liturgy. For good measure, I included a few nondenominational prayers and several inspirational songs in Hebrew and English.

The day of the first service arrived. Trying to ignore the din of ringing phones, the pervasive TV, the babble of staff and resident voices both within and outside the unit's all-purpose room, and assorted noises from the demented, I eagerly distributed the prayer booklets to the nine women seated in a circle around the TR leader and me. Facing the women, however, I was chagrined to realize that there were only a few Jews present, and even among them, not one was familiar with or alert enough to recognize the Hebrew prayers. Furthermore, few could read the English because of their cognitive or visual impairment. So much for the prayer booklet; in fact, most of it was irrelevant to the group. Yet, despite the inappropriateness of the material, the women responded enthusiastically to the gathering.

The Jews and non-Jews loved hearing *"Henei Mah Tov"* as much as *"Kum Baya."* They were visibly moved by the grand finale when I chanted the blessing of the Cohenim: "May God bless you and protect you. May God's presence pervade your life. May God's spirit bring you peace." But ultimately what was most powerful was their eagerness to share their feelings and experiences with one another about God and the role of faith in their lives. This hour gave them the chance not only to pray but also to talk about the relevance and meaningfulness of their beliefs and how their beliefs sustained them during this sad time in their lives.

Their response to the first few groups led me to believe that I was on the right track. The more I listened and observed, the easier it was for me to relinquish my prayer booklet. Over time the format of our hour together changed to consist of opportunities for them to talk to one another while the TR leader and I interjected our own thoughts, prayers, song, and blessing at what seemed to us to be the appropriate time.

With the change in content the groups became more emotionally oriented and spontaneous; ironically, the less I prepared, the more successful the sessions. These diverse women, with the occasional male participant, ranged in age from 70 to 105. They included Jews, Protestants, Catholics, atheists, Caucasians, blacks, and others. Our discussions varied—anything from relationships with parents, siblings, and spouses to constipation. More often than not their frame of reference for their families reverted to their family of origin rather than the family they raised. Topics varied from week to week and arose from the TR leader's and my elicitations and their remarks. We regularly attracted a core group of eight women, a few of whom were aphasic and a couple who were demented.

Although the aphasics did not speak, they clapped their hands, nodded, or mouthed words during singing, and they responded with a smile to blessings. As for those afflicted with dementia, some sat silently while others remained in the circle staring into space. Occasionally someone became disruptive and was ignored or removed. Those who remained for the entire session seemed to derive comfort from simply being in the same room with the talkers. Their effect during the group was indicative of at least a measure of pleasure. Quite a few who had developed bonds with others express their affection.

In response to a particular prayer or reading, some residents or patients exclaim, "That's exactly how I feel!" Rarely does a patient decline the offer of a prayer on his or her behalf or the opportunity to discuss a prayer, even if it is simply to dispute the sentiment! These prayers are "voiced or voiceless longing of the heart, the cry for God's presence."[21] Petitioning by individuals on behalf of themselves and the others in the group expresses not only connection to God but also love of neighbor. Here the "I" becomes a "we," as concern for self is transformed into compassion and empathy for others in this community.

At one group, I was touched to see a newcomer, whom I had introduced to the group, reach out to shake everyone's hand as they welcomed her, one by one. This was impossible, unfortunately, because of space constraints and the challenge of maneuvering ten wheelchairs. Since she could shake only a few hands of those on either side of her, I suggested that the others blow kisses instead.

One very poignant incident occurred following one of the first sessions. I had felt rather frustrated during the hour because of that particular group member's limited verbal ability, and I questioned the effectiveness of the group process as well as my leadership skills. On the way back to my office an Afro-American teenage male volunteer, who had been present, followed me. "Rabbi, what you did for those old ladies was really important. I'm really glad I was there. Can I ask you a favor?"

"If it's something I can do, I'd be happy to," I replied, surprised by his statement.

"Could you pray for my little brother, Richard? He's really sick."

"It would be an honor for me to pray for your brother," I responded and offered a prayer on the spot. He thanked me and continued on his way.

At that moment the power of what we had been doing during the group amazed me. I realized that we had crossed generational, racial, gender, and religious barriers to comfort and support one another. There was solace even in the moments of silence we shared. How wise Dittes (1999) is when he points out that the counselor need neither demand nor even expect a response, but only accept the counselee "as is."[22]

Following the teenager's comments, the group took on a new and deeper meaning for me. Clearly the groups were powerful for these women and were an effective way for them to utilize one another's wisdom and solace as well as the staff's.

Most human beings, regardless of their age, benefit from participating in a group with others who are dealing with issues similar to their own. The healing power of peer support and identification with others' problems has been well documented. Yalom, for example, writes, "Group therapy not only draws from the general ameliorative effects of positive expectations but also benefits from a source of hope that is unique to the group format.... Members are inspired and expectations raised by contact with those who have trod the same path and found the way back."[23]

The addition of spiritual emphasis through prayer and discussions about God broadens the dimensions of the group process. I have observed women as diverse as a sixty-eight-year-old African American maid from North Carolina, with only a sixth-grade education, reach out her hand to commiserate with a blind, eighty-nine-year-old Austrian Jewish Holocaust survivor, a professor of theology at one of New York's Jewish seminaries. The two of them, along with three others in a group of eleven, talked about losing children. The pain and empathy in the room was palpable as one after another spoke of the death of her child. One who expressed profound faith revealed that of the five children she bore, three had died.

The group process as well as the prayers allowed these strangers to open up to one another, whereas previously they had not shared these painful stories with one another nor with the staff who had interviewed them upon admission. Furthermore, they expressed great relief at discovering others in like situations. This enabled the group members to comfort one another in ways that only those who have experienced something so devastating can.

I have seen women who are initially reluctant to share their personal story participate when we read prayers, sing familiar spiritual songs, and offer blessing to others in the group. It is the rare attendee (except for the physically disabled or demented) who remains aloof throughout the hour-long process. As Yalom describes the galvanizing power of groups: "Many patients, because of their extreme social isolation, have a heightened sense of uniqueness.... After hearing other members disclose concerns similar to their own, patients report feeling more in touch with the world ... 'We're all in the same boat.' ... Patients are enormously helpful to one another ... they offer support, reassurance, suggestions, insight."[24]

Finally, the facilitator of the group should have the ability "to witness and reflect feelings.... The witnessing is an act of intense energy and focus, astute and attentive ... [that] lets the facts, the situation, the problem wash by and attends instead to the feelings implied ... passes over the content."[25] I have been as transformed by these groups as the women who participate in them.

When the participants of a spiritual support group are able to experience the sacred within themselves and feel unity with the group, they are open to the possibility of the Divine. Spiritual support groups have the potential power to help those who feel hopeless overcome their despondency, lead the way toward creating community, and make a welcoming space for the *Shechinah* (God's female presence on earth). As Buber articulates:

> The Baal-Shem teaches that no encounter with a being or thing in the course of our life lacks a hidden significance. The people we live with or meet with, the materials we shape, the tools we use, they all contain a mysterious spiritual substance which depends on us for helping it towards its pure form, its perfection. If we neglect the spiritual substance sent across our path, if we think only in terms of momentary purposes, without developing a genuine relationship to the beings and things in whose life we ought to take part, as they in ours, then we shall ourselves be debarred from true fulfilled existence.[26]

"When you pray, know before whom you stand" (Babylonia Talmud, *Berachot*, 31a).

NOTES

1. Martin Buber, *The Way of Man according to the Teaching of Hasidism* (New York: Citadel Press, Kinsington Publishing, 1994), 16.

2. Geraldine G. Hamlen, "Challenges to Preparing and Conductiong Christian Worship in Nursing Homes," *Journal of Pastoral Care & Counseling* 58, no. 4 (Winter 2004): 325–34.

3. Eugene Borowitz, *The Jewish Moral Values* (Philadelphia: Jewish Publication Society, 1999).

4. Hamlen, 334.

5. Mark Bartell, "What Is Spiritual Suffering?" *Journal of Pastoral Care & Counseling* 58, no. 3 (Fall 2004): 187–201.

6. Hamlen.

7. Ibid., 327.

8. Buber, 30.

9. Eugene Borowitz, *Studies in the Meaning of Judaism* (Philadelphia: Jewish Publication Society, 2002), 343.

10. Buber, 25.

11. Sarah Fogg et al., "An Analysis of Referrals to Chaplains in a Community Hospital in New York over a Seven Year Period," *Journal of Pastoral Care & Counseling* 58, no. 3 (Fall 2004): 225–35.

12. Maimonides, *Guide to the Perplexed*, trans. with introduction and notes by Shlomo Pines (Chicago: University of Chicago Press, 1963), vol. 2 ; Maimonides, *Mishneh Torah: Hilchot De'ot*, trans. with commentary and notes by Za'ev Abramson and Eliyahu Touger (New York: Mozanim Publishing Corp., 1989), 132.

13. Patricia Huff Byrne, "'Give Sorrow Words': Lament—Contemporary Need for Job's Old Time Religion," *Journal of Pastoral Care & Counseling* 56, no. 3 (Fall 2002): 255–64.

14. Hamlen.

15. Thomas St. James O'Connor et al., "Review of Spirituality Research in Three Health Care Databases (1962–1999): Implications for Health Care Ministry." *The Journal of Pastoral Care and Counseling* 56, no. 3 (Fall 2002): 227–32.

16. Michael Fishbane, *"Prayer,"* in *Contemporary Jewish Religious Thought,* ed. Arthur A. Cohen and Paul Mendes-Flohr (New York: Charles Scribner's Sons, 1987).

17. Ibid., 724.

18. Daniel Landes, "Prayer as Petition: The Philosophic Basis for Halakhic Prayer," in *The Amidah,* vol. 2 of *Traditional Prayers, Modern Commentaries*, ed. Lawrence A. Hoffman. (Woodstock, VT: Jewish Lights Publishing, 1998), 2.

19. Hayim Bialik, *The Book of Legends* (New York: Schocken Books, 1992), 526.

20. Buber, 41.

21. Fishbane, 724.

22. James E. Dittes, *Pastoral Counseling: The Basics* (Louisville, KY: Westminster John Knox Press, 1999).

23. Irvin Yalom, *The Theory and Practice of Group Psychotherapy* (New York: Basic Books, 1995), 5.

24. Ibid., 6, 12.

25. Dittes, 64.

26. Buber, 39.

PART III

Body, Mind, and Spirit

CHAPTER 6

Biblical Heroes as Role Models for Jewish Women

Rabbi Hara Person

The female characters in the Bible have historically been an important source of role models for Jewish women. For generations, Jewish parents have blessed their daughters with the words, "May God make you like Sarah, Rebekah, Rachel, and Leah." Girls have been taught to aspire to the qualities that Jewish tradition attributed to these biblical matriarchs, qualities like faith, loyalty, hospitality, being good homemakers, and good mothers. Other biblical women, such as Esther and Ruth, were regarded as models of courage, steadfastness, and devotion.

Biblical women also functioned as role models for Jewish women in prayers known as *tkhines*. These were a form of Yiddish prayers developed specifically for women beginning around the seventeenth century. Some are specific to the realities of women's lives, touching on topics like pregnancy, childbirth, or even *challah* baking. Devra Kay maintains that much of this literature was written by women, though the authors are generally anonymous.[1] Some of these prayers present biblical women as models of piety and proper behavior for Jewish women. From the *Seyder Tkhines* (1648) comes a prayer to be said when placing the Sabbath loaves into the oven. The prayer expresses the hope that the dough will rise and not burn, and it ends with invoking the biblical matriarchs:

> So, I make this holy blessing
> As You blessed the dough of
> Our mothers, Sarah and Rebecca.[2]

75

This blessing takes a real-life concern, that the dough rises and bakes properly, and makes a connection to biblical women. The tkhines provided worthy role models as they affirmed the importance of the activities that filled women's days.

The traditional Jewish view of the biblical women was a reflection of the rabbinic outlook on women in general, according to which there were both positive and negative behaviors. The same male textual tradition that held these women up as models of ideal womanhood also often censured or criticized them as examples of generalized female weaknesses. The rabbis called Sarah an eavesdropper, Rachel envious, Miriam talkative, and Dina a gadabout (Gen. R. XLV:5).

Rather than reading these women solely through the lenses of the classical rabbis, contemporary Jewish women are studying the biblical text closely, looking for connections that resonate with their own lives. Familiar Bible heroes or stories are being reframed as women search for their own place within the Jewish textual tradition and challenge standard interpretations. New readings are emerging that expand upon what is only suggested in the text.

Midrash, from the Hebrew root meaning "to draw out or explain," is one way that Jewish tradition has wrestled with biblical text for centuries. The midrashic enterprise is a form of creative interpretation that expands the text. Classical midrash, developed by the rabbinic sages as early as the fifth century CE, was developed in different parts of the Jewish world over many generations and does not speak in one voice. New midrash is still being developed today as modern Jews struggle to make meaning out of the ancient texts and its characters. Like midrash, commentary is also part of the canon of sacred Jewish text. In addition to traditional forms of commentary, Bible scholars today interpret the text using tools of contemporary scholarship from fields like literary criticism, anthropology, archeology, philology, and feminist criticism to find new perspectives and possibilities within the familiar narrative.

There is no lack of intriguing possibilities for role models within the Bible. The stories of the biblical matriarchs Sarah, Rebekah, Rachel, and Leah are filled with pathos, heartbreak, longing, rivalry, trickery, and tragedy. Dina, Jacob's one daughter, is the central protagonist in a particularly tragic and violent episode (Gen. 34). Tamar, Judah's twice-widowed daughter-in-law, seduces her father-in-law, gains her long-awaited children, and makes him take responsibility for his mistreatment of her (Gen. 38). Miriam, the sister of Moses and Aaron, ensures the future of Moses and is a prophet in her own right (Exod. 15:20). There is Yael, who bravely seduces, nourishes, and then murders Sisera, securing a victory for Israel (Judg. 4–5). There is Vashti, the defiant and banished wife (Esther 1:10–22). Esther, the main protagonist of the dramatic book that bears her name, undergoes a transformation from passive young woman to risk-taker and strong leader (Esther 2:1–9:32).

These women's stories were likely created, shaped, or codified by men. That premise necessitates the question of what might have been edited out of these stories. What aspects of women's lives were not considered important and are thus not reflected in these stories? What in these stories need to be repaired, reinterpreted, or re-envisioned? What new interpretations of these stories are emerging? And then, in light of these re-readings, how might these women serve as meaningful role models for Jewish women?

Sarah: The Faithful Wife, The Woman Who Laughed (Gen. 12:5–23:2)

Sarah is the first of the biblical matriarchs. She is Abraham's partner in leaving their homeland and their families in order to follow God. She is an integral part of Abraham's journeys to Canaan and throughout the region. Her laughter, upon being told that she will bear a son in her old age, seems perfectly understandable and real. Her story is also filled with other elements, such as the rivalry that develops between her and her handmaid Hagar, who has given birth to Abraham's first son in her stead and whom Sarah later sends out into the wilderness. The silences in Sarah's story also reverberate loudly; when her beloved son Isaac is taken up to Mount Moriah by Abraham, the text provides no information about Sarah's feelings or reaction.

Sarah is the model of a supportive spouse. When God tells Abraham to leave his land, his birthplace, and his family and to go out into the unknown, Sarah follows unquestioningly. As they journey, Sarah remains steadfast in her support of Abraham's decisions. The midrash teaches that Sarah was fully Abraham's partner in the spread of monotheism. As Abraham spread the word and converted men to monotheism, Sarah converted women (Gen. R. 39:14). As Dvora Weisberg points out, "Sarai serves here as a paradigm of a faithful follower of God, one who responds to God's call without the promise of a reward."[3]

Ellen Frankel creates a conversation between biblical women characters and other actors on the stage of Jewish history. Using this methodology, Frankel looks at the way in which Sarah is first introduced in the text, when her barrenness defines her.

> Sarah continues: And my barrenness. Abraham is defined by a lineage and extended family; I only by an absence.

Mother Rachel explains: Now we understand why Sarah left Ur. Unlike Abraham, who goes in quest of God, Sarah seeks a new home and with it, a change of fortune. As our bubbes teach: A change of place brings a change of luck.[4]

Frankel's interpretation sheds new light on Sarah's struggles and journey, giving voice to what is left unsaid in the Biblical text.

Just as Abraham's name is changed from Avram upon his having entered into the covenant with God, Sarah's name changes from Sarai. She too is an integral part of this relationship, though, as Susan Niditch points out, "she is included in the covenant through her capacity to procreate."[5] Abraham will have other children, but it is only through Sarah that the covenant with God can be continued. Yet Sarah suffers as she struggles with infertility, finally suggesting that her husband take Hagar as a wife and through her produce an heir. In the end, she comes to resent Hagar and eventually has Hagar and her son Ishmael sent out into the wilderness.

Sarah's qualities of faithfulness and loyalty make her an appealing role model. Her struggle with infertility also offers welcome reassurance for many women today who deal with the same pain. But her relationship with Hagar presents a challenge.

It is not only contemporary women who are bothered by the way Sarah treats Hagar. The rabbis praise Sarah for giving Hagar to Abraham as a second wife rather than just as a concubine (Gen. R. 45:1) and for encouraging Hagar to engage in sexual activity with Abraham by stressing his holiness (Gen. R. 45:3). They balance these righteous behaviors against her later treatment of Hagar, imagining that Hagar used her own pregnancy to humiliate Sarah. The rabbis go even further and state that Sarah's actions vis-à-vis Hagar were inspired by prophecy (Gen. R. 45:2; BT M'gillah 14a; BT Sanhedrin 69b), a high form of rabbinic approbation. But even so, they are critical of Sarah and underscore the idea that after being cast out, Hagar still merits divine protection (Gen. R. 45;7).

Sarah's life ends abruptly. She is absent during the entire narrative concerning Abraham's near-sacrifice of Isaac, only to have her death mentioned immediately afterward. Noting the connection between these two events, a midrash teaches that when Sarah hears that Abraham has taken Isaac to sacrifice him, she dies of grief (Gen. R. 58:5). Similarly, another midrash teaches that she died of shock upon learning that he survived (Tanhuma on Vayeira 23). Either way, her death is tied to the events on Mount Moriah.

Norma Rosen looks again at these texts and wonders, with all the midrash the rabbis created, why didn't they ask the obvious question: "How could Sarah, who taught Torah alongside Abraham, who heard God's voice clearly the first time when God announced the birth of Isaac, not know of God's ordering Abraham to sacrifice Isaac? Knowing, how could she not act?"[6] Rosen then goes on to create a midrash in which Sarah followed Abraham and Isaac up the mountain, carrying the ram with her. In this re-envisioning, she is able to stop Abraham and provide the substitute ram, but she is so traumatized by seeing Isaac bound up and Abraham ready to sacrifice him that she dies.[7]

Sarah is what Ruth Sohn calls "the mother of the covenant."[8] She is a supportive wife, a loving mother, and a partner in nation-building. She serves as a model of a woman who struggles with balancing her disappointments and pain with a sense of purpose. Her flaws are human; her faith is inspiring.

REBEKAH: PRIME INITIATOR, MATERNAL TRICKSTER (GEN. 24:15–28:5)

Rebekah is one of the women of the Bible about whom much is recounted. When Rebakah is first introduced, her beauty is immediately remarked upon. The text goes on to note that she is a virgin of marriageable age. When asked by Abraham's servant to give him water, she not only does so but also offers to give water to his camels until they are satisfied. She is shown to be hospitable, as well as generous and quite strong; providing camels with their fill of water would have required multiple trips to the well, a physically challenging task. She is thus identified right away as someone who may become a force to be reckoned with. When Rebekah has the choice of whether or not to go back with the servant and become Isaac's wife, she swiftly and decisively agrees to leave home and set out into the unknown. Tamara Eskenazi points out that the marriage arrangements stress Rebekah's active role in the negotiations. She writes, "These details emphasize the union of Rebekah and Isaac as one in which the woman is assertive and the man compliant."[9] All these qualities make Rebekah a good candidate for women looking for biblical role models. But Rebekah's story gets more complex.

Like all the matriarchs, Rebekah goes through a period of infertility. At last she becomes pregnant with twins. While pregnant she receives direct prophecy from God that the children in her womb are two separate nations, and that the older will serve the younger. From that emerges a tale of resentments, favoritism, and trickery as Rebekah works to make sure that Jacob, the younger son, receives the blessing and the birthright from Isaac, rather than the older son, Esau.

At a critical moment in the text, Rebekah steps in and uses the limited tools at her disposal to dramatically affect the flow of the narrative. While Rebekah's plan may be creative and even ingenious, it is easy to understand why some readers are uncomfortable justifying her behavior. Tikva Frymer-Kensky supports Rebekah's actions, writing,

> The biblical world valued cunning in the underdog. Only the powerful value honesty at all costs. The powerless know that trickery may save their lives. Early interpreters, both Jewish and Christian, praised Rivka [Rebekah], as did medieval and reformation writers. The censure did not begin until the end of the nineteenth century, when male biblical scholars began to condemn her as a Lady Macbeth. The pendulum is beginning to swing again as we learn more about how the disadvantaged make their way in the world and how women negotiate through patriarchy. To some contemporary eyes, the ingenuity and cunning of Rivka's plan is itself a mark of divine guidance and her role as divine helper.[10]

Without official authority, Rebekah must use the tools at her disposal to make her plan work.

The midrash credits Rebekah with a greater understanding of God's role in the story than do many of the modern commentators. That she gave Jacob the food to carry in to Isaac but did not accompany him is seen as her acknowledgment that from thereon, God would guide Jacob (Gen. R. 65:17). This interpretation recovers her role as God's helper and implies that she acted in accordance with God's plan, rather than as an interfering troublemaker. Rebekah's actions are generally accepted by the rabbis, perhaps because they were seen as necessary in order for Jacob to become the third patriarch and the father of the all-important Joseph.

For the rabbis, Rebekah is particularly righteous because she fulfilled the prophecy at the cost of deceiving her own husband and son (Gen. R. 63:6). The rabbis also justify her favoritism of Jacob over Esau, imagining that when she was pregnant, every time she went near a synagogue or school, Jacob struggled to come out, and every time she went by a place of idolatry, Esau tried to come out (Gen. R. 63:6). Also, the fact that Jacob was a good student made her love him more (Gen. R. 63:10). These explanations represent an attempt on the part of the rabbis to ascribe good motives to this matriarch rather than criticize her questionable behavior.

Frymer-Kensky labels Rebekah as one of what she calls "the victors." These are women who "appear on the scene to act powerfully to affect Israel's destiny."[11] While Rebekah's actions can be seen as underhanded and deceptive, it can also be argued that she ensured that God's will was carried out. Through her actions, Rebekah serves as the critical link in the transmission of the covenant from Abraham to Jacob. She secures the family lineage at great personal cost; Jacob leaves home to escape Esau's wrath and she never sees her beloved son again. As a role model, Rebekah can be seen as an active, determined woman who does what must be done for the greater good, however difficult or painful it may be.

RACHEL AND LEAH: SISTERS, WIVES, MOTHERS, RIVALS (GEN. 29:9–35:26)

The biblical text presents a story of two sisters bound together in a complex relationship. Upon encountering Rachel, Jacob is immediately smitten and overcome by emotion. The text reports that he kisses her and cries in a loud voice. Jacob then professes his love, but her father, Laban, tricks him and gives him Rachel's sister, Leah, as his wife. Having worked seven years to marry the first time, Jacob can marry Rachel only if he commits to working another seven years. The text reveals few details about the two sisters other than to provide a clear contrast: Rachel is beautiful and shapely, while Leah is said to have "weak" or "tender" eyes. Though this comment about Leah's eyes is unclear, either way the implication is that Rachel is more attractive. Once they become Jacob's wives, the two sisters enter into a competition based on their fertility and that of their handmaids, Bilhah and Zilpah. The unloved Leah is successful at conceiving and bearing sons, while the beloved Rachel lags behind in the child-bearing race. The text describes Rachel as being envious of her sister, while Leah resents the attention Rachel received from Jacob. They wind up striking a deal in which Leah gets to spend time with Jacob, and Rachel gets mandrakes, thought to be an aphrodisiac, after which she becomes pregnant.

As role models, their relationship of jealousy and resentment can cause discomfort, as does their apparent passivity. Their father and Jacob plot around them, while they go along with the plan but manipulate behind the scenes to fulfill their need for both love and children. For all that the text reveals, much is left unsaid. What might exist between the lines that was not made explicit in the biblical narrative? Were the sisters passive victims of their father's trickery, or was something else happening behind the scenes?

The Talmud offers a midrash in which Rachel helps Leah deceive Jacob. Rachel revealed her father's plans to Jacob and taught him special signs so that he would know it was her. But Rachel realized that by rights Leah, the eldest, should be married first. Not wanting to disgrace her older sister, Rachel taught her the signs (BT Baba Batra 123a). Thus Jacob was tricked not only by Laban but by Rachel as well. Another midrash takes this possibility even further, imagining Rachel hiding under the marriage bed so that when Jacob spoke to Leah, Rachel could respond in her own voice and maintain the pretense (Eichah R., proem 24). Both midrashim paint Rachel in an active and compassionate light as a woman who took action and placed her sister's feelings above her own. The rabbis also laud the sisters as equal partners in building up the Jewish people, who between them produced chieftains and kings, prophets and judges (Gen. R. 70:15).

Elyse Goldstein offers a perspective on the bond between the two sisters that challenges the stereotypical idea that Jacob, as the man and husband, would have been in charge of the complex relationships within their household. She writes, "Rachel's offer to pay for mandrakes with sex with Jacob shows her power in determining with whom Jacob will sleep and suggests that through the years Rachel is not only more loved by Jacob, but more sought out by him sexually."[12] The sisters are able to come together to figure out how to get what they both want from Jacob. Rachel becomes pregnant, and Leah gets time with Jacob.

In a modern midrash, Jill Hammer imagines Leah arranging to take Rachel's place. In this version of the story, Leah has a visit from an otherworldly figure, the man Israel whom Jacob will someday become. He asks Leah to marry him, explaining that although the part of him that is Jacob loves Rachel, the part of him that will someday wrestle with God and become Israel loves her, Leah. She writes:

> "But Jacob," Leah stammered, "I mean, Israel, it is Rachel you love. Don't you know? You will be wed to her tomorrow."
>
> "The part of me that is Jacob loves Rachel," he answered, "but the part of me that is Israel loves you. Jacob doesn't know it now, but he needs your depths as much as Rachel's heights. He needs your wisdom and compassion as much as her beauty and boldness. I need you in order to be the patriarch I must become. Please, Leah, be my wife."[13]

Though upset at the idea of wronging her sister, Leah heads off to fulfill her promise to her future husband, Israel. This rewriting of the biblical text creates a scenario in which Leah is not a victim but is actively working behind the scenes to bring about her desired outcome.

Norma Rosen also creates a midrash in which Rachel and Leah are united in confusing Jacob. They switch places and names continually and insist on lovemaking only in the dark, so that he never knows which one he is really with. Instead of rivals, they are united in sharing the burden of being wives and mothers, and they, rather than Jacob, maintain control over the sexual relationship. They believe that their actions are for Jacob's own good, so that he will come to understand that the only real owner of anything or anybody, even wives and sons, can be only God and not man.[14] Rosen thus provides a more positive gloss on their rivalry and gives the sisters more power than a plain reading of the text would allow.

Through re-readings and modern midrash, Rachel and Leah become not only the mothers of the twelve tribes but also models of women struggling with difficult situations. Working within the confines of their time, they are able to attain a level of control over their lives and learn how to attain what they most desire, be it children or love. Out of adversity, they find common ground and learn to work together rather than at odds with each other.

DINA: A SISTER, AN ADVENTURER, A VICTIM? (GEN. 34)

Dina is the one daughter born to Jacob in the midst of twelve sons. She is, like her mother, Leah, often overlooked. Her only moment in the spotlight is brief and tragic. Dina goes out to see the local women of the land and is noticed by Shechem, a local prince. What next ensues is most commonly understood as a rape scene, in which Dina is victimized. She then fades out of the narrative as her brothers, seeking vengeance, brutally take center stage.

The rabbis judge Dina harshly for wanting to "go out." This is the classic response of blaming the victim, in which the rabbis see Dina as a young woman who brings trouble upon herself. In one midrash, it is implied that her going out was an act of harlotry (Gen. R. 80:2). Another suggests that her going out was related to improperly exposing herself and thereby causing Shechem to notice her (Gen. R. 80:5).

Dina is imagined by Vanessa Ochs as someone hungry for contact with other women and for adventure.

> If she could only meet people outside her world, hear their languages, eat their foods, shop for red ribbon in their bazaars, wear their clothes, style her hair as they did. She would make a friend, who would reach for her hand.[15]

Ochs's sympathetic version of Dina is that of an overprotected young woman who yearns for broader horizons and friendship.

Frymer-Kensky argues that the text doesn't actually say that Shechem raped her. Rather, it says he "took her, lay with her, and degraded her" (though some translations use the word "rape," the Hebrew can be read in multiple ways). She writes,

How did Shechem approach her? The story never hints at what happened. Did he speak to her? Did she speak to him? Did he take her by
force or did he persuade her? Did he act like Prince Charming, or like
an imperious monarch stating his demands? And what about her? Was
she love-struck and happy, defiant and satisfied—or the victim of
rape?[16]

Frymer-Kensky goes on to explain that the word order of the description is
important and may provide a hint that this was not in fact rape. The degradation came after the sex, not before, which could mean that while the sex
itself was consensual, it was only in the aftermath that Dina became a victim.
She continues,

> In rape, abuse starts the moment the rapist begins to use force, long
> before penetration. In other illicit sexual encounters, the act of inter-
> course may not be abusive. The sex may be sweet and romantic. But the
> *fact* that the man has intercourse with her degrades her, and the word
> *innah* comes after the words "lay with."[17]

It is not a question that Dina is degraded. But is her degradation a result of
Shechem's actions or a result of having lost her virginity and willingly given
herself to a man without her father's permission? Laura Geller connects the
story of Dina to the practice of honor killings that continue today. She suggests that what happened between Dina and Shechem was humiliating to
her family; and though unlike typical honor killings, for it is not Dina who
gets killed, there is retributive punishment carried out by the shamed
family.[18]

What happens to Dina after this brief episode is a great source of
speculation for the rabbis as well as for women today. There is a midrashic
tradition that she became the wife of her brother Simeon (Gen. R. 18:11,
2) and another that she marries Job (Gen. R. 19:12; BT Bava Batra 15b).
A different midrash suggests that she became pregnant by Shechem, and
her daughter was given to an Egyptian priest. This daughter later becomes
Joseph's wife, thereby eliminating the rabbinic discomfort at the idea that
Joseph married an Egyptian woman rather than an Israelite (P D'R E 38).

That the patriarchal text focuses more on the men than the woman is
a given. Like Queen Vashti in the Book of Esther, who has only in recent
years been considered a role model for her defiance of patriarchal rules
and unwillingness to be controlled, Dina is being re-examined and
reclaimed by contemporary Jewish women. Ochs sees Dina as a useful
example of risk-taking: "Dina comes to tell us that just because her story
of stepping out ended poorly, we must continue to be enticed by the music

of otherness and risk stepping out. We must meet people who are different from us, people who might not like us at first, people who rattle us and leave us unbalanced. Most important, we should defy those who stand in the way of our taking risks in relationships."[19]

These expressions of renewed interested in Dina are attempts to make sense out of a troubling story and transform Dina from her status as a hapless victim or a "bad girl" into a role model of strength and self-determination. For the brief moment that Dina appears in the text she is active. She chooses to go out. She attempts to make her own choices and control her own sexuality. Her experience doing so provides a model of empowered behavior while offering a sobering reminder of the risk that these choices may not be welcomed by the surrounding society and, indeed, may carry a certain amount of danger.

TAMAR: A RIGHTEOUS RISK-TAKER (GEN. 38)

The story of Tamar serves as a counter-tale to that of Dina. Tamar refuses to become a victim, and to that end she successfully takes an enormous risk. Tamar's story begins with Judah, one of Joseph's brothers, marrying a Canaanite woman who bears him three sons. Tamar is chosen by Judah as a wife for his first-born son, Er. Er dies without producing any children, and Tamar is given to Onan, the second son. According to the laws of levirate marriage as outlined in Deuteronomy 25:5–10, if a man is to die without having produced a son, his widow is required to supply a son who will count as being the son of the late husband's. The brother is allowed to refuse to cooperate, though he must do so through an official ritual of refusal, while she has no choice in the matter and is not permitted to marry outside the family until she has produced a son.[20] Onan is thereby instructed to provide his brother with a posthumous heir through Tamar. But this plan does not work either, as Onan refuses to comply and dies. Judah, meanwhile, still has no new generation to carry on the line, and Tamar has no child. As a childless widow, Tamar is vulnerable. She has no standing in the community, and no one who is obligated to care for her in her old age. Judah sends her back to her father's house, reinforcing her helplessness and dependency.

Tamar comes to realize that Judah has no plans to give her his third son and enable her to have both a husband and children. At that point Tamar takes matters into her own hands by taking off her widow's garb and disguising herself as a prostitute to attract her father-in-law. Seemingly unaware that she is his daughter-in-law, Judah has sex with Tamar after giving her his personal items as a guarantee of future payment. Tamar becomes pregnant with twins, and when Judah criticizes her wanton behavior and calls for her death, she shames Judah into admitting that he has not treated her well and that it is he who is to blame.

Tamar is a classic underdog, a vulnerable childless widow who resorts to subterfuge when no other avenue of redress is open to her. Susan Niditch notes that prostitutes are "liminal characters, outside the social order."[21] A prostitute, a woman by definition not tied to any one man, presents a danger and a threat to the society. So too the childless widow. As such, Tamar had already fallen between the cracks of comfortable societal norms.

The biblical text praises Tamar and presents her as a positive model.

When Ruth is married, she is blessed with the wish that she may be like Tamar (Ruth 4:12). Tamar is the outsider who allows Judah to be redeemed and have sons to carry on his lineage. One of her twins becomes the ancestor of Boaz, with whom Ruth, another outsider, will conceive Obed, who leads to King David. Without Tamar, and without Ruth, there would be no King David. The actions of both of these bold women, therefore, are seen as necessary means to an end.

While such a tale, hinging as it does on prostitution, might have presented serious problems for the rabbis, Tamar merits great praise. The rabbis see Tamar's actions as pure (Gen. R. 85:2). Rashi credits her with taking special care not to shame Judah, echoing Talmudic portrayals of Tamar in which she is seen as being more righteous than Judah (BT Sotah 10b). The rabbis also connect Tamar to Rebekah. Carol Bakhos writes, "For the rabbis, Tamar's heroic actions display the wherewithal, foresight, and fortitude of a matriarch such as Rebekah. They allude to this association in B'reishit Rabbah 60.15 and 85.7: 'Two covered themselves with a veil, and each gave birth to twins—Rebekah and Tamar.' Tamar's behavior is considered a praiseworthy response to a situation of injustice."[22] The veil is also significant in midrashic readings of Tamar because it allows her to be viewed as a modest woman, a positive attribute in the rabbinic value system. In this interpretation, her modesty was what merited her a place in the messianic line (BT Megillah 10b).

Bakhos points out that *Biblical Antiquities,* a first-century Jewish commentary, calls Tamar a role model for the Israelites in Egypt because of her determination to perpetuate the line of Judah despite the risk.[23] She similarly finds Tamar to be an example of righteous behavior. She writes, "Judah railed to have Shelah impregnate her, but now she has caused him to impregnate her himself. She is therefore more righteous, in her commitment to continuing the line through the levirate, than Judah has been."[24]

Frymer-Kensky points out that Tamar is rewarded for her actions by God. Tamar's hard-won children are her recompense for risk-taking, despite the deception and potentially dishonorable behavior. But this story serves to rehabilitate Judah as much as it makes a heroine out of Tamar. Frymer-Kensky continues, "Her boldness, initiative, and willingness to defy society's expectations have enabled God to provide Judah with two new sons after the death of his first two sons. By continuing to consider herself a member of Judah's family and insisting on securing her own future within its parameters, she has made it possible for that family to thrive and develop into a major tribe and eventually the Judean state."[25] Tamar transforms the history of this people as she transforms Judah. For this reason, Ochs calls Tamar a teacher of ethics.[26] Having gotten himself into a morally questionable situation in chapter 37 vis-à-vis his brother Joseph, Judah has shown that his character is in need of redemption. Tamar's actions create a situation in which he first appears to be in the wrong, and then at the climatic moment he acknowledges his wrongdoing and in so doing is seen as having repented. Just as Rebekah's actions serve the ongoing needs of the narrative, so do Tamar's. She gets her desired children but is essentially never heard from again. Judah, on the other hand, gets a full makeover and achieves a kind of immortality through the importance that his tribe will come to have in the history of the children of Israel.

Debra Orenstein writes about Tamar as a forgotten woman, one whose story is easy to miss in the middle of the ongoing story of the matriarchs and patriarchs. But Orenstein goes on to suggest that Tamar is also a model of a co-conspirator with God, writing, "Some of the most maligned and mistreated women of the Bible—Tamar among them—are also, when one scratches the surface, some of the bravest, most independent, and most spiritually evolved."[27] Tamar puts a plan into action that will not merely help herself but will get the larger narrative back on track. She takes matters into her own hands while also assuring that Judah's line will continue, leading all the way to the Messiah. Tamar is thus a model of risk-taking and assertiveness. Refusing to be a victim in a system set up against her, she is a strategist who fights for her rights and makes those around her accountable for their actions.

MIRIAM: WISE WOMAN AND PROPHET (EXOD. 2:4–10; 15:20–21; NUM. 12:1–15; 20:1; 26:59)

Moses' sister first appears in the narrative as a young girl who has the wherewithal to save his life. She arranges for his adoptive mother to hire his biological mother as a wetnurse, ensuring his connection to his community of birth. Though unnamed in that episode, she is understood by

Jewish tradition to be the same sister later identified as Miriam. Unlike other women in the Torah, Miriam is never associated with any man other than her brothers, Moses and Aaron, and she bears no children. She is seen as a leader of the people and is associated with water and its life-sustaining properties. Yet even so, when Miriam speaks out against Moses, she receives a harsh punishment from God.

Miriam is called a prophet by the text, leading the rabbis to wonder why she should merit this great honor. They create a midrash in which she prophesies that her father would have a son who would bring the Israelites out of slavery (Mehkilta d'Rabbi Ishmael, Shirata 10:58–65; BT Sotah 12a). When Pharaoh decrees that all newborn Israelite boys are to be killed, the husbands and wives divorce and refuse to procreate. Because of her prophecy, Miriam convinces them to get back together and have children, thereby ensuring that Moses will be born.

One of Miriam's defining moments comes when she leads the women in joyous song after the crossing of the sea. Ochs pictures Miriam as an inspiring visionary. Not only was she able to see that the Israelites should continue to have children, but even in the rush of leaving Egypt she had thought to bring instruments as well as the more obvious necessities. When they crossed the Sea of Reeds, Miriam led them in song as they danced with their hand drums. Although they faced the terrifying unknown, she was able to give them hope. Ochs suggests that Miriam provides an example of "inspiration, courage, and reassurance."[28]

Midrash HaGadol, a thirteenth-century Yemenite midrash, is based on the text extolling a Woman of Valor (Prov. 31:10–31). In the midrash, each verse represents a biblical woman worthy of praise. Its praise of Miriam is based on the verse "She girds herself with strength and performs her task with vigor" (Prov. 31:17), connecting this to the midrash of Miriam convincing her father to remarry her mother and conceive Moses. In her commentary on this midrash, Marsha Pravder Mirkin emphasizes the fact that Miriam is never anyone's wife or mother. She is a sister and a prophet. Commenting on the midrash's connection of Miriam and strength, she writes, "The strength that I see rising from her is spiritual, emotional, and psychological. It allows her to challenge the powers of her time and to celebrate in the midst of uncertainty."[29] Mirkin goes on to create a new midrash in which Miriam inspired an army of resisters, Israelite and Egyptian women working together to save babies without Pharaoh's knowledge. When the Israelites left Egypt, these resisters went with them.[30]

Mirkin's midrash plays on the traditional reading of Miriam as a source of community strength. The rabbinic midrash creates a tradition about wells of water that follow Miriam wherever she goes (BT Shabbat

35a). In this way she is able to provide for the people and be a nurturer. The biblical text itself recounts Miriam's death, and the next verse goes on to report that the people are suddenly without water. Rashi comments on the juxtaposition of these two verses, noting that the one is a consequence of the other. Drawing on this same connection, a modern practice has developed of placing a cup of water on the Passover seder table alongside the traditional Elijah's cup. Called "Miriam's Cup," this new ritual harkens back to Miriam's role as the provider of water and serves to remind a new generation of women's important contributions to the survival of the Jewish people.

Along with reasons for celebration, Miriam's story also provides challenges for contemporary women. She was a leader, a prophet, and a wise woman, but ultimately she was not *the* leader. Did that fact assert itself like a glass ceiling for Miriam? When Miriam and Aaron speak out critically against Moses, it is only Miriam who becomes afflicted with scaly disease and has to be outside the camp for a week until she heals. Her story thus poses another question: how can we speak out in ways that will get us heard but not punished?

Miriam is a model for the necessity of speaking out and taking action at critical moments despite the risks. She was a rebel who saved Moses' life, thus ensuring a future for her entire people. Miriam provided inspiration, guidance, and hope to the people. Loyal to her brother, her family, and her people from the time she was a young girl, she was both wise and generous with her wisdom. For contemporary women, Miriam provides an often too-realistic model of leadership, with both its attendant joys and challenges.

THE DAUGHTERS OF TZELOPHECHAD: A STRONG SISTERHOOD (NUM. 27:1–11; 36:1–12)

Mahlah, Hoglah, Tirzah, Noa, and Milcah, the five daughters of Tzelophechad, have a brief starring role in the Book of Numbers. The fact that they are all named is itself noteworthy. These five sisters are the daughters of a man who has died without sons. They challenge Moses and ultimately God for the right to inherit land and thus carry on their father's name. They boldly claim what should be theirs, and they are granted the right they desire. Their success comes at a price, however. Once their request is granted, the men from their tribe complain that when the daughters marry, their inheritance will pass out of the tribe to their husbands or children. Their inheritance right is affirmed, but they are limited to marrying within the tribe.

For the rabbis, these women are considered models of righteousness. The motivation for their actions is understood to be not personal gain but, rather, to honor their father and his legacy. They are credited with being wise and righteous also because they knew the right moment to speak up. Judith Baskin points out that they are additionally praised by the rabbis for showing faith in God and God's ability to make a just judgment on their petition. Their challenge is seen as positive and merit-worthy because it pushes Moses to clarify the law. The Torah itself approves of their behavior, which makes it easy for the rabbinic tradition to extol the sisters, going so far as to credit them with being knowledgeable in Jewish law.[31]

The sisters provide a model of women who understand how to deal with power structures and emerge victorious. Ochs writes,

> The daughters show us how women can work together to effectively be heard in settings that have traditionally privileged male styles of leadership and expression. The daughters show us that we can teach men to recognize and respect the different but highly effective ways that women working together can lead and make important changes.[32]

They are examples of cooperative problem solving, risk-taking, leadership, and strategizing. They are empowered, assertive women who are not intimidated by the seemingly intractable power structures they encounter.

Hammer creates a midrash in which each sister has a voice, allowing their separate personalities to emerge. Mahlah is the planner. Noa is a determined strategist. Hoglah lives in the world of the spirit. Milcah is a poet. Tirzah is deeply in love but still practical. This midrash emphasizes not only the strength and determination of these sisters but also the challenge of having their independence tempered by the requirement to marry within their tribe. In doing so, Hammer acknowledges that for contemporary women, this condition diminishes the triumph of the sisters' victory. Hammer thus creates a scenario in which this limitation can be overcome. In her retelling, it is Tirzah who has the most to lose by this secondary ruling, as she is in love with someone outside the tribe. Hammer finds a creative solution in which this sister arranges for her lover to be adopted by her uncle, thereby becoming part of the tribe. In Tirzah's voice she writes, "I hope no one decides to oppose me. I do not intend to let my cousins, or even Moses, decide whom I marry. My sisters and I are getting used to choosing for ourselves."[33]

Ora Horn Prouser sees the five daughters as an example of the necessity for communal change. She writes, "In periods of transition, new realities arise and need to be addressed—including realities specially related to women's rights."[34] In this story, women see a need for change that applies directly to them. They work respectfully but forcefully within the system, attempting not to threaten its foundations but challenging it to adapt. She argues that this is a useful model of change for the Jewish community today, writing, "Our own generation must be willing to step forward like the daughters of Tzelophechad and to redress wrongs. We also must be willing, like Moses, to accept that change is inevitable. New situations, challenges, and solutions are the natural outgrowth of a vital, living tradition. Such evolution does not threaten our tradition but rather, strengthens and solidifies it."[35] Frankel makes a similar claim. In the voice of Beruriah the Scholar she writes, "We can understand this story as a valuable lesson for us all, teaching us that Jewish law has the flexibility to expand and embrace women, giving us increasingly more rights and a fairer share of our common legacy."[36]

For Jewish women today, the limitation placed on these sisters is all too evident. Yet the fact that they spoke out and gained rights at all was remarkable in its context. These learned, strong, independent women were not scared to demand justice. As such, they serve as early models of women who spoke out and worked as a sisterhood to fight for their rights. Whereas most of the biblical women operate within the personal sphere of the family, the power of these women as role models was that they worked in the public sphere, and the ripple effects of their actions were felt by the whole community for generations to come.

YAEL: A COMPLEX HEROINE, A DOMESTIC WARRIOR (JUDG. 4, 5)

The story of Yael is a short and self-contained unit, told once in chapter 4 of the Book of Judges in prose, and again in chapter 5 in poetry. Like so many of the biblical women, Yael is a woman who steps into a story and changes the course of events. A battle ensues between the Israelites and Yavin's army, led by Sisera. Barak, at the heeding of Deborah, leads the Israelites and appears to be winning, despite the fact that Sisera's troops are better equipped. He pursues Sisera, who flees and seeks refuge in the tent of Yael. She seizes the opportunity and, disguising her true intentions in the guise of hospitality, lulls Sisera into a false sense of safety. She covers him with a blanket, gives him milk, and when he is truly relaxed she kills him. Like Judah, who saw in Tamar only what he wanted to see, Sisera does not see the threat and danger behind Yael's hospitality.

This narrative plays on the familiar bifurcated image of woman as both nurturing mother and sexual seductress, which Yael uses to her advantage. The Bible seems to praise Yael when the text states that she is blessed among women, an indication that her act was seen as justified. Tikva

Frymer-Kensky points out that this verse can also be read "Blessed be Yael **by** women," which she takes to mean that the Bible sees Yael as a role model for other women.[37]

Yael is generally praised by the rabbis. The rabbis of the Talmud commented on the sexual undertones in this tale, teaching that it was with her voice that Yael inspired lust (BT Megillah 15a). The rabbis count the expressions of sinking and falling in 5:27 and determine that this represents seven times that Yael had intercourse with Sisera. However, instead of criticizing her for adultery, they conclude that the end justifies the means. Just as they refrain from censuring Tamar for her act of harlotry with Judah, they decide that Yael did not derive pleasure from the intercourse but, rather, performed these transgressions with an ulterior, and in their minds more positive, motive of killing him (BT Nazir 23b; BT Horayot 10b; BT Yebamot 103a).

The story of Yael, with its overt sexuality and violence, may make contemporary readers uncomfortable. Is Yael strong and assertive, or is she overly aggressive? How much violence is too much violence? A modern interpretation by Andrea Cohen-Keiner views the story as one in which Yael is threatened by Sisera, who is planning to rape her. In this interpretation, her act of violence toward him is justified as self-defense.[38]

Susan Niditch finds Yael to be a model of self-determination and active decision making. She writes, "The Jael [Yael] tale read by modern women provides an alternate symbolism. One is not suggesting that women become men-slayers in some simple-minded reading, but rather that this tale is rich in images of directed action, self-assertion, and consciousness on the part of the underdog. The archetype expressing on many levels male anxieties can thus become a powerfully charged model for all marginals, in particular women."[39] Like Rebekah's and Tamar's, Yael's status denies her access to official authority. Yael is a woman who stays in the tent; she is not out in the heat of the battle. Yet she is able to use her limited power to change the course of events. She uses domestic, feminine tools like milk and a blanket, as well as male assumptions about female behavior. Rather than a sword, she uses what is readily at hand, a tent peg. Nevertheless, her covert actions have an enormous impact. Yael is a reminder of the hidden reserves of creativity, strength, and courage that even the most powerless women can call upon in moments of crisis.

VASHTI AND ESTHER: A TALE OF TWO QUEENS (BOOK OF ESTHER)

The Book of Esther has much in common with classic fairy tales, including a befuddled king, good guys and bad guys, a beautiful queen, and a happy ending. Featured in this biblical book are two women, Vashti and

Esther, who represent opposing models of womanhood. Vashti is the "bad" wife, the queen who refuses to do the king's bidding and is banished. Esther, in contrast, is the "good" wife.

Esther is an orphan being raised by a relative, Mordecai. After Ahasuerus, the king of Shushan, has his queen Vashti banished for disobeying him, he instructs his advisors to search his kingdom to find the most beautiful virgins in the land. Those women would be brought into his harem, and the woman who most pleases the king will become his new queen. Esther is chosen to join the king's harem and, eventually, to be the new queen. Mordecai warns her not to reveal her identity, and Esther obediently complies. Meanwhile, the king's second-in-command, Haman, arranges to have all the Jews in the kingdom killed by order of the king. Upon learning of this plan, Mordecai asks Esther to reveal her identity and beg for the king's intervention. Unwilling to take the risk, Esther at first demurs. But in the end she takes action and manages to save her people. Esther is thus the heroine of this dramatic story, a woman who risked her life to save others.

Esther has long been a role model for Jewish girls and women. She exemplifies beauty, obedience, and bravery. During Purim, the holiday commemorating the events in the book of this tale, Jewish girls traditionally dress up as Esther, each trying to outdo the others as the most beautiful queen. The midrash reinforces the biblical idea of Esther's great beauty (Esther Rabbah 6:9). In contrast, Vashti is presented as a negative role model in the Bible as well as in the rabbinic literature. The Bible explains that she could not be allowed to refuse the king, as that would cause other women to disobey their husbands. The Talmud calls Vashti's beauty false and surmises that the reason she won't appear as summoned is that she has a tail (BT Megillah 12b).

These two women are inextricably linked and can't escape being compared. Vashti is the disobedient woman who says no, whereas Esther is compliant and obedient, at least to a point. Vashti defied her husband, for which the classical texts show no support, whereas Esther saves her people. Yet, both are more complex characters than their images in popular folklore would suggest.

In her rewriting of the story, Ochs creates an Esther who is less passive than the plain sense of the biblical text allows. In this version it is Esther herself who chooses to compete to become the new queen, not Mordecai who chooses her. Ochs's Esther is a young woman not only beautiful but wise, who recognizes that her beauty will give her an opportunity to fulfill a yet-to-be-revealed mission.[40]

For Tamara Cohen, Esther is a model of a woman with a personal connection to God. Cohen writes, "Esther is a spiritual innovator and had faith that sustained her ability to work in partnership with a God she couldn't see or hear directly. She asks for opportunity to fast and pray before going in to the king. She established a fast day that continues even until today. She knew how to draw strength from many sources—herself in prayer/meditation, from the community who she asked to fast/pray with her, from Mordecai with whom she worked as a team, and with God."[41]

Parallel to the attempt to find new ways of reading Esther, Vashti is being reclaimed as a role model of a woman who refused to acquiesce. Mary Gendler writes, "If women would begin to identify also with Vashti, as I am proposing we do, we could discover our own sources of dignity, pride, and independence."[42] Vashti has become an example of positive refusal, the woman who was able to say no and be heard.

Esther, like many of the biblical women, took action when it was necessary to do so. Although it may have been against her nature, when there was no alternative Esther stepped up, spoke out, and saved her people. Esther, the beautiful queen, is an example of a woman defined not solely by her looks. Working subversively from within the system, she was able to use her status to effect positive change. Vashti appears only at the beginning of Esther's story as a counterpoint to all of Esther's positive qualities. Yet modern re-readings of Vashti argue that she herself is worth viewing as a role model rather than simply as a Not-Esther. Together, Esther the faithful insider and the defiant outsider Vashti model two different ways of fighting against abuses of power.

THE CHALLENGE OF FINDING ROLE MODELS

The Bible is rich in women who represent potential role models for Jewish women. In addition to those explored here, there is Deborah the Judge, a military strategist. Michal, one of David's wives, is the only woman in biblical text said to be in love with a man, who saves David's life by helping him escape. Abigail is a shrewd strategist who goes behind the back of her then-husband Nabal to align herself with David and become his wife. The young widow Ruth faithfully follows and cares for her bereaved mother-in-law, accepting both her mother-in-law's fate and faith, ultimately remarrying and bearing a child who will become a progenitor of the Messiah. And there are many, many more, some named, like the harlot Rahab who helps Joshua, and some, like Noah's wife, Lot's wife, or Jepthah's daughter, who remain unnamed other than by their relationship to a man.

Identifying role models for Jewish women among the bible heroes is not without significant challenges. None of the biblical women presents a picture of idealized perfection or even consistency. They are, like their male cohorts, flawed heroes. These flaws make them more human and thus easier to relate to. Yet it can be difficult to aspire to their strengths while also coming to terms with their weaknesses.

The search for role models is a complex task that requires study, interpretation, and sometimes reinterpretation. For the rabbis, these women characters represented paradigms of femininity, examples of behavior to emulate or to avoid. Either way, this polarized view ignores the texture of their individual stories and overlooks the depth of their unique characters. Today Jewish women can employ both the traditional Jewish tools of study and interpretation as well as contemporary methodologies to probe the biblical text and even expand upon it. Just like Jewish women in previous generations, they are able to find inspiration, affirmation, and a sense of purpose through their encounters with the lives of the biblical women.

NOTES

1. Devra Kay, ed., *Seyder Tkhines: The Forgotten Book of Common Prayer for Jewish Women* (Philadelphia: Jewish Publication Society of America, 2004), 10–11.

2. Ibid., 152.

3. Dvora Weisberg, in *The Torah: A Women's Commentary,* ed. Tamara C. Eskenazi and Andrea L. Weiss (New York: URJ Press and WRJ, 2008), 79.

4. Ellen Frankel, *The Five Books of Miriam: A Women's Commentary on the Torah* (Philadelphia: Jewish Publication Society of America, 1996), 14.

5. Susan Niditch, in *The Torah: A Women's Commentary,* 76.

6. Norma Rosen, *Biblical Women Unbound: Countertales* (Philadelphia: Jewish Publication Society, 1996), 43–44.

7. Ibid., 44.

8. Ruth Sohn, in *The Torah: A Women's Commentary,* 81.

9. Tamara Eskenazi, in *The Torah: A Women's Commentary,* 127.

10. Tikva Frymer-Kensky, *Reading the Women of the Bible: A New Interpretation of Their Stories* (New York: Schocken Books, 2002), 19.

11. Ibid., 3.

12. Elyse Goldstein, *ReVisions: Seeing Torah through a Feminist Lens* (Woodstock, VT: Jewish Lights Publishing, 1998), 66–67.

13. Jill Hammer, *Sisters at Sinai: New Tales of Biblical Women* (Philadelphia: Jewish Publication Society, 2001), 73.

14. Rosen, 81–92.

15. Vanessa Ochs, *Sarah Laughed: Modern Lessons from the Wisdom and Stories of Biblical Women* (New York: McGraw Hill, 2005), 76

16. Frymer-Kensky, 182.

17. Ibid., 183.

18. Laura Geller, in *The Torah: A Women's Commentary,* 204–5.

19. Ochs, 76.

20. Richard Kalmin, "Levirate Law," in *Anchor Bible Dictionary* (New York: Doubleday, 1992), 4:296.

21. Susan Niditch, "The Wronged Woman Righted: An Analysis of Genesis 38," *Harvard Theological Review* 72 (1979): 47.

22. Carol Bakhos, in *The Torah: A Women's Commentary,* 227.

23. Ibid.

24. Ibid.

25. Frymer-Kensky, 274.

26. Ochs, 75.

27. Deborah Orenstein, *Lifecycles: Jewish Women on Biblical Themes in Contemporary Life* (Woodstock, VT: Jewish Lights Publishing), 28–29.

28. Ochs, 26–30.

29. Marsha Pravder Mirkin, "Miriam," in *Praise Her Works,* ed. Penina Adelman (Philadelphia: Jewish Publication Society, 2005), 58.

30. Ibid., 63.

31. Judith Baskin, *Midrashic Women: Formations of the Feminine in Rabbinic Literature* (Hanover, NH: Brandeis University Press, 2002), 144–45.

32. Ochs, 42.

33. Hammer, 144.

34. Ora Horn Prouser, "Living in Transition: A Biblical Perspective," in *Lifecycles: Jewish Women on Biblical Themes in Contemporary Life,* ed. Debra Orenstein and Jane Litman (Woodstock, VT: Jewish Lights Publishing, 1997), 253.

35. Ibid., 254.

36. Frankel, 236.

37. Frymer-Kensky, 51–52.

38. Andrea Cohen-Kiener, "Yael," in *Praise Her Works*, ed. Penina Adelman (Philadelphia: Jewish Publication Society, 2005), 78.

39. Susan Niditch, "Eroticism and Death in the Tale of Jael," in *Women in the Hebrew Bible,* ed. Alice Bach (New York: Routledge, 1999), 313.

40. Ochs, 57–64.

41. Tamara Cohen, "Esther," in *Praise Her Works,* ed. Penina Adelman (Philadelphia: Jewish Publication Society, 2005),188.

42. Mary Gendler, "The Restoration of Vashti," in *The Jewish Woman: New Perspectives,* ed. Elizabeth Coltun (New York: Schocken, 1976), 247.

CHAPTER 7

Women of the Holocaust: Whispering Heroes

Pamela Treiber Opper

I am a clinical social worker and fortunate to have worked with a group of women who are survivors of the Holocaust. With this chapter, I wish to honor my friends and heroes by telling their stories as they were told to me. They are locked in my memory. It is my hope their stories will be told for generations.

These stories are about their experiences in the camps, the forests, and the ghettos. Their stories reach into their lives before the war and after. Their stories reveal the secrets of their survival. We will never know what it was like to be them, nor will we ever fully comprehend the level of despair they carry with them every day. We can, however, continue to be inspired by their lives.

We can learn to have faith, we can learn to be brave, and we can learn to love life and the gifts it brings with it. We can learn to teach our daughters and our granddaughters to be fearless in the face of evil. We will never know how they found the courage to go on after what they experienced. As they move closer to their loved ones and further away from our lives, they will continue to be our giants, our heroes, our myths, and our dreams. The following stories reveal how one weaves straw into gold, how one can take a sad song and make it better.

We are blessed with every story a survivor of the Holocaust entrusts with us. With each story we become the custodians of memory; we store these memories deeply in our souls. No two stories are ever the same, and the women's stories often differ in mysterious ways from the stories told by men. A male survivor shared, "What kept me alive was the smell of freshly baked bread and the hope that I would one day be able to eat it again."

While men dreamed of food, women used the exchange of recipes to distract them. "Our greatest wish was to work in the bakery. Even though we could not eat the food, we could speak among ourselves about how we used to bake. This kept our mind off our hunger and our focus on the food." These quiet exchanges of domestic life created a bond between women and helped them to create a sense of family within the ghettos and the camps. The ability to stay focused on the future was their key to survival. "My secret of survival was that I never lost the hope that the day would come when I would be standing in my kitchen once again, preparing a Shabbos meal." This image generated hope and strength under impossible conditions.

Life for women during the Holocaust years was like living a life turned inside out. Mothers proved their love and attachment for their children by giving them away. Mothers calmly held their children's hands as they walked their children to strangers' homes. The door would open as they watched their child step in. They turned away, knowing they may never see their children again.

Childbirth and child rearing became a nightmare rather than a time of greatest joy. Terror and fear swept through camps and hiding places each time a baby cried or a woman's belly began to grow. Women were faced with the dilemma of either having to kill their newborns or watch them slowly starve and die from infection. There were some who chose to accompany their children to the gas chambers rather than desert them. Women bravely walked their children to the gas chambers, soothing their children with song.

Women bartered for food and for their lives with their sewing, their cooking, and their bodies. A fourteen-year-old sister tried to drown out the sounds of her older sister having sex with a Nazi officer in the bunk bed above her. "My sister was a flirt. She kept our names off the deportation lists with flirtation." She acknowledged that her sister saved their lives each time she had sex. Women who became partisans in the forests knew that there was a great chance that they would be raped while they slept in the woods. Partisan camps were raided often; women were the most vulnerable and could not fend off the attackers. "My best friend was my shotgun. The rest, I can't talk about. I don't even remember. I only knew that we hid in the woods and I lived."

The reason the women who survived stayed alive was because they bonded with one another. These friendships created great strength and solidarity among Jewish women in captivity. Friends gave food to starving friends; the strong did the work for the weak and ailing.

They have left behind their diaries, their poetry, their art, their songs, their children, their grandchildren, and their stories. Their lives inspire us to love deeply and with dignity, to live fully and completely, and to honor their courage. We are humbled by the love they offered to one another, to their children, and to all who have come after them.

LEAH

Leah was an only child born to an established Hungarian family. She worshiped her father and was devoted to her mother. She was to find out after she was liberated by American soldiers that her father died within days of the liberation of Mauthausen. She never knew where the Germans had taken her father. She knew only that he was forced from their home and never returned.

After this incident, Leah and her mother were taken to the ghetto. Her fiancé was in a labor camp and had heard that if people got married, they received preferential treatment. They made a plan, and she met the young man whom she had met and loved from the time she was fourteen years old. He was waiting for her outside the ghetto, escorted by a Nazi guard. They went to the synagogue and married. She then went back to the ghetto to join her mother, and he went back to the labor camp. Every Thursday the young husband fasted to honor his wife in the ghetto. He had heard that people were taken to Auschwitz on Thursdays. He kept her picture in his pocket and was able to keep this picture with him his entire life. She shows the folds from his pocket. The young girl proudly stares into the camera with a yellow star on her blouse.

Leah and her mother were taken to Auschwitz. As she rode with her mother in the cattle car, she could not comprehend what was happening. She could not breathe. There was no air and people were dying all around her. The smell of human excrement filled whatever air there was to breathe. People stood on each other to help get one breath of fresh air from the only window. She held her mother's hand so that they would not become separated. When the doors finally opened, she and her mother got off the train and were ordered to stand on a line.

A man looked her mother up and down and signaled for her to go to the line on the right. When she followed her mother, the man ordered her to step back into line. He evaluated her strong young body and pointed his finger to the left. She watched as her mother walked in the direction of the smoke stacks. The smoke smelled of human flesh as she watched her life, her mother, move closer and closer to the monstrous stacks. She never saw her mother again. She was completely alone among thousands, numb with grief.

Leah never gave up hope that she would see her mother, and she looked for her everywhere, every day. She saw a fence that bordered the camp and assured herself that her mother was on the other side. "I saw the smoke stacks, and I knew what they had done to my mother. I knew that they had killed her in there, and yet I could not comprehend it. It was impossible, so I continued to look for her every day."

When Leah was taken from Auschwitz to a labor camp, she found her aunt, who had heard that her own two sons were alive and were living in Hungary. They were living with the young bride's husband. After the Americans liberated the labor camp, Leah and her aunt left the camp for Hungary. They rode on top of a train for fear Nazi officers would hurt them if they saw them. When a group of Nazi soldiers climbed on top of the train, the aunt and niece clung to each other in terror. The Nazi soldiers never saw them.

Miraculously the young married couple found each other and were reunited. They were now both orphans forced to face their future without their loving parents. "I could never accept that my mother was dead. I looked for her in Hungary. I looked for her every day for a very long time. I could not believe she was dead. When I was liberated, I could feel that my body was filled with hate. I did not know what to do with this hate because I had never felt these kinds of feelings before the war. I had to do something with this hate. I made the decision to heal people instead of hate them. My husband and I went to medical school and became doctors. We paid for our schooling by selling the jewelry his family had hidden before the Nazis captured them."

Leah and her husband immigrated to America, where their son was born. He was born into a home with the sound of classical music, with beautiful art on the walls, and with all the love his parents had been given by their parents. Their son became an artist. One of his paintings is a portrait of his father, a doctor and musician, who played swing music in the camps. The father died after a long illness and thankfully lived long enough to know and enjoy his grandson.

Today Leah grows plants in her garden, plays classical music, and wears pearls during the day. We meet on Fridays to sip what she calls "pink wine" and attempt to eat what she calls food. She makes fun of herself and her inability to cook. When she laughs, she laughs with the abandonment of a young girl.

At eighty-three she has taken up pottery. Beautifully colored ceramic flowers are placed all over her home. Her friend whom she calls *"Beal"* (Bill) is proud of her work and boasts to friends about her talent. She beams, she flushes, and she has found the courage to love again. She has an incredible sense of humor and wonder. Her blue eyes still sparkle, and she is stunningly beautiful.

In the year 2005 we travel together to Israel to join survivors from all over the world. It is the sixtieth anniversary after liberation. We are on Mt. Herzl with our friends surrounding us: Golda Meir and Yitzhak and Leah Rabin. We come across a tribute to Hannah Senesh, a sacred place that houses her remains. We stand together in silence, looking down on Hannah's grave. Filled with courage, she parachuted into enemy territory to find and rescue her mother. Even after being tortured, she never revealed the names of her comrades to the Nazis. She died before a firing squad. Shortly before her execution she wrote the poem "Eli, Eli, I pray that these things never end, the sand and the sea, the rush of the water, the crash of the heavens, the prayer of the heart."

MANYA

It is Manya's funeral; it is 2008. Her daughters weep when the rabbi states that she died on the eve of Yom Hashoah (Holocaust Remembrance Day). Each year at the local commemoration her husband had read the narrative as the procession of survivors lit the candles when their name was called and their story was told. He passed away three years ago; he was the love of her life and her witness to the atrocities. Her fiery red hair lives on in both her daughter and her grandchildren, as they bend their heads at her graveside. When someone comments on their beautiful red hair, they reply: "At least no one can say that we were not her children!"

She was proud and at times brazen about the fact that she had lasted longer in more concentration camps than anyone else in the group. "How long were you in camps?" She would demand of others. She would challenge other group members to respond to her question. No matter how many years they would answer, she would throw her hands up in the air and tell them in her husky voice, that was nothing. She was tough, she was funny, she was charming, and she was abrasive. Her directness could be, at times, overwhelming.

She survived too many camps to mention. She towered over most survivors. She was strong and lived life with a passion. She was still playing poker, four games at a time, the last days of her life.

Manya embraced life, courage, and survival with a vengeance. Her laughter shook the world, and there is a huge hole where she left us. The world will never be quite the same because she embraced it. There was nothing she could not face, endure, or conquer. She was a whispering and roaring hero who roared as she told her story to children. She was determined that the Shoah (Holocaust) would never be forgotten. No matter how many times it took to tell the story, no matter how many hours she had to spend telling her story to children, she was tireless and she was courageous. She confided that it tore her apart each time she revisited her nightmares, but she had to tell her story, or Hitler would win.

She delighted people with her sense of humor. One day she told a funny story. "We had gone to America. I had a cousin in New York and we were at the beach. Even after everything, I still had a good figure. When my cousin eyed my shapely, tall frame, she went into her beach house and came out with a huge bathing suit. It was so large that when I put it on, it floated around me like a tent! I wore it anyway. And I still looked good. She didn't seem too happy about that."

If they play poker in heaven, then she is playing there. If there is laughter in heaven, then the heavens are laughing with her. If there is love in heaven, then she has found the love of her life, she has found her youth, and she has found her family. She is beaming at her husband. They are looking down lovingly on the beautiful family they created together. She is moved from despair to joy as she leaves them.

GERDA

Gerda was the youngest of the group and perhaps the most vulnerable. At the age of six she was chosen by a philanthropist from Philadelphia to come to America. His stipulation was that fifty children would be chosen from Vienna based on their intelligence. As she stood with her mother to take her first intelligence test, Nazi soldiers stormed the synagogue and shot into the group of children and their mothers. People fell all around her. She looked up at the staircase where her religious school used to be. Sky was all she remembers, where the ceiling used to be. She looked at her mother in silence as her mother stared blankly ahead. She was determined to save her daughter. "Stay in line," she calmly told her. "Soon it will be your time to take the test."

She took a battery of tests for one week and was chosen to be one of the fifty children. Her father had found someone to sponsor him in America and waited for the rest of his family to join him there. Her older sister became a Zionist and escaped to Israel. She was alone in the world with her mother. Her mother was her world: it was a world filled with terror.

They stand on the platform at the station; she grasps her mother's hand with one hand and clutches her brand-new purse with the other. The purse has on it a black Scottie and a white Scottie. "Be a good girl" are the last words she hears from her mother. As Manya tells the story, she glances at the small black and white Scotties placed on the desk in front of her. If one were to close her eyes and listen, she would hear a six-year-old crying—a child trapped in a woman's body, forever.

In America Gerda's father lived in a little house in a cemetery. A brilliant, educated man, he was grateful to be a groundskeeper and to be joined by his little daughter. They waited for the papers to come through for her mother. Something was holding up the process. It was only after her death that they discovered the answer: A social worker from the Jewish agency had put her papers in his drawer and gone on vacation. The Nazis caught Gerda's mother as she waited to join her family. She was taken to Mauthausen and murdered.

Now Gerda trains dogs to assist people with disabilities—people who are unsteady on their feet, the dizzy, the disoriented, those who walk in darkness, or those too weak to walk alone. How does one be a good girl in a world that is cruel and unforgiving, a world that opens up and swallows mothers whole? In session, I give Gerda a set of her own black and white Scotties as a token of friendship. They are a small attempt at healing. They are a memory. They are words.

EVA

Eva was born to an elegant Warsaw family. She was filled with grace, with beauty, and with sophistication. Her handsome young husband studied painting at the Sorbonne in France. Her parents were vacationing in Chicago at the World's Fair when the Nazis invaded Poland.

She passes around the photograph taken of this stunning young couple on their honeymoon, days before they were captured by the Russians and taken to labor camps. "They were no different than the death camps. They worked you to death anyway, or tried to. Most people died. The living conditions were not good enough for animals, let alone people. We were not people to them."

Eva did not know what to do with the beloved little dog she had taken with her on her honeymoon. She hid him in her fur muff and kept him for days until she realized she had no food to feed him. She wandered into the countryside and begged a kind woman to take her little dog. Because she was a privileged young woman, this was the worst thing that had ever happened to her. The loss of this little dog was the loss of everything. Little did she know what was ahead of her, and little did she know what she was going to have to endure.

Prior to their being captured, the couple had conceived a baby. Eva did not know this. She noticed that each day she grew weaker, that each day the work became harder, and that each day the food became scarcer. The freezing wind would rip right through her, and each day she became hungrier. She marched through the cold, slept on rocks for beds, and was fed only enough food to keep her barely alive. She carried her baby full term.

Eva managed to hide her swelling stomach and gave birth to her first child, an infant son whom she named Earnest. The baby's identity remained unknown to the officers. Eva continued to work as hard as she did before with her baby left behind in the barracks to wait for her. She was able to sustain both of their lives for one and a half years. Then measles and starvation took him. She watched as he fought for his life. She remembers begging for a crumb of bread, anything to sustain him. She also remembers the people in the camp refusing. "Do I believe in a God who could do such things? No. Do I believe in humanity and people's ability to do the right thing? Never. They watched my child starve before them and did nothing to help."

Eva's husband never knew his baby. Eva and her husband were separated when they were captured by the Russians and taken to work camps in Siberia. After the war, Eva somehow made her way back to Poland. She went to their brand-new apartment, where they had planned, before their world was shattered, to begin their new life together. He was waiting for her there. The apartment had been stripped bare. She glanced through open doors into the homes of neighbors and saw wedding gifts: Shabbat candlesticks, a silver menorah, beautiful china dishes. The neighbors acted as though they had never left, as if she and her husband were just returning home from their honeymoon.

Eva and her husband left Poland and moved to America, where Eva gave birth to a daughter, and later a son. But there was always the presence of the other. The children sensed this and moved both emotionally and physically away from their parents.

In their beautiful home with towering plants and her husband's paintings hanging on their walls, she stands in her kitchen, the epitome of elegance with her silver-white hair, her cashmere sweater, and her strand of perfect pearls. She takes out a gold locket with a lock of baby hair, one golden curl. "I can still feel his fingers on my cheekbone where he touched me," she whispers, so that her two grown children in another room cannot hear. She begins to cry and turns away. She collects herself and turns around again. She smiles. She walks into her living room and asks if anyone would like any more of her perfect Polish pastries. Her children decline as her husband steps toward her.

When they are at the end of their lives, she eighty-five and he ninety, she calls out for help, but her children are not there. They are used to her independence, to her strength, and to her power. They do not see the frail person with an imprint on her cheekbone, the stunning young woman posing for a picture in front of a ski slope, the smile on her face that is eternally gone. The couple dies within months of each other. They pass with the help, love, and support of other survivors. Their journey is finally over.

They will join their baby. They will go back to Warsaw before the war, and they will go home.

HANNAH

Her mother passed away long before the war. Hannah lived with her dashing, handsome father, who managed the most prestigious hotel in Budapest. She was very proud of him and beams when she describes his charm. When the Nazis invaded Poland, she and her father would ride the trains all day and come back to the hotel at night to be hidden by his staff, who worshiped her father. They were never caught. The secret was to keep moving. She tells her story with no elation, no expression, no detectable emotion on her face.

Hannah is quiet now. She has stopped moving. Her husband is dead. She is disconnected from her children. Both children live far away in different states and never come to visit. Her daughter refuses to talk to her and will not explain why. She is a psychologist. There are secrets in this family that perpetuate shame. Hannah lives in the mountains in the desert, isolated and alone. People rarely visit. What ghosts did her children grow up with that scattered them far from home? She watches as her sharp mind starts to forget things, like numbers and words. She was a bookkeeper in her younger years and fears the onset of dementia more than she feared the Nazis. Once again she is forced into a situation where she has no control. The trains keep moving in her memory, but her mind is grinding to a halt. She reaches to her children for comfort but receives no response.

MIRIAM

Miriam's father had gotten his papers and had immigrated to Cuba. The plan was for his wife and two adolescent daughters to join him in Cuba after they received their papers. "My mother thought of everything. She was a sharp cookie. She wanted to leave Germany the minute she heard the rumors. She arranged for our papers as soon as she heard the rumors. My father wanted to stay. He was, after all, an upstanding citizen. The Germans always protect their own."

The day came, and the youngest daughter was excited. "We were on a huge ship called the St. Louis. We were going to be with our father! It was all very exciting. I did not understand what was happening in Germany, I was too young." The mother and two daughters made a successful crossing. When they came into the harbor they could see Cuba. They saw their father waving at them as the ship moved toward the shore. But then something happened. They were not allowed to get off the ship. They waited there for hours watching their father on the corner of the platform. He stared at his wife; he was anxious to join his family at last. The girls did not understand why they could not run and greet their father. "The captain of the St. Louis tried in vain to convince the Cuban government to let the Jewish passengers in. He was a very good man. He tried to help us." As the ship left the harbor, heading for Florida, the girls remember the way their father and mother looked at each other as the ship pulled away. They knew this would probably be their last time together.

When the ship arrived in Florida, the same thing happened. "We were not allowed to get off the ship. The captain pleaded. America refused. Nothing happened. It was clear that we, the Jews, were not welcome in America." The ship pulled away from American waters and headed back to Germany. "They took our mother off the ship and to the death camp. We never saw her again."

"My sister was a real beauty. A regular movie star. I was the scrawny one; no one paid attention to me. She flirted with the Nazi officer who was putting people's names on a list. He did not write our names down. She bought us some time; he did not send us to a death camp; we went to Bergen-Belsen."

The sisters shared a bunk bed. The younger sister would hear the Nazi soldiers enter the barracks. One by one, they would climb past the bottom bunk to reach her sister. She could hear noises in the cot above her. She would try to drown out these sounds from her young head. Miriam knew that her sister was trying to save them.

When they were liberated, they made their way to America. They were joined with their father, never again to be a complete family. The two sisters lived in the same city. They rarely spoke. There was an unspoken code between them. If they acknowledged their past, it would haunt them.

"Here is a book written about us. You can read all about it. Here we are on the decks of the St. Louis. See the skinny one? That's me. My sister was always using her beauty. I was the scrawny sister that got in the way."

SARA

Sara was frail, gentle, and giggled nervously during group time. She disliked attention drawn to her and tried to remain invisible. This was difficult, as she was the only survivor who had been a partisan during the war. It was easy to still see the partisan in the tiny, fiery, woman. Her hair still shone with fire. One could still conjure the brazen young girl, fearless about living in forests, blowing up railroad tracks, and shooting her gun.

When asked about her experiences, Sara shrugs and claims it was nothing. When asked if she was afraid to go to sleep for fear that someone would attack her, she insists she knew she was never alone. She would refuse to share her experiences in the resistance. She raised her hand into the air, as if to brush it away. "It was nothing," she would respond, always in the same manner. "I was just staying alive, that is all."

CHAYA

When Chaya tells her story, her eyes light up; she is animated. It is as if she were standing in front of her sisters, as if they were still there. They stand vividly before her. She sees their children, who perished, her parents and friends. Her poetry and paintings tell her story. The trip in the cattle car, the humiliation of a young girl who walks past the neighborhood boys and squats over a bucket, her face turned away in shame. She paints the despair on people's faces, the gap between the teeth in the Nazi Dr. Mengele's face. She can still feel his touch on her shoulder, she can see the demonic look on his face as he points to the right and left, deciding people's fate.

As Chaya tells the story, she becomes a young girl again. "There was a horrible stench in the air of burning flesh. We watched as our mother disappeared into the smoke. We knew she would soon be ashes. We begged for bread to save our sister, a cube of sugar, a cup of coffee, anything to build her strength."

Soon after they were taken to Auschwitz, the youngest sister contracted an ear infection. Enduring lice, disease, freezing conditions, and hard labor, the sister could not hold onto her strength. Her sisters did her work for her; they hid her in her cot to let her sleep. They begged for anything that could sustain her and held her between them in the ice and snow when they were forced to walk shoeless on the death march out of Auschwitz.

Each time a person faltered on this walk, he or she was beaten and then murdered in front of everyone's eyes. The sisters bolstered their youngest sister between them, never letting the Nazi officers see that her feet barely hit the ground. They survived the march. In Chaya's painting one can see flurries of snow everywhere.

Chaya recalls when her sisters were liberated by the British army. Too weak to walk, she crawled to a British officer and begged him for a cube of sugar to give her sister strength. She carried this treasure back and placed it in her sister's mouth. "I was determined to keep her alive." The British officers had to pry Chaya's fingers off her sister. The officers assured Chaya they would take her sister to the hospital, where she would receive needed care. Chaya pleaded with them not to take her sister away. Within hours, the ailing sister died alone in the hospital, never to see her sisters again.

ANNA

They go to a marriage counselor for counseling. His wife does not love him, he claims, after fifty-five years! Anna wants a separation. He is perplexed. He and their children do not understand. When she is alone with the counselor, she explains.

"I was taken in the cattle car to Auschwitz. When the doors opened, it was my sixteenth birthday. Nazi officers were running. The war was over. The Russians had come to liberate us."

Anna went back to her village. Most of her family was gone. She searched the streets for the boy she had been in love with before the war, the boy she left behind. "He was not Jewish," she whispers, as if her parents can still hear her. This was her great secret. He was her true love. She looked for him everywhere. She never found out what had happened to him.

In the village she met the man who would become her husband. Their meeting had been arranged. He was significantly older than she was. So few Jews remained. He spoke loudly, with great animation. She went through the motions of life but never lived it. She did not have a strong bond with her children. At seventy-six, she announces that she wants to go live with her mother. "Is it the young man?" her therapist asks. She nods. "I never stopped loving him."

LIVIA

Livia is standing in line after being taken to Auschwitz. The line is three-hundred-people long. She needs to relieve herself. She looks around; there is nowhere to go. She steps out of line and walks to the far corner of the camp. She comes back to discover the Nazi soldiers had run out of ink. The numbers were not tattooed on her skin.

She survives and gives birth to two children—two daughters who love their mother and are very protective. Their mother is a quiet and gentle woman. She embroiders beautiful images of Judaism on prayer shawls, marriage canopies, and tableclothes.

Livia turns every nightmare into beauty. Her gentle presence soothes anyone who is near her. Her peaceful face always smiles. When she tells the group about her experience, one of the more sarcastic members asks her, "So, nu? Should we take you back to Auschwitz for your tattoo? We would hate to think you missed something." She laughs with the others.

Her daughters heal and teach people. They are often with their mother even though they live far away. They travel with her to Israel on the sixtieth anniversary of liberation. Their children carry their mother's light inside them. Her goodness shines everywhere.

OLGA

To every group session Olga brought her food carefully wrapped from her kosher kitchen. At eighty-five she is as strong as ever. "I still have about thirteen [people] for Shabbat dinner every Friday." When asked what her secret of survival is, she states, "Keeping a kosher kitchen."

Her faith and traditions remained intact during the Holocaust years. She is proud that at sixteen, she outsmarted the Nazi officers. In Germany, where she and her brother lived, the Nazi captured her brother and took him in for questioning. She knew that there was a good chance that she would not see her brother again.

Olga also knew that mental instability both frightened and unnerved Germans. She ran into the police station screaming. She appeared to be mad, screaming at the officers with words that made no sense. She continued to rant and rage, pointing to her brother, screaming obscenities at the Nazis. They believed she would have to be out of her mind to run into the headquarters and behave this way. They became increasingly uneasy as they attempted to deal with this unbalanced girl. Her intensity was increasing. They moved her to her brother's cell to appease her. They finally let him go. As the brother and sister escaped the clutches of Nazi occupation, she was still screaming obscenities.

LIVIA

There were simply not enough locks to keep the enemy out. A judge, Livia's daughter moved her from apartment complex to apartment complex because she was constantly being evicted. The sweet, elegant, and articulate old woman accused her neighbors daily of breaking and entering her home.

When one enters Livia's beautiful home filled with family portraits, it is hard not to notice that every door and window has at least three or four locks. After speaking to Livia about her safety, I realize that a person can never have enough locks to keep the enemy out.

Livia tells the story of her children and siblings, who were murdered by the Nazis. She speaks of the visits her brothers make to her each night.

In her dreams, they are still children and look exactly the same as she last saw them.

The Nazis murdered all three of her children. What she does not know is that her infant was smothered by her husband in order to keep their hiding place secret. Her daughter, who was born after the war, has had to live with this secret. Livia dreams of the siblings she will never know.

CONCLUSION

Elie Wiesel once said that we must become the custodians of the stories that have been told to us. And yet, I believe that it is these stories that house us. When we place ourselves within their walls, we can hear the voices of the women who have trusted us with their words. What we hear is their determination to live. We hear their determination to honor the families left behind, the children they will never hold again, and the parents they will never see grow old. Their stories house us, and they shape us. When we are faced with life's incomprehensible turns, we remember them and they give us strength. What their stories give us is the belief that the human spirit can rise above the unimaginable, that even the most fearsome foe cannot win. Not everything. Why do we tell these stories? Because they are our greatest gift. These stories birth us. They open the doors to a courage we thought we could never attain. They stand behind us and gently move us forward. They are our history. They are our armor. They are our gold.

CHAPTER 8

How Women Integrate Judaism with Other Spiritual Technologies

Rabbi Sheila Peltz Weinberg

I was born in the Bronx in 1946 and grew up there. I lived in a totally Jewish neighborhood as a child. My entire life has been spent absorbed with Jews and Judaism. I have worked with Jews, studied and taught Judaism, celebrated our festivals and life cycles. I have worried about the future of the Jewish people and their traditions for as long as I can remember. I have been a rabbi for the last twenty years.

The bookshelves in my home office tell the story. To my right are several large bookcases filled with commentaries on the Hebrew Bible, rabbinic literature, Jewish history, philosophy, literature, and culture. To my left, on my desk, is a copy of the *Middle Length Discourses of the Buddha: A Translation of the Majjhima Nikaya*—a hefty hard-back volume in a brown-and-gold jacket. I am a practicing Jew with an abiding interest in the dharma and in the teachings of the Buddha. That is the simple and not so simple truth.

Every few months, without fail, someone in my life, somewhere on the planet, sends me an e-mail with the subject of Zen Judaism. Usually my correspondent writes a short apologetic note saying, "You've probably seen these before . . . but I couldn't resist." Then comes the litany:

- If there is no self, whose arthritis is this?
- Be here now. Be someplace else later. Is that so complicated?

- Drink tea and nourish life. With the first cup, sip ... enjoy. With the second ... satisfaction, with the third ... peace. With the fourth, a Danish.
- Wherever you go, there you are. Your luggage is another story.
- Accept misfortune as a blessing. Do not wish for perfect health or a life without problems. What would you talk about?
- The Tao does not speak. The Tao does not blame. The Tao does not take sides. The Tao has no expectations. The Tao demands nothing of others. The Tao is not Jewish.
- Let your mind be as a floating cloud. Let your stillness be as a wooded glen. And sit up straight. You'll never meet the Buddha with such rounded shoulders.
- Be patient and achieve all things. Be impatient and achieve all things faster.
- To find the Buddha look within. Deep inside you are ten thousand flowers. Each flower blossoms ten thousand times. Each blossom has ten thousand petals. You might want to see a specialist.

My usual impulse is to immediately delete these jokes. I find them offensive to two of the things in the world that I most love. In one fell swoop these jokes dismiss the dharma and demean the Jews. They do express a certain dichotomy that is fairly prevalent, however. What do the jokes say about the Jews? We are impatient, hypochondriacal, anxious, demanding, blaming, food-oriented, complainers. We have embodied the irreverence, aggressiveness, and materialism of secular culture and would be the least likely to open to the poetic sensibilities of Zen. These poems do not identify Jews as spiritual seekers or Judaism as a source of wisdom or compassion.

The Zen jokes reflect cultural stereotypes of an immigrant nation. Jews who came to America were by and large looking for economic and political security rather than spiritual fulfillment. They were quite willing to leave behind the centers of Jewish learning and devotion in Europe for these golden shores. Life here was tough and, like other immigrants, Jews worked hard to give the next generation the advantages their parents did not have. They wanted Jewish identity and tradition to survive, but they also embraced the individualism and secularism of their new home.

My parents were children of immigrants. The Jewish cultural identity that they lived was very powerful, but it had shallow roots. Life was more about "making it" in America than living a life of connection to spirit. I knew I was supposed to be a good person, and I grew up hearing Yiddish spoken, but concepts like spiritual practice, self-reflection, or sacred community were as foreign to me as Latin or Greek. I was well fed and clothed enough to be able to dismiss "things" as the source of meaning. I needed something else. I yearned for something. That very yearning has been at the core of my love affair with both Judaism and the dharma. I was also a child of my times born in the twin shadows of Auschwitz and Hiroshima. I was one of that generation who needed to seek the light of meaning through these shadows.

What were the primary motivations operating in my search and struggle? There are two that may be really one. First is the aspiration to be part of sacred community, to find relationships that celebrate and embrace the infinitely mysterious life force within all creation. The second is the urgency to face and heal the broken, frightening, and wounded aspects of the soul I encounter in myself and others.

THE SEARCH FOR SACRED COMMUNITY

What is the sacred? It is that which cannot be fully named and yet lies underneath all efforts of naming. It is the spirit or energy that unites everything in the cosmos. It is the direction of our evolution. The sacred dispels confusion and aimlessness. It serves the true and the wise.

The sacred cannot be attained without sharing it with others. It cannot be hoarded or stockpiled. It cannot be bought or sold. In many ways it is the greatest longing of our technical-materialist age. It is a hunger in the heart that rages when the hunger in the belly has been satisfied. The capacity to touch the sacred is not that different from being able to be present, to sit quietly with whatever is hurting and just breathe. The sacred is not about fixing or making whole. It is about seeing wholeness wherever we are.

The sacred is talked and written about in every culture that human beings ever produced. It always has a personal and a communal dimension. It sparks literature, dance, music, and art. It is probed by philosophers and theologians. The search for the sacred has built temples and monasteries, gardens and monuments that dot the globe and bear infinite shapes, colors, and smells.

The sacred is about the dance between separation and union. It calls on us to make choices. It is nourished by leave-taking and homecoming. It lives in the in-between times and places. But we can also know time that is filled by the sacred. We can draw the boundary lines around the eternal flow of time. Just as we dedicate space to the sacred, so we can dedicate a moment, a day, or a week.

My interest in sacred community was sparked, I believe, by attending Camp Ramah from the time I was nine until sixteen. I was introduced to a new language, Hebrew, to the Torah, to daily prayer, and to the Sabbath.

These were not tools to master like English and mathematics. They were special, different. They were meant to connect us as a Jewish community, to our ancestors, and to the sacred—something deep, lasting, and precious. I remember feeling that the text and the language and the other practices that I learned in those summers were pure and purifying, were dedicated to a higher goal, than the usual affairs of the day in my regular, non-camp life.

I have never stopped being passionately interested in sacred community. I have worked professionally as a rabbi and Jewish leader to realize that passion. I have been a part of a sacred community of Jewish feminists, women's support groups, and interfaith clergy groups. I have also sought out teachers from many paths and practices to hear their wisdom—psycho-therapists, Sufis, Buddhists, Christian mystics. I have been a member of a twelve-step group for two decades.

In 1990 I was introduced to mindfulness or insight meditation. I was curious about the possibility of sitting in silence for a long period of time. I was exhausted in my job as rabbi. There was always more to read and study. There was always more to do and prepare and write. In particular I felt weighted down by the words—the many wonderful but also burden-some words of our tradition. I craved space that might surround the words and illuminate them anew for me and those I served. I was intrigued and also frightened by what would emerge in the silence.

The first ten-day silent retreat I attended at Insight Meditation Society (IMS) in Barre, Massachusetts, was a powerful and difficult experience. I was asked to be with the contents of my own mind-body without distrac-tion and just to notice what arose. What I noticed was a microcosm of the world in which I live. There was great judgment and fear, a desire to do well and compete, a desire to attain and obtain, to know for sure that I was safe because I had that elusive "something." I saw that I was always planning the next moment. I saw that I was frightened of the sacred, frightened of the present, frightened of stillness. What a dilemma. Here I was, a spiritual teacher and my mind was pandemonium. It was racing around without a home, afloat in a sea of chaos and desire. This was not the totality of that experience, however. I was given a glimmer of how to be with what I saw. It was enough of an opening to cause me to return for another retreat, and another, and to begin to sit in meditation myself.

At first I was terribly confused because as a rabbi, the last thing I was looking for was a new religion. I did not want to become a Buddhist, not that there was any pressure from the retreat leaders for me to do so. How-ever, fairly soon I realized that the teachings, or dharma, at these retreats were nothing other than the teachings of Torah, teachings leading me to-ward sacred community and healing. I realized that as my mind settled in silence, the wisdom that arose was none other than the inner teachings of

Judaism. Since then, as I have come to understand the nature of my mind more deeply, I see how these teachings could be practiced and integrated into sacred Jewish community. I meet, in the stillness, again and again, pain, fear, and confusion and learn that awareness itself is the key to the ongoing healing.

In Deuteronomy 30:11–14 it is written: "For this commandment which I command you this day, is not concealed from you, nor is it far away. It is not in heaven, that you should say, 'Who will go up to heaven for us and fetch it for us, to tell [it] to us, so that we can fulfill it?' Nor is it beyond the sea, that you should say, 'Who will cross to the other side of the sea for us and fetch it for us, to tell [it] to us, so that we can fulfill it?' Rather, [this] thing is very close to you; it is in your mouth and in your heart, so that you can fulfill it." This summarizes the approach of mindfulness practice. We learn the reality that our capacities to live a spiritual life do not reside in some far away place. They reside within our own experience. We are each endowed with an essence that is sacred and pure. The qualities that we seek to expand and express are already part of our nature. This is the meaning of being created in the image of the Divine, as I understand this core teaching in the Book of Genesis. If we want to access compassion, it is within our capacity to be present in the midst of pain. We simply need to do it. We need to practice, again and again. We need to train or retrain our mind and heart in the way that is wholesome, life affirming, nonviolent, and loving. We need to see how deeply connected we are to life and to each other and practice acting on the basis of that reality. This also teaches us that we cannot work to reform something external when we are not in internal alignment. If we are angry and spiteful, that will be the results of our actions even if we speak about generosity and goodwill.

What really hooked me? What was it at Camp Ramah in my teens that I found again in Barre in my forties? It comes down to three things: the teachings, the teachers, and the practices. But mostly it is the non-separation between these three.

TEACHERS AND TEACHINGS ARE ONE

Reading or hearing sacred teachings does not have the impact of experiencing a teacher who embodies the practice and who can, herself, speak about her experience of transformation through practice. This is an integrated transmission. We are inspired by this living model to accept that there is something we can do for ourselves. We do not depend upon the teacher to "do" for us. The practices will become the teacher and teaching for each person in her unique way. At the same time, the universality of the human mind and heart is revealed as the teacher points to how similar we are in our wounds, our conditioning, in our longing for wholeness, and in our desire to be seen, known, and loved.

In some ways the nearly seventeen years since that first retreat have been for me a working out of the relationship between the Torah and the dharma. It has been a bumpy and beautiful journey. The public part of the process began with small gatherings at the Barre Center for Buddhist Studies. It was made up of Buddhist teachers who had Jewish origins and of Jewish teachers who were interested in mysticism and meditation. Through these events I met Sylvia Boorstein, who became a mentor and beloved friend. As we began teaching together, at first she was the dharma teacher and I was the rabbi. As time went on, those boundaries dissipated. I started giving instructions for meditation, and Sylvia started chanting Torah. Eventually, joined by Rabbi Jeff Roth, we offered rabbis and other Jewish leaders retreats where we taught mindfulness in a Jewish idiom. We understood mindfulness as a nondenominational way to practice Judaism in thought, speech, and action. We realized that Jewish stories, rituals, songs, and teachings were accessible vehicles to impart the dharma. We also discovered that fostering conditions where people could practice paying attention to their own experience moment to moment helped expand their understanding of prayer, learning, and action in the world immensely. Eventually this work culminated in the creation of the Institute for Jewish Spirituality, which brings rabbis, cantors, Jewish educators, and lay people together to learn mindfulness and its relationship to Jewish learning and practice, to renew their spiritual lives and the lives of their sacred communities (see http://www.ijs-online.org).

I do not have any trouble translating fundamental Jewish ideas and images into the language of dharma. I think we are all talking about the same thing. Well-known scholar of Jewish mysticism Arthur Green puts it this way: "The job of each human being is to teach every other human being that we are all One, and to find ways in our behavior as well as our thought to include all other creatures within that vision of Oneness as well."[1] This is not so different from the language bell hooks quotes Sharon Salzberg using in her book *Faith*: "This is the essential question we must bring to any belief system. Can it transform our minds? Can it help reshape our pain into wisdom and love?"[2] It seems to me that if we really could see that we are all One, then we could not help but to function with greater wisdom and compassion toward each other and the earth.

MUSINGS ON TORAH AND DHARMA

Over these years I have written some poems that reflect my love of dharma and Torah. They emerge from intensive retreat practice when I come face to face with my own stumbling blocks to seeing clearly, to wisdom, and to kindness. In the quiet I have a chance to see how full the ego is of itself and how false ideas of being separate and different, of being less than or better than, obscure the truth of oneness and connection. What happens to me frequently on retreat is that a word or phrase from Jewish liturgy or narrative will pop into my head. That language speaks through my experience and gives it contours in a miraculous way. I thought I would share a few of those musings (could I call them poems?) to illustrate the way an integration of experience and tradition occurs for me.

This is the practice,
This is how the heart gets purified,
This is how we get to know God.
Again and again and again—
Ill at ease
Distant
Separate
Uncomfortable
Critical thoughts of self and other
Race in the mind,
Inadequate, not quite okay, just off-center
Like mice in a maze.
The mind is the
Mice and the maze.
Again and again,
Until a moment of—oh, yes—
This is suffering, non-dramatic,
Relentless, underground,
And again and again and again,
It is protecting something,
Which turns out invariably
To be "ME."
Then comes the grace, the mindfulness, the compassion.
Warm attention to the frozen and contracted, tender light on the shad-
    ows of delusion.
And then a moment of freedom.
Relax the heart.
You are home.
Empty
Happy
One.

I am reminded of a verse in the Sabbath prayer book *"V'taher libaynu l'avdecha b'emet"* (Prepare or purify our hearts to serve you truthfully): We ask that our heart be purified, the obstacles removed, the blockages melted.

In yoga we would say, may all hindrances to the flow of prana be removed. Breath is the grossest manifestation of prana, the life force. In Hebrew we call this *chiyut*. We must be able to train our attention in order to see what the blocks are. We must become sensitive in order to notice when we are constricted. To the extent that these knots can be loosened, our potential is released to do the work of service to creation. This comes out in our unique creativity and in causing less harm to ourselves and others. When we are free of the blockages, we are able to manifest the divine attributes of goodness, love, kindness, patience, generosity, and gratitude.

> *The Kaddish is about opening the window*
> *Not looking through the glass, but opening the window.*
> *The window of the heart, the window of not knowing.*
> *Opening the window on fear and love.*
> *Opening the window on all time and space—l'olam ulolmei olmeia.*
> *Just that.*
> *Opening the window*
> *To the kingdom that is just this.*
> *Opening the window to the name. The great name.*
> *No name.*
> *Amen.*

The Kaddish is probably the most well-known Hebrew prayer, and it is not even in Hebrew. It is in Aramaic, the vernacular of two thousand years ago. The prayer begins with the hope that the great name of God be made greater and holier in all the dimensions of time and space. It ends with an aspiration for peace in all the worlds. The practice of mindfulness allows one's mind to grow more spacious. This invites a connection with a wider and broader way of seeing. I identify this with the mind of God or the name of God, which can never really be known. Mindfulness practice is about expanding beyond pettiness toward relationship, beyond self-centeredness toward peacefulness, and beyond duality to a wholeness that holds multiplicity and paradox.

> *Nowhere to run from these feelings.*
> *Watching them spill into tears and sobs and then make their way to*
>   *the great open sea.*
> *Hoping to be cleaner and emptier from the secrets—Menistarot*
>   *Nakayni—*
> *I have asked for this and now there is no place to hide, no place*
>   *to run.*
> *This too is part of your kingdom.*
> *This too is a face of your light.*

This too is arising and ceasing in your realm.
This too is ready for your mercy, in your transparent gaze that makes
all the difference.
Vayagale libi b'yeshuatecha—
My heart rejoices in your freedom, oh merciful one.
All I can do is sing praises.
L'maan shemecha—
For Your name's sake.
Because this is who You are.
Because the essence of existence is one.
And we are called upon to be unifiers of the name.
Opening in our small and feeble way in whatever way we can to the
underlying relatedness, oneness.
Call it whatever you like—trust, love, generosity, surrender.
You are One.
Your name is One.
For Your name's sake.
There is no other possibility,
However we might rebel, resist, and run.
We come back to this.
Shma Yisrael Adonai Elohaynu Adonai Echad.

We are told that Judaism and Buddhism stand in conflict over the existence of God. Judaism says yes and Buddhism says no. However, when I am quiet, whether in prayer or meditation, I recognize that everything is arising and passing. Not only is this so, but everything is caused by something else and in turn causes something else. This means that everything is connected. The whole of this is without beginning and without end. And it is mostly empty space. The fact that my tiny dot of consciousness can connect with this much is an occasion for deep amazement and gratitude. The Jewish God that I know is called "IS/WAS/WILLBE." It cannot be named or pictured. Any effort at depiction or final naming is considered idolatry. Idolatry is attachment. The Buddha taught that attachment is the source of suffering and ignorance. Human liberation is tied to a sense of the unlimited, unpossessable nature of this mysterious, ever-changing existence. This was what I was seeing when I wrote this reflection on the verse used in Jewish prayer services when we replace the Torah scroll in the ark—"She is a tree of life to all who cling to her"—

Etz Chayyim He.

It does matter what you cling to, what you hold on to.
Call it God, Life, Torah, Dharma, Wakefulness, the One.

And when you truly connect, hold on, trust,
Then all other clinging is revealed
As a shadow, a garment, an echo.

T'SHUVAH: RETURNING TO OUR INTENTION

Among the many extraordinary gifts I have received from mindfulness
practice is a deeper understanding of the concept *t'shuvah*. This is the
process whereby we set an intention and, when we invariably stray, we
remember and return to the initial intention. This is the basic instruction
in sitting or walking meditation that I was introduced to at IMS. I find
that it is a paradigm for all spiritual work, all training of the mind and
heart, all education of self and others. T'shuvah makes human life, beset
by so many mistakes and missteps, truly possible. The Jewish tradition
teaches that is so and that t'shuvah existed before God created the world.

T'shuvah is a Hebrew noun derived from the three-letter root that
means "turn" or "return." It presumes that our lives have a direction and a
purpose. It also presumes that we frequently forget this truth, lose our
way, or actually move in the opposite direction. The days surrounding
Rosh Hashanah and Yom Kippur ask us not only to reflect on the meaning
of t'shuvah but also to do some actual turning and returning—to put our
lives on course.

Several questions immediately arise: What, indeed, is the desired
direction of a life? What keeps us from moving in that path? How do we
reorient the vehicle of our lives? Jewish language speaks in terms of dwelling in the presence of the Divine, purifying our hearts, harmonizing our
will with God's will, and rectifying the harmful acts that we do to others
and to ourselves. Ultimately, we are intended to become ever more open
hearted, generous, patient, loving, wise, and caring. As we touch these expansive qualities, we feel deeply connected to the great web of existence.
In this genuine belonging, we discover true happiness and peace.

In order to accomplish t'shuvah, we need to see and touch the patterns and habits that have been constructed in the scaffold of our minds
that turn us around and lead us astray. One way to encounter our own
minds is through meditation. It is easy to ignore or evade one's inner life
in the daily rush of life. We tend to fill all pauses and spaces with activity
and chatter, electronic or human. When we take the time to pause and be
still, the mind settles like a muddy pond. The simple practice of silence
reveals an unfamiliar terrain. It can be surprising and frightening. It is a
powerful tool for the practice of t'shuvah.

I have often marked the few days prior to Rosh Hashanah by going on
a mindfulness retreat. The goal is to simplify one's life as much as possible

and avoid distractions. This can best be done in the context of a structure where silence is embraced. The schedule consists only of periods of sitting, walking, eating, sleeping and personal hygiene—the basic rudiments of life. The teachers offer instructions that consist mostly of telling us to pay attention to our experience in the present moment. "Just notice the breath as it enters and leaves the body," they will say, or, "Pay attention to the sensation of each step as you lift, move, and place it on the ground," or, "Allow the various pleasant, unpleasant, and neutral sensations to arise and pass through your body. Watch them change." Our thoughts are treated in the same way as our breath or bodily sensations, and we are encouraged to watch them arise and disappear. Amazingly enough, I have experienced a profound process of t'shuvah in just such a setting.

In the absence of external stimuli and distractions, after a while, one begins to notice the content of one's own mind. I have been shocked, dismayed, and outraged by mine. On one retreat I kept noticing a man who particularly annoyed me. Bear in mind that I had no contact with and no knowledge of this person. I just did not like the way he looked or acted. Every time there was a chance to ask a question, he invariably had a question. This annoyed me. He seemed restless when sitting and made more noise than I thought necessary when he breathed. I also noticed him in the dining room pouring huge quantities of honey on his cereal. This annoyed me also. While there was no smoking on the retreat, there was a smokers' hut. I would see this man frequently coming in or out of the hut. He always smelled of tobacco. As a former smoker, I disdained this behavior.

Meanwhile the teacher urged us to focus our attention on our experience in the moment. As my mind settled, I realized that my experience was one of annoyance and judgment. Perhaps hate is too strong a word. But I was having an aversive reaction to a person who was not only a total stranger but also someone who was not hurting me at all. I came to realize that this man irritated me because he made me afraid. I was most afraid that I was like him—out of control, hungry, addicted. I saw and felt my own fear under the irritation. I could explore how painful that felt. The structured and safe silent environment allowed me to explore this rocky terrain without experiencing another reaction of guilt and punishment—namely, of thinking, "Bad girl for having such thoughts." Rather, my mind was spacious enough to hold these thoughts and feelings and the grief they contained. Again and again, returning to the simple truth of the moment brings a soothing wind of calm. Awareness of the truth allows mercy to arise. Call it the sweetness of Divine grace and forgiveness. Call it release from a habit born of fear and separation.

One thing became clear. My reactions had nothing to do with the man I disliked. I had uncovered the process in my mind that casts blame outside myself. I had explored its raw edges and its oozing heart. In the light of that quiet, loving awareness it began to melt on its own. As it melted, I returned to my purpose. I regained my footing on the path to wholeness and connection. Again and again, this kind of movement is t'shuvah. That is the point. Again and again I witness moments and patterns of mind and heart that have hurt me and others. Again and again I try to unlock incidents where wrong was done, where an amends is in order. How different this is than believing that the man was indeed evil or hateful or the cause of my pain in some objective way. Moving to this recognition feels like bold and courageous work.

However, this work cannot be done effectively if I judge myself unworthy. Just as the liturgy of the High Holy Days repeatedly urges us to experience a God who is gracious and filled with compassion, kindness, and patience, so the process of t'shuvah, moral transformation, assumes an unceasing source of love and forgiveness, contained as a seed in each moment of pure awareness.

JEWISH FEMINISM AND SPIRITUALITY

I am a daughter of the second wave of feminism. When I finished college in 1967, it was inconceivable to question that women could not be rabbis. I had the second Bat Mitzvah in my synagogue without any of the boys' privileges, and I fought for that. In 1983 when my daughter Abby became a Bat Mitzvah, I was in rabbinical school and she could not believe there ever was a time when there weren't women rabbis.

I love being a woman rabbi. I see women's contribution to all religious life as beyond measure. The life experiences, voices, approaches, minds, and hearts of women are transformative. I think my willingness to see the connections between dharma and Judaism is connected to my life as a feminist and a woman in a public religious role. I want to tell people: It is about practice and about the heart, not just about what you think or know. Spirituality is about being alive and knowing that—being awake in the world, not just in the mind or the book. Spirituality is about telling the truth, talking about what you feel and know. It is about bringing in the margins, taking in the lost, forgotten, and weak, not just pretending to be sure and certain. I don't reject the learned, the rational, and the linear. I just want to bring in the possibility of dancing in prayer, crying out to God with real tears, and not being sure what I am going to say before I say it because I am so in this moment. The inclusion of women is the inclusion of the earth that has been rejected. It signals the inclusion of the body that has been scorned. It is the inclusion of the non-white, the non–straight, the non–rich, and the non-privileged. It is the heart of the dharma, the Torah, the wisdom of life. It is the goddess aroused and filled with juice.

Bell Hooks said that every woman engaged with Buddhism is asked at some point how she can support a patriarchal religion. The same can be said of Judaism. I am not blind to patriarchy. I see it everywhere. But I do not surrender to it. I realize that our cultures and our conditioning emerge from dualism and hierarchy. I know that our world is riddled with unspeakable gaps of wealth and resources, degradation and oppression. As a Jew I am heir to a past heritage of marginality, suffering, and victimization and a contemporary situation of power, wealth, and privilege. That makes for some complex choices. I am also aware that all religions—including Buddhism and Judaism—can build bridges of the heart to one another or be vehicles of hatred and violence. I do not turn my back on the light and wisdom of the past. But I am emboldened to challenge what I have received, especially as a woman, and ask: is this practice sacred? Is this sacred community? Is this for the sake of healing and wholeness or for the sake of power, possession, and prestige?

What do I have to offer as a woman, as a Jew, and a lover of dharma? I have each moment the willingness to live with an open heart. I have the capacity to love and to forgive. I have the wish to pursue the truth and not to hide or pretend or deceive. I have the goal to remember the stranger, the one who is different than I am, and know we are not separate. I aspire to honor the earth as I enjoy her bounty. I can try to be gentle with myself for not knowing as much as I would like to know or being as good at some things or for remembering all the things I would like to remember. For wholeness is not about reaching perfection. And above all I can keep practicing. I can practice qualities of heart that I associate with the divine abodes or with the image of God—loving kindness, compassion, joy and peace, generosity, gratitude, equanimity, courage, and patience. And when I am lost and I know I am lost, I can come back.

NOTES

Reprinted from *Women Practicing Buddhism: American Experiences* with permission from Wisdom Publications, 199 Elm Street, Somerville, MA 02144. http://www.wisdompubs.org. Copyright © Peter N. Gregory and Susanne Mrozik, 2008.

1. Arthur Green, *Ehyeh: Kabbalah for Tomorrow* (Woodstock, VT: Jewish Lights Publishing, 2003), 134.
2. Sharon Salzburg, *Faith: Trusting Your Own Deepest Experience* (New York: Riverhead Books, 2002), 62.

PART IV

Sexuality, Power, and Vulnerability

CHAPTER 9

Women in the Double Life
of *The Song of Songs*

Debra Band

Of all the love poetry that humankind has sung, the brief 117 verses of *The Song of Songs* have offered us the words most often engraved on wedding rings and hearts for thousands of years of Jewish tradition, verses beloved also within Christian traditions. One of the reasons we are endlessly drawn to this poetry is its double life. In Jewish tradition, not only do the verses sing of the compelling physical passion of the young lovers, but they have also become the essential paradigm of the love between God and Israel. This religious passion, in turn, underlies the concept of the Chosen People that permeates every aspect of Jewish identity. In Christian theologies, *The Song of Songs* has been viewed as the love song between Jesus and Christendom.

Within both the literal poetry and the Jewish religious allegory that has grown around it, women play prominent roles. Through a close reading of the text we will discover the young woman lover to be an active and independent person, relating to her lover, her family, and the chorus of the "daughters of Jerusalem" to whom she defends her love and explores her attitudes toward sexuality and sensual expression. We also examine the role of the woman in the early rabbinic allegorical interpretations of the poetry. Through this close reading of the text we will glimpse the double life of women in the literal and allegorical readings of *The Song of Songs*, as active participants in the daily life of the community at the times the poems were written and redacted as well as allegorical symbol of the community of Israel in its tumultuous love affair with God.

THE LIFE OF THE YOUNG WOMAN

In my illuminated manuscript, *The Song of Songs: The Honeybee in the Garden,* I treated the biblical book as the daydreams of a single young couple set within a walled garden.[1] This device offered an effective framework for fusing the narrative and allegorical interpretations of the poetry. Indeed, many commentators from different traditions have treated the poetry as the utterances of a sole couple. However, *The Song of Songs*, composed as it is of numerous diverse poems likely written and rewritten at different times, cannot be regarded as the story of a single specific woman. Rather, it is an anthology—literally a bouquet of beautiful flowers—of short poems possibly written by different people at diverse times and places, then probably redacted at some time following the late sixth century BCE end of the Babylonian Captivity. Consequently, we cannot assume that circumstances inferred in one passage necessarily apply to the woman mentioned in another. All we can conclude is that these circumstances were conceivable in the eras and places in which the particular verses in question were composed and later redacted. For convenience, however, we will nonetheless often refer to the young woman lover as a single individual, but the reader should be aware of the limitations of this assumption.

Who is the woman whose voice we hear in *The Song of Songs*? A cursory reading leads us to believe that she is young enough to be unmarried yet mature enough to be sexually desirable; she is obviously being courted. We note that the poems allude to neither encumbrances, such as a previous husband, children, or property of her own to be managed, nor any urgent need to marry quickly.

She almost certainly lives in Jerusalem. Many interpreters have regarded *The Song of Songs* as rural poetry; for instance, the twelfth-century Spanish Jewish commentator Ibn Ezra considered that read literally, the poetry expressed the love between a shepherd and a rural maiden.[2] It is certainly possible that the passage describing shepherding and vineyard cultivation in the second chapter was composed in an agrarian community and eventually folded into the anthology. However, most often the poems reflect urban life; they record numerous snatches of conversation with the "daughters of Jerusalem" and encounters with the "watchmen of the wall"—who of course would only patrol a city. Thus it may be that the occasional references to agrarian life largely relate to folk memories, in much the same way that our urban, electronic culture retains phrases such as "till the cows come home." Alternatively, even urban dwellers might actually catch sight of agrarian life and reflect those glimpses in poetry. One might well imagine young people in Jerusalem seeing sheep grazing in the nearby Judean hills, observing them from a city gate or a high rooftop, or perhaps during trips into the countryside, or even hearing accounts of these graceful sights from visiting travelers, merchants, or herders. The poems thus strongly link the young woman with Jerusalem. Whether her Jerusalem actually was as rich and powerful as its portrayal in biblical sources is of course controversial today. Nonetheless, the redactor's strong association of the girl with the beloved, idyllic city of his post-586 BCE imagination lends luster and importance to the poetic character.

We cannot quite know precisely when she, or they, lived, or whether "they" even lived at the same time, or exactly when the discrete poems were first composed. *The Song of Songs* is traditionally attributed to King Solomon, who flourished in the tenth century BCE, and it is indeed possible, even probable, that fragments of the poems date to that period. However, the presence of occasional Persian or Aramaic-influenced words makes it highly likely that it was rewritten into its current form after the Babylonian conquest of Judea in 586 BCE, or after the Persian conquest of Babylonia in 539 BCE. This theory derives from the specific descriptions of grand objects in the royal palace and the ease with which Tirzah, the town that became the capital of the Northern Kingdom following Israel's split after Solomon's death, is mentioned in the same breath as Jerusalem. So, let us begin to search the poems for details about the life of young, unmarried women in the idealized urban, wealthy Jerusalem of King Solomon's day and perhaps even in the years following the restoration of Jewish leadership to Jerusalem.

THE FAMILY SETTING

Our woman, or women (with the possible exception of the Shulamite dancer in the seventh chapter), lived in a family setting dominated by a strong maternal presence. In verse 2:9, the woman compares her lover to a gazelle, standing behind "our wall," indicating a family home. The mother's influence—and absence or irrelevance of a resident father—is revealed when the young woman declares that

> when I found the one I love. I held him fast, I would not let him go till I brought him to my mother's house, to the chamber of she who conceived me.

Similarly, in 8:2, she tells her lover that "I would lead you, I would bring you to the house of my mother, of her who taught me," again with no mention of a father's presence or influence.

In three instances the presence and influence of brothers are mentioned. In verse 1:6, the woman, who in this case may live not in the city but in an agrarian setting, blames her sunburn on her brothers:

> Don't stare at me because I am dark, because the sun has gazed upon me. My mother's sons quarreled with me, they made me guard the vineyards; my own vineyard I did not guard.

However annoying those brothers might be, 8:1 infers that public displays of affection with brothers were socially acceptable. She tells her lover,

> If only it could be as with a brother, as if you had nursed at my mother's breast: then I could kiss you when I met you in the street, and no one would despise me.

At the same time, the brothers might feel a responsibility for guarding their young sister. The woman relates her brothers' anticipation of the moment when she reaches marriageable age:

> *What shall we do for our sister when she is spoken for?*
> *If she be a wall, we will build upon it a silver battlement;*
> *If she be a door, we will panel it in cedar.*

Thus, we can infer from the text that young women of the poems might have lived in a maternal-dominated family setting that might also include brothers.

OUTSIDE THE HOME

The Song of Songs offers only scant inferences about young women's activities outside the family home. Let us review the aforementioned passage in the first chapter that describes the woman's dismay at her sunburn:

> [6]*Don't stare at me because I am swarthy,*
> *Because the sun has gazed upon me.*
> *My mother's sons quarreled with me,*
> *They made me guard the vineyards;*
> *My own vineyard I did not guard.*
> [7]*Tell me, you whom I love so well;*

Where do you pasture your sheep?
Where do you rest them at noon?
Let me not be as one who strays
Beside the flocks of your fellows.
[8]If you do not know, O fairest of women,
Go follow the tracks of the sheep,
And graze your kids
By the tents of the shepherds.

We learn from these verses that women might engage in some activity out-side the home, in this case, relating perhaps to women in an agrarian setting, working in vineyards and shepherding. A verse quoted earlier, 8:1, tells us that it was acceptable for a young woman to walk through the busy daytime streets, but the sight of a woman running through the streets at night might cross the bounds of social acceptability. In 5:6, panic-stricken when her lover suddenly bolts from her door, she flies into the streets to chase him. There she is caught by guards who evidently consider her an outlaw:

I sought, but found him not;
I called, but he did not answer.
[7]I met the watchmen
Who patrol the town;
They struck me, they bruised me.
The guards of the walls
Stripped me of my mantle.

While women might participate in the daytime street bustle, apparently a lone woman in the dark street might be presumed to be a thief or a prosti-tute. We should also note here that such a lone figure might also encounter the guards without such violence. In chapter 3 the restless woman walks out into the town to search for her absent lover, asks the night watchmen whether they had seen him, and is left to move on without further reported incident.

AMONG FRIENDS

The poems offer us many small glimpses of relationships among a society of young Jerusalem girls. While the verses never mention a particular friend or confidante, the young woman often addresses the "daughters of Jerusalem," or "daughters of Zion." In the early verses of the book the woman defends herself—in this case, as we have seen, explaining her sun-burn to the surrounding girls: "I am dark, but comely, O daughters of

Jerusalem." In a later poem (5:9) that same crowd challenges her to tell them what's so special about her boyfriend: "How is your beloved better than another, O fairest of women?"

We learn from a refrain repeated three times in the book (2:7, 3:5, and 8:4) that her friends might be out and about in the city enough to encounter her lover, and so she begs them:

> *I adjure you, O maidens of Jerusalem!*
> *If you meet my beloved, tell him this:*
> *That I am faint with love.*

ROMANCE AND SEXUALITY

The Song of Songs offers evidence of young unmarried women engaged in romantic and sexual relationships with no mention of betrothal or marriage. The love expressed by the young man and woman focuses entirely on sexual desire—we find nothing in the verses about sharing common values or dreams or a sense of humor! Confident of her physical appeal, the woman boasts not of her sensitivity or commitment to a meaningful relationship but, rather, of her statuesque and desirable body. She knows that she is as strong as a city wall and as luscious as a vineyard, more desirable than even the vineyards and treasure of the storied king:

> [10]*I am a wall,*
> *My breasts are like towers.*
> *So I became in his eyes*
> *As one who finds favor.*
> [11]*Solomon had a vineyard*
> *In Baal-hamon.*
> *He had to post guards in the vineyard:*
> *A man would give for its fruit*
> *A thousand pieces of silver.*
> [12]*I have my very own vineyard:*
> *You may have the thousand, O Solomon,*
> *And the guards of the fruit two hundred! (8:10–12)*

What do we learn about the nature of the love the couple shared? Whereas contemporary Egyptian and Mesopotamian love poetry explicitly portray their lovers' physical arousal,[3] these Israelite poems use metaphors relating to the natural world as a delicate veil for the highly charged eroticism implicit in their encounters. The woman anticipates the sensuality of one night's lovemaking (4:16):

¹⁶Awake, O north wind,
Come, O south wind!
Blow upon my garden,
That its perfume may spread.
Let my beloved come to his garden
And enjoy its luscious fruits!

None of the liaisons referred to in *The Song of Songs* involve marriage. Although one might speculate that a wedding might follow sometime later, these relationships are not yet sanctioned by marriage. Throughout the poems, no woman speaker ever refers to a husband, and only in a long passage stretching between the fourth and fifth chapters does a man refer to a marriage in the phrases "my sister, my bride" and "my bride." The endearment *kalati*, which unequivocally means "my bride" in modern Hebrew, may not have indicated marriage at all in the idiomatic Hebrew of that era. We thus have no convincing evidence that the couple is married.

The young woman's excited evocation of spring (2:8–13) anticipates the arrival of her lover—she mentions neither betrothed nor husband—who clearly lives apart from her and is coming to whisk her away from her home to enjoy the delights of the season:

⁸Hark! My beloved!
There he comes,
Leaping over mountains,
Bounding over hills.
⁹My beloved is like a gazelle
Or like a young stag.
There he stands behind our wall,
Gazing through the window,
Peering through the lattice.
¹⁰My beloved spoke thus to me,
"Arise, my darling;
My fair one, come away!
¹¹For now the winter is past,
The rains are over and gone.
¹²The blossoms have appeared in the land,
The time of pruning has come;
The song of the turtledove
Is heard in our land.
¹³The green figs form on the fig tree,
The vines in blossom give off fragrance.
Arise, my darling;
My fair one, come away!

In another poem, when the woman recounts how she longed for her lover and ventured out into the city streets in the middle of the night to find him, she could not rest until she brought him to *her*—not *their* shared—home:

> [4]*Scarcely had I passed them*
> *When I found the one I love.*
> *I held him fast, I would not let him go*
> *Till I brought him to my mother's house,*
> *To the chamber of her who conceived me.*

Indeed, in the very last verse of the anthology, the woman urges the man to run off into the hills. As many scholars have noted, the lack of either angst or anger in the verse leads the reader to surmise that although dawn has begun to light the sky and the unmarried couple dare not be caught together after their night of love[4] they nonetheless look forward to meeting again.

THE WOMAN AS ALLEGORICAL SYMBOL OF ISRAEL

The Song of Songs has survived for us to enjoy today not solely because of its inherent delight but also because of the allegory attached to it by the early rabbis. The first line's attribution to the wise and holy King Solomon led the rabbis of the late Roman and Byzantine periods to regard it as a mirror reflecting the love between God and Israel. One might ask why we need attend this allegory at all, nowadays when many readers focus solely on the literal meaning of biblical texts. However, it is precisely the allegory in which the early rabbis wrapped this love poetry that has remained, consciously or unconsciously, an important expression of "the Chosen People," the principle that ties together diverse Jews across the world, connecting the People and Land of Israel with God. Throughout the allegory the figure of the woman becomes the embodiment of Israel, eternally bound in adoring love to God.

Why, we might ask, did the rabbis compare Israel's relationship with God to a pair of young lovers? The scholar of Jewish mysticism Arthur Green suggests that

> in the search for the kind of intimacy, tenderness, and warmth that such people wanted to express in talking about the relationship between God and Israel, they could not remain in the domain of the all-male universe where they lived their public lives. There is no way, without turning to images of the feminine, or without thinking of the relationships between

men and woman, that most men can express the degree of love, passion, and warmth that the spiritual life may arouse in them.[5]

Yet, the woman portrayed in the allegory does not express any real woman's thoughts, words, or actions. Rather, as Green notes, in the rabbinic interpretations of *The Song of Songs,* we find a construct, "women as created by men, women in the fantasies of men, albeit sacred fantasies." As we examine the early rabbinics on *The Song of Songs*, we will look for evidence of what part the rabbis saw the woman lover playing in the relationship.

The allegory surrounding *The Song of Songs* has flowed through two discrete courses, each with its own tributaries. The earliest interpretation is the *midrash,* or commentary, in which the early rabbis developed the allegory to explain the history of Israel from its foundation during the Exodus through their own late Roman and Byzantine eras.[6] In this allegory, the rabbis construct an image of a young woman, ripe for marriage but not yet wed, who exists as a symbol of the nation of Israel in its unique relationship to God. Apart from the historically oriented midrash, however, a second stream of interpretation developed in Jewish mysticism from about the thirteenth century. The mystical literature attempted to explain, not the course of worldly Jewish history, but instead, the flow and play of attributes of unity and separation within the Divinity itself. The young woman lover is embedded in Jewish mystical traditions as the figure of the *Shechinah*, the emanation of God closest and most accessible to the mundane human world.[7] Arthur Green notes that while the Zohar, the most comprehensive single work of medieval Jewish mysticism, has no section per se on *The Song of Songs,* references to it abound throughout.[8] Here, however, we will focus on the image of the woman in the historical interpretation embodied in the midrash and Targum, or interpretive Aramaic translation, on *The Song of Songs.* It is this interpretation that has become the essential expression of the concept of the Chosen People in all its religious, social, and political ramifications.

THE MIDRASH AND TARGUM ON *THE SONG OF SONGS*

The allegory that compares this body of erotic love poetry to the love between God and Israel stretches deep into Jewish history. This interpretation seems to have been well established by the early second century CE discussions over canonizing problematic books such as Kohelet (Ecclesiastes), Ezekiel, and Esther. Whereas the Mishnah preserves evidence of serious discussions about the sanctity of *The Song of Songs* and these three other books, and records debate about removing Kohelet, Ezekiel, and Esther from the body of accepted revelation, no discussions about excising

The Song of Songs from among the approved sacred texts have been recorded. However, doubt nonetheless lingered. In a discussion recorded in the Mishnah, the first codification of Jewish law redacted by the end of the second century, when some rabbis questioned the wisdom of including *The Song of Songs* in the canon of the Hebrew Bible, Rabbi Akiva, the celebrated sage and political activist of early second-century Jerusalem, famously exclaimed:

> God forbid: no man in Israel ever disputed the status of *The Song of Songs* saying that it does not defile the hands, for the whole world is not worth the day on which *The Song of Songs* was given to Israel; for all the writings are holy, but *The Song of Songs* is the holiest of the holy."[9]

The main collection of midrash that explains the value that Akiva and others found in the poetry is Song of Songs Rabbah (hereafter Song Rabbah),[10] part of a larger collection of midrash on many biblical books called Midrash Rabbah. Notably, the midrash on this exceptionally brief biblical book is at least as lengthy as the midrash on any other except Genesis. Song Rabbah was likely rewritten—for it is a compilation of several hundred years of discussions—in the land of Israel around 600 CE. The detail and length with which these rabbis approached the allegorical exegesis of the poetry reflect the seriousness with which they approached the task of supporting Jewish identity and life in the decades and centuries following the two traumatic Roman destructions—that of the Second Temple and much of Jerusalem in 70 CE and also the complete razing of the city following the Bar Kokhba Revolt of 133–135 CE—and the later challenges posed by subsequent Roman and Byzantine rule. These same circumstances underlie the approach offered in another major source of rabbinic allegorical commentary on *The Song of Songs,* the Targum, or Aramaic translation probably completed in Palestine by around the eighth century.[11]

And why was *The Song of Songs* considered so important? The rabbis considered the book to be the essential finishing touch for the Jews' wardrobe of revelatory writings:

> Judah ben R. [Hiyya] (220–250) said: Your cheeks are comely with circlets (Song of Songs 1:10): This refers to the Torah. Your neck with beads: this refers to the Prophets. We will make you circlets of gold: this refers to the Hagiographa. With studs of silver: this refers to *The Song of Songs*—something complete and finished off.[12]

Indeed, the entire Hebrew Bible, the very Torah itself, was considered incomprehensible to one who did not already appreciate the love between

God and Israel expressed in *The Song of Songs*. According to an enduring rabbinic principle, *The Song of Songs* should be read only as allegory; one who valued its literal romantic content merited only scorn. The denial of the literal meaning of the verses was so thorough that the midrash entirely avoids recognition of their earthly sensuality and sexuality—for instance, in interpreting the sweet fragrances described in 4:6:

> ⁶*When the day blows gently*
> *And the shadows flee,*
> *I will betake me to the mount of myrrh,*
> *To the hill of frankincense*

The rabbis convert the perfumed breezes to the sweetness of Abraham's and the people of Israel's devotion to God. Soon afterward the woman invites to the man to join her to enjoy sensual pleasures (4:16):

> ¹⁶*Awake, O north wind,*
> *Come, O south wind!*
> *Blow upon my garden,*
> *That its perfume may spread.*
> *Let my beloved come to his garden*
> *And enjoy its luscious fruits!*

The midrash likens the fragrant winds to the aroma of burnt-offerings rising from the Temple, and to the eventual reunification of the northern and southern reaches of the Land of Israel in the days of the Messiah.[13] Today we might wonder at the rabbis' evident discomfort with the poetry's sensuality, yet, as scholars have remarked, their need to reinterpret it was "inherited from the old biblical struggle against cultic sexuality."[14]

The first sections of Song Rabbah include a series of tales that explain the role of the brief book in the greater body of the Hebrew Bible, including the following. The Torah—whose values the wise Solomon embodied—was like

> a cask which was full of precious stones and pearls, but which had a tight-fitting cover and was put away in a corner, so that no one knew what was in it, until someone came and emptied it, and then everyone knew what was in it. So the heart of Solomon was full of wisdom, but no one knew what was in it, but when the Holy Spirit rested on him and he composed three books [including *The Song of Songs*], all knew his wisdom.[15]

Solomon's act of setting down *The Song of Songs* thus enabled the People of Israel to comprehend the love between God and Israel (just as reading Kohelet and Proverbs offer other kinds of wisdom), opening their eyes and hearts to the value of Torah. In the midrashic view—which remained the normative Jewish religious approach to this text—the miraculous crossing of the Red Sea was God's seminal act of love for the Chosen People; *The Song of Songs* was first composed at that moment and only later revealed to Israel through Solomon. Song Rabbah thus provides phrase-by-phrase exploration of the allegorical (and thus sole correct!) meaning of the poetry. Song Rabbah treats the poetry as the history of Israel's relationship with its divine lover from the Exodus through their own day, continually looking forward to the lovers' ultimate reunion at the time of the coming of the Messiah. Throughout the midrash, the rabbis struggle to reconcile the adversity that their community faced with their unfailing conviction that God's love would ultimately prevail, attributing their troubles to Israel's own repeated failure to comply with divine law expressed in Torah. Within this exegesis, the figure of the woman lover almost always symbolizes Israel, passionately in love with, necessarily subordinate to, but not always obedient to its ever-just divine lover.

The midrash likens Israel's disobedience to the sunburn that the girl mentioned, as we saw in 1:6. The midrashic comment that begins the discussions of this passage explains the girl's assertion that even though sunburned, she is nonetheless desirable to her lover:

> **I am black but comely**. I am black through my own deeds, but comely through the works of my ancestors. **I am black but comely**. The community of Israel said: I am black in my own sight, but comely before my Creator ... Another explanation: I was black in Egypt, as it says, But they rebelled against Me and would not hearken unto Me (Ezek. xx, 8). And I was comely in Egypt with the blood of the Passover and the blood of circumcision.[16]

Israel's obedience to God in Egypt, its sacrifices on the night of the Exodus, became evidence of its love of God. We see here an example of the rabbinic view that the Exodus was the moment when the love between God and Israel was revealed. However, Israel violated God's law throughout Jewish history. The next passage we quote here traces Israel's disobedience in episodes far later than the Exodus. Here, a prominent rabbi interprets the girl's complaint about her sunburn in the light of a statement in Jeremiah, showing that implicit in the woman's words was Israel's admission of sin during the days of the Temple:

That the sun hath tanned me. R. Abba b. Kahana said in the name of R. Hiyya the Great: It is written, For my people have committed two evils (Jer. 11,13). But did they not neglect many precepts? What this teaches is that they committed one sin which was as bad as two: they worshipped idols and turned their backs on the Sanctuary.[17]

Although the midrash continually recognizes Israel's propensity to sin, it also stresses Israel's ability to trust in its divine lover to rescue it from adversity. Here again the Exodus is the moment of that revelation. Let us examine the rabbis' interpretation of the man's plea for the woman's trust implicit in verse 2:14. Here, the man pleads to the woman:

> [14]*O my dove, in the cranny of the rocks,*
> *Hidden by the cliff,*
> *Let me see your face,*
> *Let me hear your voice;*
> *For your voice is sweet*
> *And your face is comely.*

In Song Rabbah the rabbis use the poem's comparison of the woman to a dove to express Israel's trust in God to deliver it from both the perils of Egyptian vengeance and drowning at the Red Sea:

> It was taught in the school of R. Ishmael: When Israel went forth from Egypt, what did they resemble? A dove which was fleeing from a hawk and flew into the cleft of a rock, found a serpent lurking there. When it tried to turn back it could not because the hawk was hovering outside. What then did the dove do? It began to cry and beat its wings so that the owner of the cote should hear and come to its rescue. This was the position of Israel by the Red Sea. They could not go down into the sea, because it had not yet been divided before them. They could not turn back, because Pharoah had already drawn near. What did they do? And they were sore afraid; and the children of Israel cried out unto the Lord (Ex. xiv, 10). Then straightway, Thus the Lord saved Israel that day (ib. 30).

The rabbis compare the woman, likened to a frightened dove, to Israel at the Red Sea and use the comparison to demonstrate Israel's ability to trust in divine deliverance from ultimate peril. Israel's trust in God was rewarded at the Red Sea; embattled Jews forever after might similarly trust in divine deliverance from peril.

The midrash acknowledges that although God would ultimately deliver Israel from its enemies, the Chosen People might nonetheless need to persevere through long periods when, because of their sinning, its divine lover might hide himself. A long series of comments on the beginning of the third chapter,

> [1]*Upon my couch at night*
> *I sought the one I love—*
> *I sought, but found him not (3:1)*

interprets the "night" as periods when God absents himself as punishment for Israel's sin. Whereas Israel, the rabbis reasoned, had enjoyed God's light and favor between the Exodus and the Babylonian Exile, since then God had withdrawn those gifts, leaving Israel in the perpetual night of successive oppressions by Babylonia, Media, Greece, and Rome. "Now that I sleep neglectful of the Torah and precepts," the rabbis wrote, "one night follows immediately on another,"[18] while Israel longs for her lover's deliverance. From midrash we learn that the allegorical woman Israel may be beautiful and desirable, and indeed a worthy covenantal partner for God, but, inevitably in the relationship between humanity and God, her real virtue lay in her ability—however inconsistently realized—to obey her divine lover's Torah.

The Targum on *The Song of Songs,* its vernacular Aramaic paraphrase, also presents the poetry as an allegory of the history of the love between God and Israel. *The Song of Songs,* it tells us, is the ninth in a series of ten great songs to be sung in the course of pre-messianic human history.[19] In synagogues of Byzantine-era Israel, for whose worshippers Aramaic had long replaced Hebrew as the vernacular, during ritual readings of *The Song of Songs,* passages of the Hebrew biblical text would be read aloud alternating with the corresponding passages of the Targum. Thus the allegorical paraphrase became the normative popular understanding of the poetry. The Targum's prominence extended far beyond the Land of Israel itself; the eleventh-century commentator Rashi based his own commentary on *The Song of Songs* very closely upon it. It is worth noting here that Rashi's own significance in the history of Jewish biblical interpretation is such that even today, traditional Jewish approaches to text study consider his commentaries the single most essential tool for understanding any biblical text.

The Targum offers a striking interpretation of the final verse of *The Song of Songs* (8:14):

> [14]*Hurry, my beloved,*
> *Swift as a gazelle or a young stag,*
> *To the hills of spices!*

As we saw, the "good-bye" in this passage is likely an "au revoir," as the woman seems to anticipate another meeting. The Targum paraphrases the verse, applying a similar scenario to the relationship between God and Israel: "O Beloved Lord of the Universe," the elders of Israel plead,

> flee from this polluted earth, and let your Presence dwell in the high heavens; and in times of trouble, when we pray to You, be like a gazelle, which, while it sleeps, has one eye closed and one eye open, or like a fawn of the hinds, which, in running away, looks back. So look upon us and regard our pain and affliction from the high heavens, until such time when You will be pleased with us and redeem us, and bring us up to the mountains of Jerusalem, where the priests will burn before You the incense of spices.[20]

Just as the young woman and man in the literal text tacitly look forward to their next embrace, Israel looks toward the time when it will merit final reunification with its divine lover.

Thus, we see in these two allegorical explorations, not a portrayal of an actual Jewish woman, but a construct developed by male religious leaders who seized upon the most profound relationship they knew to describe their devotion to the Divine. While they might have compared the passion between Israel and God as a tempestuous marriage, one cannot expect the allegory to reflect realistic relationships and expectations among men and women.

In a human relationship, the woman might enjoy some degree of independence, but in the relationship between Israel and its divine lover Israel could only be the subordinate partner. In a human relationship love might be founded on sensuality, but in Jewish religion, which from its inception had rejected religious sex rites, erotic expression needed to be sublimated into longing for union with the Divine. While one might wonder about the motivations of a lover who suddenly and inexplicably flees, when God seemingly turned his face away from his Chosen People, only Israel could have possibly erred, since God is eternally just. Yet just as the young woman's last words urge her lover, "Hurry, my beloved, Swift as a gazelle or a young stag, To the hills of spices," while looking forward to embracing him again, in the rabbinic allegory that has preserved *The Song of Songs* place in Jewish tradition, the woman Israel knows that she will one day be forever unified with her divine lover.

NOTES

1. Debra Band, *The Song of Songs: The Honeybee in the Garden* (Philadelphia: Jewish Publication Society, 2005).

2. Ibn Ezra offered three "expositions" of the poetry: first, a study of the meaning of each word; second, understanding the poetry as the love songs of a rural maiden and shepherd; and third—and, as he stated, the only really valid reading—an allegorical interpretation as the love song between Israel and the Shechinah, or the divine presence.

3. See the chapter on "Form Criticism and Canticles" in Marvin Pope, *The Anchor Bible: Song of Songs* (New York: Doubleday and Company, 1977).

4. Ariel Bloch and Chana Bloch, for instance, regard the final verse as "an ending that looks forward in anticipation to another meeting." Ariel Bloch and Chana Bloch, *The Song of Songs: A New Translation* (New York: Random House, 1995), 221.

5. Arthur Green, "Bride, Spouse, Daughter: Images of the Feminine in Classical Jewish Sources," in *On Being a Jewish Feminist*, ed. Susannah Heschel (New York: Schocken Books, 1995), 250.

6. *Midrash* is the collective term for rabbinic commentary on the meaning of biblical verses, wherein a problematic word or phrase is considered, and its significance determined in the light of similar phrasing elsewhere in the Hebrew Bible, in other stories or legends, in Jewish written or oral traditions, or even in the commentator's own experience.

7. See Arthur Green, "*The Song of Songs* in Early Jewish Mysticism," *Orim: A Jewish Journal at Yale* 2, no. 2, Spring 1987.

8. Ibid., 59.

9. Sid Z. Leiman, *The Canonization of Hebrew Scripture: The Talmudic and Midrashic Evidence* (New Haven: Connecticut Academy of Arts and Sciences, 1991), 104.

10. See note 6.

11. After the Babylonian captivity (586–538 BCE) Aramaic, and later Greek also, became the dominant vernacular of the Land of Israel and Hebrew remained the language of sacred texts. Thus, Jews who no longer spoke or read Hebrew fluently required that an Aramaic translation accompany synagogue readings of biblical texts; such a translation is referred to as a "Targum." In many cases, such as with *The Song of Songs*, the Targum is not a literal translation but an interpretive paraphrase, giving the reader a symbolic understanding of the text at hand instead of a literal translation. Even such an interpretive Targum is, however, *traditionally* considered to be close enough to the accepted meaning of the text that it is not considered to be midrash, where allegory is acceptable, but instead is considered *p'shat*, or a direct translation. The Targum in this way established the allegorical reading of *The Song of Songs* as the normative understanding. Nonetheless, because the Targum on *The Song of Songs* is highly interpretive rather than literal, here we consider it separate from, but closely akin to, the midrash.

12. Leiman, 68.

13. Song of Songs Rabbah, 227.

14. Green, "Creating a Feminist Theology," 251. See also Robert Gordis, *The Song of Songs: A Study, Modern Translation and Commentary* (New York: Jewish Theological Seminary of America, 1961), 27.

15. Song of Songs Rabbah, 55.

16. Ibid., 51.

17. Ibid., 57.

18. Ibid., 143.

19. A. J. Rosenberg, trans. and ed., *The Books of Esther, Song of Songs, Ruth* (New York: Judaica Press, 1992), Song of Songs: 2.

20. Ibid., 103.

CHAPTER 10

The Book of Ruth through New Eyes

Joy Silver

Many ideas and interpretations regarding the Book of Ruth have emerged through the ages. Almost all of them revolve around the concept of welcoming the "Other"—that is to say, having tolerance and acceptance of the outsider. This acceptance traditionally sets the stage for the story of the outsider, Ruth, in the Book of Ruth, and her conversion to Judaism. The importance of the story of Ruth lies in the acceptance of the Torah and its people by a single individual, signifying an act of conversion to Judaism. It will be the scope of this chapter to show that the Book of Ruth is rooted in the acceptance, and even encouragement, of same-gendered marriage. The story of Naomi and Ruth provides an example of how that acceptance, in the context of social responsibility, advances and fulfills the destiny of the Jewish people.

Judaism itself has historically been a progressive, evolving way of life. It endured a freezing of its evolution by the years spent in the ghettos. This kind of Judaism is considered by its adherents as the one and only true Judaism. The historical openness of Judaism, however, makes for alternative suppositions as to what and who is Jewish. This openness has made interpretation, and the study required to interpret, a central activity of the Judaic religious and spiritual process. The evolution of progressive interpretation has a traceable history.

Rabbi Akiva Ben Joseph (AD 50–135) taught that textual teachings are to be expanded upon and that the covert lessons in the Torah have far

greater weight than the overt. Akiva initially generated the idea, now considered a Judaic tradition, that adjustment of the law should be made for
the times. This idea was further advanced by Rashi (Rabbi Schlomo Itz-
haki, AD 1040–1105), who declared that communities are entitled to can-
cel decisions made by the ancients according to the needs of current
times. Rabbi Mordechai Kaplan (AD 1881–1983), founder of Reconstructionism, has added to this evolving concept in our more contemporary
times. He has said that each generation has the responsibility to keep Judaism alive by finding new meanings that are relevant. We call, then, on
these evolving traditions and their authorities to add to and create contemporary *midrashic* and Talmudic works. The particular interpretation of the
Book of Ruth found here relies on this authority.

THE OUTSIDER

The Book of Ruth is about acceptance of the outsider, and about conversion. Conversion, and the acceptance of converted women by the community, may have been deemed essential by writers of the period to support
the survival of the Jewish people. Ezra (10:2) and Nehemiah (13:23) both
identify the issue of Jewish men marrying foreign women, then following
the god(s) of their wives rather than the God of the Hebrews as a challenge to the survival of the Jews. Ezra additionally condemns intermarriage
as the reason the Hebrews fell out of relationship with their God. The
story of the Book of Ruth, written in support of marriage to women who
would convert, may be seen to reinforce the good that comes out of
accepting converts. The story's ending fully underscores the importance
of accepting the converted woman, for it leads to the birth of the greatest
of all Jewish kings, David.

Since the Book of Ruth ends with the lineage leading to David, it may
be assumed that the story was written after that of David. Take into con-
sideration that "The Songs of Songs" appears between the Book of Ruth
and David and Jonathan's story, found in Samuel. "The Song of Songs"
also makes a case for accepting the Other. It is a love song between a
black woman and a non-black man, simultaneously depicting the relationship between a human and God. This shows the power of accepting the
Other, by illustrating the strength and pleasure of divine marriage. A number of relationships are referred to in the Book of Ruth, all of which depict
non-mainstream unions. However, an interpretation of the Book of Ruth
based simply on acceptance of the outsider doesn't go far enough.

It is true that the acceptance and tolerance of the outsider is a critical
aspect to the Book of Ruth's lesson, but for reasons other than those usually studied. The interpretation to be found herein proves the following

case: Ruth never actually accepts the Torah or Judaism for its innate truth or spiritual teachings; rather, it is her love of the woman Naomi that is her sole reason for conversion. There is no mention of the Jewish God or her love of the Torah. Further, the story teaches that love between people of the same gender holds a place in responsible Jewish community life. This is evidenced specifically by references to non-mainstream or seemingly questionable sexual and domestic relationships involving other biblical characters—all resulting in the furthering of the existence, aiding in the survival, and even in the subsequent greatness, of the Hebrew people-including King David's relationship with Jonathan.

The story centers on the journey of two women, Naomi and Ruth, who are in desperate straits. It appears to be told from the viewpoint of a woman. I maintain that we may read the Book of Ruth as a love story between these two women. For all intents and purposes, they are married in the eyes of both the community and God. Acceptance of the relationship and its parameters is clearly portrayed by the community's acknowledgment of the child Ruth bears, known as Naomi's child, for Naomi becomes the child's other mother, or perhaps even its father in name. The birth of this child, Obed (Servant), historically leads to the lineage of the one known as the Greatest King of the Jews, David. It isn't a coincidence that we also find in the David story a parallel or at least similar case of same-gender love in the relationship he has with Jonathan. We could say that the acceptance of the Other—here the Other being same-gendered love—has led to the continuation of the Jews' greatness because it has produced a leader through Naomi and Ruth. King David is aided in meeting his destiny through the relationship he has with the son of King Saul, Jonathan. In our contemporary political and social culture, these relationships would be seen as gay, although not named as such given the times of these stories, but certainly understood.

THE NAMES OF GOD

Another aspect worthy of exploration in this story is the actual concept of the Hebrew God in the context of its time, as well as references found therein to earlier definitions of God. The definition of God and the ability to envision or experience God as inclusive of the feminine gender becomes important in the Ruth story. Such conceptual inclusion informs the historical authority called upon by the story to enhance accepting the pairing of community responsibility and conversion. Baruch de Spinoza (AD 1632–1677), an influence on the advent of Reconstructionism, teaches that God cannot have a personality, and, for sure, there is no personified God in this story. We do, however, find in this story a concept in a name for God, although God does not appear, nor does he speak to anyone in this story. The name referred to is *El Shaddai*, that is, "God with many breasts." Although there remain some scholars who refuse to translate *shaddai* as "breasts," the language used in Jacob's blessing, Genesis 49:25, emphasizes that this is the correct translation: "El Shaddai who blesses you ... with blessings of the breasts and womb"(10). This name is a pre-Moses term for God, indicating that the idea somehow pre-dates when God appeared to Moses. The God of Abraham, Isaac, and Jacob was known by this name (Exod. 6:2–3) and again in Job, whom Naomi is likened to when she recites her trials and tribulations. We find this name used forty-eight times in the Tanach, often in reference to a god that promised fruitfulness. So why, after Moses, do we find this name of God in the Book of Ruth, and linked to a name that is of the divine feminine? The use of this name suggests that the union of Naomi and Ruth has the blessing of God, that is, of the god or goddess harkening back to the Hebrew people at the time of their origin—ancient even to the people who would be reading the Book of Ruth when it was contemporary. The god name "Yahweh" was not used until the days of Moses, for the Book of Exodus records that God said to Moses, "I am YHWH [or Ehyeh Asher Ehyeh]. I appeared to Abraham, to Isaac and to Jacob as El Shaddai, but by my name of YHWH I did not make myself known to them" (Exod. 6:2–3).

The word *Elohim* is also used as a name for God in this story. The plurality shows that female and male genders are included in this name, suggesting that here we refer to a God of Unity. Naomi and Ruth together, in their fruitfulness with their many breasts as two women together, find themselves and their relationship parallel to an earlier aspect of the god of their people. This serves to show us that a desirable union, in the eyes of God and the community, is taking place between them.

THE STORY

Since the Book of Ruth may not seem overtly lesbian to the mainstream reader, let us explore the points taken in this context so that they become more evident. The bare bones of the Book of Ruth might commonly be viewed as a story in three acts. It begins by moving from the relationship with Naomi as mother-in-law, which includes the conversion and declaration of love, to the budding relationship or strategy for community acceptance between Naomi, Boaz, and Ruth, through to the marriage of Boaz and Ruth. The epilogue relates Naomi's joy at the turn of events, and then the proclamation and acknowledgment by the community that Ruth and Boaz's baby is to be known as Naomi's. We end with the patrilineal list of Naomi's descendents, leading to King David.

We are told that the story begins in Moab. The land of Moab itself is problematic, as are its inhabitants, the Moabites, and to the reader this signals that there are deeper issues that are meant to be considered. In earlier Books, we have been told that we are to understand that neither Ammonites nor Moabites are to be considered friends of the Hebrews, yet Moab is precisely where Ruth hails from. Interestingly enough, the reasons for the antagonism have to do with these groups' inhospitality to the Hebrews and with a rather unacceptable incestuous sexual act. The Ammonites' and the Moabites' ancestors are those issued through the resulting incest committed by Lot and his daughters. The story of the Moabitess Ruth, beginning in Moab, may be considered the first clue to our understanding the underlying story that is about to take place. Central to this interpretation is the exploration of how sexuality and procreation outside acceptably mainstream relationships support the definition and survival of the Hebrew community. It also helps us to understand how individuals outside mainstream relationships need to be welcomed for the greater good of the community.

Naomi as Mother-In-Law

Evidently, Naomi follows her husband, Elimelech (My God Is King), out of Bethlehem (ironically, House of Bread) because of famine, sometimes said to have happened because he didn't want to share his wealth with his tribe's people in the homeland. Perhaps because of this, Elimelech dies, leaving Naomi, who was basically doing her wifely duty by following her husband's plan for the family, destitute in Moab. Although Naomi no longer has a husband, and she doesn't remarry for some unknown reason, during her marriage she has had two sons, who are, by the way, married to non-Jewish women. Maybe that is why she stays another ten years in Moab, since she is still being provided for by her sons, Mahlon and Chilion (Consumption and Sickly). Additionally, by staying, she may still enjoy the company of her daughters-in-law, Orpah (Back of Neck, inferring needing to flee) and Ruth (Sweet). But when Naomi's two sons die, leaving her with no provider, she makes a decision that it's time to go back to the land of her origin, Judea. Her two daughters-in-law, Orpah and Ruth, want to stay with her and petition her to do so. Naomi doesn't think this is a good idea, and she tells the two Moabite women to go back to their mothers. One of her arguments is that she certainly cannot have any more sons for them to marry—at least not in the timeframe that will do them any good. If they stay with her, Naomi doesn't see how this will help any of them, since they all will certainly be without providers.

Significantly, Naomi has not remarried over a ten-year period, and refraining from marriage is not considered holy among the Hebrew people. Genesis 2:18 says, "It is not good for man to be alone," thereby underscoring that companionship, love, and intimacy rather than procreation are the primary purposes of marriage. This is an important distinction for the purposes of understanding the nature of the relationships in the Book of Ruth. Let's look further into the Hebrew concept of marriage.

Exodus 21:10 says that marriage is about providing food, clothing, and sexual relations. The Laws of Marriage tell us that three things are to be found in a relationship in order to make a marriage. Any one of the following completes that which is known as *kiddushin* (betrothal) and makes the marriage legal: (1) a contract or declaration, (2) the establishment of identifying a provider, and (3) intimate (or sexual) relations. The process of full marriage, or *nisuin,* is to be completed only after the "husband" brings the "wife" into his (or her) home and they begin their married life together. We can identify these specific elements in the context of the relationship between Ruth and Naomi. These elements point to the possibility that they had established a relationship that might then be considered a community-sanctioned, recognized state of marriage, as defined by and in accordance with Jewish law.

THE CONVERSION: "UNTIL DEATH DO US PART"

... Where you die, I shall die,
And there I shall be buried.
Thus may YHWH add
If even death will separate me from you (Ruth 1:16–17)

Ruth's declaration to Naomi signals to Naomi, as well as to the reader, that she is ready to accept Naomi as a "wife" would accept a "husband." We know this because the "wife" must show her willingness to accept her "husband's people" and to live among them. This declaration may be found in the text commonly referred to as "The Conversion."

In The Conversion, we find Ruth pledging lifelong commitment to Naomi. These words are some of the most famous and beautiful marriage vows found in Western history and are still used in weddings today. Not only does Ruth pledge to stay with Naomi "until death do us part," but she also pledges to accept her family and people. This presents us with another clue to the relationship between Ruth and Naomi. Considering that Ruth has already married into Naomi's family and that her status is that of widow to Naomi's son, why would she need to declare that she accepts Naomi's family and people? Isn't Ruth already Naomi's family by marriage? The only reasonable conclusion is that she needs to say these words to begin the process of marrying Naomi by fulfilling the declaration requirement, in accordance with the Jewish Laws of Marriage. The words also signal to Naomi that Ruth is available and willing to be her "wife."

The traditional acknowledgment pinpointing the moment of conversion happens when Ruth tells Naomi, "Your God shall be my God." Ruth wants to leave Moab with Naomi and converts for the love of her. It's important to understand that Ruth has not converted because she loves the God of Israel. In fact, Ruth never speaks of God; she speaks only her love of Naomi. An additional aspect to this conversion may also be that she converts so that Naomi's people will accept her, and therefore their "new" relationship, since her desire is to travel back to Naomi's homeland. This seems to be a radical move on Ruth's part, since Ruth has had years to convert. Certainly she did not even after she married a Jewish male. Ruth's declaration serves as evidence that this so-called conversion has a different meaning to these two women in this context, and it certainly signals more than conversion, if it even signals conversion at all. We can see that this declaration serves the double duty of not only the Act of Conversion but also the Marriage Contract. It is this declaration that fulfills the first Jewish Law of Marriage.

IDENTIFYING A PROVIDER

Until now, Ruth's declaration has been determined independently of male authority. The actions taken to establish this new relationship between Ruth and Naomi have so far been taken by Ruth. Once Naomi realizes that Ruth is not to be dissuaded, she rethinks her position. She certainly is not happy with circumstances that will require her to move and start over, but this passionate declaration from this younger woman holds potential. We know this because Naomi's response is to accept the responsibility of the opportunity, and she makes her move to fulfill the second Jewish Law of Marriage, which is identification of a provider. The situation needs a response, and this action shows her acceptance. Naomi constructs a plan, one that includes taking care of Ruth as well as herself, effectively accepting the role of provider and "husband." She will return to her people and look up relatives of hers so that she can redeem the land owned by her deceased husband so that it might be worked to provide for both of them.

INTIMATE RELATIONS

Things are not going to be particularly easy for any of the women in this family. Naomi has at this point successfully convinced Orpah to return to her mother, but Ruth has declared herself to Naomi for life. Do Naomi and Ruth seal this contract with the act of sexual intimacy at this point, before venturing off to Bethlehem? It would seem so, and intimacy may be identified as such in the story when the story tells us that Ruth "clung" to Naomi, after which Naomi is convinced and argues no more. The use of this word is one of the factors that may be further explored as defining the relationship between the women.

> Therefore shall a man leave his father and his mother, and shall cleave unto his wife and they shall be one flesh. (Gen. 2:24)

Ruth 1:14, referring to the relationship between Ruth and Naomi, tells us that "Ruth clave onto her." The special relationship between Ruth and Naomi is indicated by the word *davak,* which means "cling" or "cleave." The Hebrew word translated here as *clave* is identical to that used in the description of a heterosexual marriage in Genesis 2:24: *"Therefore shall a man leave his father and his mother, and shall cleave unto his wife: and they shall be one flesh."* At the end of the story, to underscore this point, the root *a-h-v* (love) is used by the women of Bethlehem to describe Ruth's feelings for Naomi, "for he is born of your daughter–in-law, who loves you and is better to you than seven sons (4:15)," and this is the only instance in the Bible where this verb is used to describe a relationship between one woman and another. We may conclude, then, that this act fulfills the third Jewish Law of Marriage, completing kiddushin.

To explore the context of sexual relations between women, one needs to clarify and contextualize the issues of the times. The concern with the issues of survival and generation are responsible for the Torah's seemingly contradictory attitudes toward male and female homosexuality. A people continually threatened with extinction must be concerned with producing as many strong and healthy children as possible, making the spilling of seed in male homosexual practice wasteful. Conversely, it seems that as long as a Jewish woman bears children to a Jewish male and does not commit adultery with another man to interfere with the confirmation of lineage, a woman might seek emotional and even sexual fulfillment with another woman without penalty in this culture. This may be evidenced by the fact that there is no direct prohibition placed on the practice of female homosexuality.

EXPANSION OF THE BOUNDARIES OF INTIMATE RELATIONSHIPS

From the text of the story, we are alerted numerous times to the issues of when the expansion of sexual boundaries may be acceptable and may even be considered positive. We are definitely outside the boundaries that constitute the usual infrastructure—an infrastructure, by the way, that allows polygamy and the begetting of offspring by concubines, or "hand-maids," and not necessarily only by those who have converted to Judaism. Let's take a closer look at the character of Boaz, for example. Boaz, whose name means "strength," is a relative of Naomi's, her peer, and a "prominent rich man," albeit, for some reason, unmarried. The "whole town was stirred" by Naomi's return, and the women of the community are informed of her status when Naomi tells them she "came back empty" and calls herself Mara, or "bitter." Gleaning the fields for leftover grain is the accepted welfare system for these people, and when Ruth says she will take on the job for the two of them, Naomi agrees. Boaz, being a man of means, owns part of the field and no doubt Naomi knows this. He notices Ruth in the field, asks about her, finds out she is working for Naomi, and protects her as his family for Naomi's sake. Rabbi Dr. Meir Levin confirms the opinion that Boaz is concerned about Naomi, and he points to how much of Boaz's activities are about Naomi.[1] Boaz has been well informed as to Naomi's situation, as well as Ruth's and their relationship. Naomi has been accepted by Boaz, and this is signaled by how much grain Boaz instructs his workers to allow Ruth to bring home to Naomi. Naomi now proceeds with her plan to provide permanent security for Ruth and to continue her own lineage. Remember, lineage is identified through males, and as the "husband" Naomi sees the potential for securing her own line through Ruth, and through Boaz, who is a carrier of her line. I liken this to a present-day situation in which two women, wanting to secure family lines, choose one partner as the birth mother, with the biological "father" being the other partner's male relative.

There are two other sets of relatives mentioned in the Book of Ruth. First, we see that two women, Rachel and Leah, live together in a child-rearing situation. Although there is no indication that they are sexual with each other, they are mentioned by the women of the village when they say, "May God make the woman [Ruth] who is coming into your home like Rachel and Leah" (Ruth 4:9). Second, the same women reference Judah and Tamar: "And may your house be like the house of Perez whom Tamar bore to Judah" (Ruth 4:11–12).

Family and marriage styles other than those simply consisting of one man and one woman entering a committed monogamous relationship are certainly explored in the Bible, and specifically referenced here is the non-conventional relationship between Rachel and Leah. The stories show that God sometimes blesses family structures that are quite different than the norm. This story is found in Genesis 29 and 30. It involves Jacob, who ended up creating a very large family with the help of not one but two wives and two female slaves. Additionally, it was through trickery in marriage and sex that the birth of Judah resulted. Leah becomes Jacob's wife through deception by Laban, Jacob's father-in-law, who made plans for his daughters, since he is the father of both women. Jacob clearly wanted Rachel, and loved her more, and so it is said that God gave Leah children to open Jacob's heart to her. Judah, the critical character in the genealogical line to the story of Ruth and beyond, was born of this deception. Boaz's direct ancestors are Judah and Tamar, through Perez.

Why does the particular reference to Judah and Tamar by the women of the village have meaning in the Ruth story? In Boaz's own family, the idea that a child is the result of a marriage between in-laws and Levirate marriage is clearly part of his family history, and we are reminded with this reference. Judah was father-in-law to Tamar, who had married Judah's older son. By the law of Levirate marriage (Deut. 25:5–6) Onan, Judah's younger son, should have married Tamar but did not. Unfortunately, Tamar's brother-in-law refused to have sexual relations with her, and God killed him for this. Had this marriage taken place, her offspring would have continued the name and inheritance of the deceased. Judah would not give Tamar to any of his other sons, so with the use of alcohol and her brain, Tamar tricked Judah into sex for procreation purposes and her own survival; otherwise, she would have been childless and hungry (Gen. 38:6–30). She did so by pretending to be a Temple prostitute. The result of the union between Judah and Tamar led to the birth of Perez. The house of Perez eventually celebrated the birth of Salmon, father of Boaz.

Another supporting "outside the boundaries" reference concerns Salmon and Boaz's mother, Rahab. Salmon married an actual prostitute, Rahab, and that union produced Boaz. She became "acceptable" because her actions benefited the Hebrew people and their survival. In Joshua 2:1–24, we are told that Rahab was a harlot who lived in Jericho. She hid the spies of Joshua. Because of this, the Israelites spared her life when they conquered Jericho. She later became the wife of Salmon and the mother of Boaz. Rahab's faith was later commended (Heb. 11:30–31). Rahab has been "redeemed" for her actions being right in the eyes of the Hebrew God.

Although Boaz redeems Ruth, or actually redeems Naomi so she gets her land and the continuation of her lineage, through a form of Levirate marriage, the interesting part of this history is that it shows that in-laws of differing ages can and do produce important and acceptable offspring. Judah (Tamar's father-in-law) marries Tamar, even though he does so through "alternative means," such as Tamar's trickery. The result to the community is that their marriage establishes the lineage for David, serving as a signal that this relationship has worked in the interest of the people's survival and is therefore a greater good. Likewise, Naomi (Ruth's mother-in-law) for all intents and purposes marries Ruth through "alternative means," such as two women together, and it, too, sets up the lineage for David, likewise signaling that this relationship has worked out for the greater good of the community.

REDEMPTION

But what, then, is this idea of redemption? The story suggests that Naomi needs a male to redeem her own land, ostensibly because she doesn't have the resources to work the land she owns, and because she needs a male to redeem her husband's lineage, since her own sons have died and left her without issue. Ruth also needs a redeemer in order to bear a child. I suggest, however, that there is yet another way to look at the ideas of "the redeemer" and the concept of "redemption" in the context of this story.

Expressly listed in the Laws of Forbidden Sexual Relations, law 25 says that Ammonites and Moabites shall not be permitted to enter the (Israelite) community by marriage with born Jews. There seem to be two specific reasons: (1) the Moabites did not offer the Israelites bread and water when they left Egypt and so failed to practice hospitality by welcoming the stranger, and (2) the original incident at Sodom offended Jewish sensibilities. Not welcoming the stranger, or certainly not having compassion, begins the legacy of the story regarding the demise of the people of Sodom.

Classical Jewish texts do not stress the homosexuality of the inhabitants of Sodom as much as their cruelty and lack of hospitality to the "stranger."[2] To have Ruth be Moabite is a direct reference to the Lot-Sodom story in that the Book of Ruth is traditionally interpreted to underscore the lessons of hospitality, "welcoming the other" (*chesed*), and general compassion. How is it, then, that Naomi's sons, and now Naomi through Boaz, were all able to marry Moabites? Why would this be so, if Moabites would not be acceptable even ten generations in the future?

What of the Moabites and Ammonites? Aren't they already Jewish? Actually, there is a case for answering yes. The story begins with Lot, Genesis 11–14 and 19. Lot was Abraham's nephew, son of Abraham's brother Haran. Lot used to travel with Abraham until they found that their flocks grew too large and their shepherds were quarrelling. Abraham gave Lot the option to live on the plains near the cities of Sodom and Gomorrah. When the cities came to their demise, whether from inhospitality, excess of lifestyle, lack of compassion, or the men of the cities wanting to rape the angels sent by God, only Lot and his daughters were left alive in the world, as far as they knew. Lot's wife had turned to a pillar of salt after being expressly told not to look back. Lot's daughters assumed that it was their responsibility to bear children and enable the continuation of the Jewish race. After getting their father drunk, they had sexual relations with him and each bore a son, named Moab and Ammon. Since Lot was Jewish and his daughters were Jewish, wouldn't these sons be Jewish? Wouldn't the resulting people of these sons, the Moabites and the Ammonites, also be Jewish? The answer is yes. Why make Ruth a Moabitess? Was it okay to marry females from Moab, but not the men? Although some say it was, it doesn't answer why Ruth never converted until she left Moab with Naomi.

The inhospitality of the Moabites and Ammonites would have to be the major issue between people who were basically from the same tribes. The failure of the Moabites and Ammonites to "act like family" during a crisis carried with it great consequences, particularly that of "expulsion" from the family and tribe. Not welcoming the other made them into the Other. Community, and therefore family, can be bestowed by accepting the terms of tribe, and this would include conversion, and the doing of deeds or participating in ways that helped insure the existence of the family, community, and tribe. Ruth had not participated by having children until she became the primary partner of Naomi. To do this, she became involved with Boaz.

It has been written that Boaz died the day after marrying Ruth. He was an older man and must have realized that if such a young woman wanted to marry him, when she could have younger men, there was more to this request than simple redemption of land and lineage. He agreed to forming the family of choice that his kinswoman, Naomi, suggested and helped Naomi to complete her role of becoming a proper husband to Ruth by seeing that the women had land, food, and a child—and then by dying so the women could live together and finalize the final step of marriage—nisuin.

Redemption, then, is not only about lineage or obtaining fields. When Naomi urges Ruth to visit Boaz after he is drunk and then has her offer herself to him for sexual reasons, Boaz accepts Ruth and so redeems her and her entire Moabite lineage, as well as his own direct lineage. Boaz does something historically different than any of the males mentioned in this story have done. We have Laban's deception of Jacob, which is inferred by the mention of Rachel and Leah. Next comes the story of Judah's drunkenness and Tamar's deception, followed by mention of Lot's drunkenness and his daughters' deception, and finally, we see Boaz's own direct parental history—all setting up scenarios with which to compare Boaz's actions.

Boaz's own mother Rahab's earlier history of prostitution was redeemed through acts that insured the survival of the Jewish people (without, by the way, converting). In the Book of Ruth, Boaz was going to get the chance to act differently. Naomi provided Boaz with this opportunity. She instructed Ruth to go to Boaz when he was drunk and to offer herself sexually to him. Did Naomi know that Boaz would not have sex with Ruth? The answer could be yes.

Let's say that she knew that he would understand what she was asking him to do. Maybe she was counting on his age, or maybe she understood that there was another reason he wasn't married. That reason might have been that he himself was what we today call "gay." He understood Naomi's signal and accepted this chance to be a father and continue his lineage, especially given that Naomi was his own relative. By behaving differently, Boaz changes the course of his family history, not taking advantage of the drunkenness excuse but, instead, doing what was necessary in the community by going through a rendition of levirate marriage. Redemption was possible because one man did something differently, something publicly, and so paved the way for the outsiders to participate as good community members. The case for this is underscored in the story when we are shown that God gave Ruth a conception, and all of this led to the birth of King David.

It is surely no coincidence that King David has his own story of same-sex love and that his birth is the final, exalted result of the union between Naomi and Ruth. The relationship between Jonathan and David is quite erotic in its telling, replete with sexual and love language reserved for heterosexual unions. One of the most famous expressions of David's deep emotional commitment was uttered after Jonathan's death. David's love for Jonathan "surpassed that of women." Jonathan was the son of King Saul, from the tribe of Benjamin. David was a shepherd boy from the tribe of Judah. David was enabled to gain entrée into the world of King Saul, and stay there, because of Jonathan's love for and commitment to, him.

Ultimately, if David hadn't had his relationship with Jonathan, he would not have had the chance to prove himself ready to be king when the opportunity arose. In fact, today all descendants of Israelites might have been known as Benjamish, rather than Jewish (for Judah). Let us not forget that David, too, had issues in his own direct lineage story. Questions regarding his origins were also shrouded in a deception similar to that of Leah and Rachel. David's mother, Nitzevet, conceived him by deceiving her husband, Yishai (Jesse), grandson of Ruth and Boaz, by switching places with Yishai's Canaanite handmaid. She did this because Yishai had problems accepting his lineage and the fact that his grandmother Ruth had been a Moabitess, indicating that accepting converted Moabites was still an issue for Jews. Having this issue come up again, in the parentage of David, was one last opportunity to put the Moab question to rest. The righteousness of the act of accepting a converted Moabite is proved by the magnitude of David's greatness. There is no doubt that it is from the

lineage of Naomi and Ruth that David, known as the greatest king of the
Jewish people, descends.

CONCLUSION

The simple mainstream interpretation of the Book of Ruth teaches that
faithfulness to God may be demonstrated by acts of caring, commitment,
and acts of loving kindness. A greater case has been made here, in the
scope of this argument that God is brought into our lives by our each
being responsible to our community. Ruth and Naomi's relationship was
accepted by their community. This acceptance laid the foundation for
present day welcoming of outsiders and nonconventional unions. Their
relationship is considered a legitimate marriage through the multiple references made in the text of the story. Additionally, the acceptance of Ruth
by both Naomi and the Jewish people is a reminder that the Jewish people
are meant to welcome those who choose to become part of, and responsible to, the community. The Book of Ruth is an exploration of the relationship between Naomi and Ruth, first as lovers, then as marriage partners.
They do their duty, in the political and economic context of their times,
and produce an heir to their union.

By this reading of Ruth through new eyes, we may sufficiently conclude that the Book of Ruth has made the case of inclusion for gay and
lesbian people into our community as it relates to our contemporary political and social culture. All this happens without change in the context or
definition of the story. Community is the expression of God, and love for
both God and community unifies us so that we are no longer the Other.
Social justice and responsibility keep us related, now, and in the future,
just as it has since the time of Naomi and Ruth.

NOTES

1. *Naomi and Ruth*, Project Genesis, www.torah.org.
2. Julius H. Greenstone, Emil G. Hirsch, Solomon Schechter, *Hospitality*,
http://www.JewishEncyclopedia.com.

CHAPTER 11

Becoming a Jew from a Woman's Perspective

Judith Willmore

The path to conversion to any religion is bound to be difficult; for a woman to convert to Judaism, it can be a very long and winding road. To convert to a religion of a persecuted people would give anyone pause; and Judaism, like the other religions of the Book, has a reputation of being male-dominated. Then, once the decision is made, many rabbis follow the tradition of denying potential converts three times, just to make sure they are sincere and know what they are getting into. But that is just the final part of the journey. Like the Israelites, the future convert can spend years wandering about in a spiritual desert trying to find home. Many never quite fit in with the dominant culture, and they spend much of their lives feeling like outsiders.

But the Jews too are the quintessential outsiders, the Other, the convenient target. They were monotheistic when all around them were worshipping idols, and when the prevailing theological wind blew toward Christianity, then Islam, they stubbornly refused to change. They drew strength from Torah and took heart with stories of underdogs and flawed human beings who were blessed by God and became founders of a great nation.

But not all the heroes of Torah are male, and not all the heroines of this patriarchal religion are consistently presented in a subordinate role. The earliest writings praise strong women—outsiders like Tamar, Rahab, and Ruth—as having the courage to turn conventional morals upside down in order to fulfill their destiny. Canaanite Tamar was compelled to seduce her father-in-law, Judah, in order to conceive a child and regain her value as a woman. Rahab the harlot of Jericho saved the lives of Joshua's spies because she had heard about the crossing of the Red Sea and she was in awe of the Israelite God. Ruth, the Moabite, left her native land out of devotion to Naomi and love of Naomi's God. It was only later, under Greek influence, that women's status shifted to a lesser position. Sexuality became suspect, especially out of marriage, and virginity honored. Another kind of convert was glorified: Asenath, the Egyptian wife of Joseph, was portrayed in a popular tale as a sinful idol worshipper who was redeemed by her love of him and the Israelites' God.

Tamar, Rahab, and Ruth have received a lot of attention lately from both Jews and Christians. The three converts are among the legendary ancestors of King David and, by extension, Jesus. They have been featured prominently in three articles in *Bible Review*,[1] as well as in a book of biblical heroines based on the Midrash HaGadol,[2] proving that even in the area of biblical scholarship, sex—and sexual politics—sells.

Today, women of all types, gay and straight, continue to be drawn to Judaism whether or not they plan to marry a Jew. Some, like Asenath, struggle with feelings of worthlessness until they find a God who loves them just as they are. Others, like Rahab and Ruth, meet the right people at the right time and realize what they wanted all along. All have experienced *teshuvah*. While *teshuvah* in Hebrew is usually translated as "repentance," it actually means "turning." These women turned from their wanderings in a spiritual desert to a new direction, and found home. I have interviewed three remarkable women who came to Judaism in middle age after years of searching. They all agree that instead of finding a new religion and identity, they instead recognized that they were Jews all along.

Following are the stories of these Jewish women, ancient and modern; those who blazed the path and those who followed.

TAMAR THE CANAANITE

Tamar did not technically convert, but her story as an outsider winning by courage and trickery links her with Rahab, and the two were considered proselytes in post-biblical Judaism.[3] Through Judah, she is also related by marriage to Asenath, the wife of Joseph. Joseph's brothers, including Judah, had conspired to get rid of him by staging his death and then selling him into slavery.

Tamar's story is told in Genesis 38. Judah had married a Canaanite woman who bore him three sons. When the oldest (Er) had grown, Judah selected a Canaanite wife for him, Tamar. "But Er was displeasing to the Lord" (Gen. 38:7), and he died. Judah then gave Tamar to Er's brother Onan so that the next son could provide offspring for his late brother. (This is the custom of the levirate, observed in several tribal cultures.) But Onan, knowing that the children would not be his, let his seed go to waste. That made him displeasing to the Lord, and he died also. Judah now had lost two sons and was not about to lose his last one. He told Tamar to wait until the third son, Shelah, had grown up, so she went to live at her father's house.

Tamar waited. She watched Shelah grow up to be a man, but she still was not given in marriage to him. Her status was that of a childless widow and a bad luck charm to boot. Even if she couldn't marry Shelah, she was still under Judah's control. No other man would consider marrying her, and she was destined to die childless and worthless. When she was sure that Judah would never give her Shelah in marriage, Tamar decided to take action. She had learned that Judah's wife had died, so perhaps he wouldn't refuse female companionship. When she heard he was on the road taking his flocks to be sheared, she dressed up as a Temple prostitute, covered her face with a veil, and waited for him.

Judah took the bait, and he asked the alluring Tamar to sleep with him. She agreed, but she asked for a kid in payment. Since he didn't have one with him, she demanded a pledge—his staff, seal, and cord—until payment was delivered. He agreed, they had sex, and he went on his way. When Judah later had someone take the kid back to her as promised, she had disappeared with his belongings. Three months later, Judah was told that his daughter-in-law was pregnant; therefore, she must be a harlot. "Bring her out," he declared, "and let her be burned!" (Gen. 38:24). But Tamar was ready. She sent a message to him along with his staff, seal, and cord: "I am with child by the man to whom these things belong." Judah recognized his possessions and must have felt humiliated. "She is more in the right than I," he admitted, "inasmuch as I did not give her to my son Shelah" (Gen. 38:26).

Tamar was pregnant with twins. When she was in labor, one of them put out his hand. The midwife tied a scarlet string around it to signify that he had been born first. However, he withdrew his hand and out came his brother instead. The midwife exclaimed, "What a breach you have made for yourself!" so the firstborn was named Perez, and his brother with the red string named Zerah (Gen. 38:29). Perez went on to found a dynasty: he was ten generations before King David. Tamar had legitimized her status by carrying on the line of Judah, even though she apparently never married either Judah or Shelah. By carrying on Judah's line, Tamar—a Canaanite—also fulfilled the promise of the covenant.[4]

RAHAB THE HARLOT

Rahab was a Canaanite like Tamar, but unlike Tamar she really was a prostitute. Her courage, quick wit, and faith in the God of the Israelites helped to bring down Jericho and assure her lasting fame.

Rahab's story is found in the Book of Joshua. As the Israelites were slowly invading Canaan, Joshua sent two spies to reconnoiter the area of Jericho. They found Rahab's establishment—which Spina quips was "the best little whorehouse in Jericho"[5]—and spent the night. But they hadn't been very discreet, and Jericho's king heard there were Israelite spies in Rahab's house. He sent his agents over to demand their surrender. However, Rahab heard they were coming. (Being a madam, Rahab probably had better sources of information than the king himself.) She quickly hid the spies on her roof under stalks of flax, then ran back downstairs to greet the agents. She admitted to them that the spies had spent time with her, but when night fell they left and she had no idea where they went. "Quick, go after them for you can overtake them!" she urged, and the king's agents took off toward the Jordan River, even though they didn't know which way to go.

After the agents left, Rahab pleaded with the spies to spare her and her family when they invade Jericho, just as she was protecting them:

> I know that the Lord has given the country to you, because dread of you has fallen on us, and all the inhabitants of the land are quaking before you. For we have heard how the Lord dried up the Sea of Reeds when you left Egypt, and what you did to Sihon and Og, the two Amorite kings across the Jordan, whom you doomed. When we heard about it, we lost heart, and no man had any more spirit left because of you, because the Lord your God is the only God in heaven above and on the earth below. Now, since I have shown loyalty to you, swear to me by the Lord that you in turn will show loyalty to my family. Provide me with a reliable sign that you will spare the lives of my father and mother, my brothers and sisters, and all who belong to them, and save us from death. (Josh. 2:9–13)

The spies promised Rahab and her family mercy as long as they were not discovered, and Rahab lowered the men from her window to the outside of the wall. They worked out a signal to Joshua's invaders to leave this house alone: Rahab would tie a scarlet cord to her window on the outside of the city wall and bring her family inside to await rescue. At her urging, before returning to their camp the spies hid in the hills for three days to make sure the king's agents weren't in the vicinity. The spies reported back to Joshua what Rahab had said, especially the part about the citizens of Jericho being terrified of the Israelites. And so, when the walls of Jericho came tumbling down, Joshua remembered the promise and Rahab and her family were rescued. Not only that, but rabbinic tradition holds that Rahab was a righteous gentile who converted, married Joshua, and became the ancestor of ten prophets and priests.[6] Rahab's faith in the God of Israel and her charity toward Joshua's spies saved her.

As for the scarlet cord: Samuels notes the Midrash HaGadol finds the link between Rahab and Tamar through the red thread on Zerah's hand.[7] She cites Isaiah 1:18: "Be your sins like crimson, they can turn snow white; be they red as dyed wool, they can become like fleece." Samuels points out further that in the days of the Temple in High Holy Days a red thread was tied outside the Holy of Holies. If the High Priest was successful in his prayers for forgiveness of the people, that scarlet thread would turn white. Samuels states that by tying that red thread to her window, Rahab was atoning for her sins and "paralleling the actions of the High Priest" who would come long after her and might even be one of her descendents.[8]

But had Rahab sinned? Did she feel guilty or humiliated because of her profession? Did she turn (*teshuvah*) toward God because she repented, or because she recognized the power of the Israelites' God? The first description of her is "Rahab the harlot," but by the end of the tale she is described as an innkeeper. More to the point, Rahab owned an establishment that could have been both inn and house of prostitution. In Canaanite society, such things were part of normal life and nothing to be ashamed of. Further, Rahab knew everything that went on in Jericho, so she must have had some very powerful customers. Finally, when she asked the spies to protect her family, she never mentioned a husband or children. Rahab was owned by no man and able to make her own decisions, including casting her lot with the Israelites and trading El, the chief god of the Canaanites, for YHWH.

Tamar and Rahab point the way for modern women who also find themselves on the fringe of society, not quite fitting in anywhere. Here's one of their stories:

Chaya—A Contemporary Story

Like many converts, Chaya had spent much of her life on the outside, looking in. Even though she was raised without a religion, her Christian environment instilled in her the belief that God rewards and punishes people. She was always different from her peers, who bullied her, and she had few friends. Her father, a mentally ill alcoholic, had done his best to convince her that she was bad. Once she learned that she was gay, her entire community reinforced the message. "I had gone my whole life thinking God hated me because I was gay. I was very self-destructive. I thought I was being punished because I was unlovable, hateful, evil." After her mother died, she spiraled downward into addiction and abusive relationships. By the time she was twenty-four, her liver was failing from alcoholic hepatitis and she was trapped with a woman who beat her, threatened her, and had almost killed her. "Miraculously," she said, "I was able to escape and find my way home." Even more miraculously, she got a job at a hospital for alcoholics, where she was required to learn about the disease. "There it was in front of me, the reason I was so terribly sick. The hospital helped me recover, and so did AA [Alcoholics Anonymous]. Through AA I developed a relationship with a Higher Power, and my relationship with this Higher Power brought me slowly back to health."

But then, cruel irony: she came down with an untreatable and painful chronic illness. First she had to give up all her interests, and finally her job. Her illness worsened every year. "It was true, then: God hated me. Why else would I have been punished as I had been for all these years? It had to be something evil and rotten inside me that I couldn't even see. How could I be good enough for God?"

She had spent her life exploring other faiths, including Buddhism and Wicca. "I wanted nothing to do with a God that hated people for loving." She had finally developed an idea of who God was, but she thought she was the "only person on the planet who believed in this God." She had no guidance, no teachers or community, and that bothered her.

One day she picked up a book on world religions and opened it to a chapter on Judaism. "What's that?" she wondered. All she knew about Jews at that point was their ethnicity, and she didn't have a clue about Judaism. She learned that Judaism was based on what the Christians call the Old Testament. She picked up her Bible, and it opened to Proverbs 6:16: "Six things the Lord hates; seven are an abomination to him: a haughty bearing, a lying tongue, hands that shed innocent blood, a mind that hatches evil plots, feet quick to run to evil, a false witness testifying lies, and one who incites brothers to quarrel."

"Is that all?" she thought. "Here it was spelled out—and it wasn't me! I kept reading and found that the values my mother had taught me, that I had tried so hard to stick to through everything, were in what I learned later was Torah. Suddenly I had a parent! Though flawed, I was a good person—and God loved me."

Chaya had thought that she hadn't known many Jews, but when she reflected on that, she said that it slowly dawned on her that most of her favorite people in her life had been Jews. She kept reading and found that Jews were worshipping the same God she had spent her life seeking. She spent months studying. Finally, she approached a rabbi and begged him to allow her to convert. "I'm supposed to deny you three times," he said—but he didn't. He questioned her thoroughly, then assigned her a teacher and welcomed her to the congregation.

"My friends were horrified! But what could I do? The gaping hole in my chest disappeared. I was home. I had spent my life feeling like a complete outsider. Even though I was technically a WASP [white Anglo-Saxon Protestant], I had nothing in common with them—but neither was I anything else." Chaya's conversion, especially the *mikvah* and holding the scroll at the temple ceremony, was transformative. "I found my people, my home, my God. I found a religion that gave me deep, soothing healing instead of hurt. Judaism has given me a prescription, a plan for living— even with pain—that has worked as nothing else had. I had discovered a whole new world, one that had been closed to me, filled with clarity, joy, and love. Torah has taught me, and is still teaching me, how to live."

Chaya's struggle to find God and belonging is echoed in another ancient tale from first-century CE Egypt.

ASENATH THE EGYPTIAN

Asenath is mentioned only twice in Torah (Gen. 41:44, 51) as the wife given to Joseph by Pharaoh. She became the mother of Ephraim and Manasseh, whom their grandfather Jacob blessed. She is the star of a popular tale, "Joseph and Asenath," circulating among the Jews of Egypt and Palestine around the first century CE. The story is not exactly *midrash* because it is written, not in Hebrew, but in *koine*, biblical Greek. (This may account for the variant spelling of Asenath's name, Aseneth.) Six copies have been found scattered around the Middle East, attesting to the story's popularity with the Jews of the Diaspora.

"Joseph and Asenath" is found in *The Old Testament Pseudepigrapha*,[9] a collection of poems, wisdom literature, odes, and prayers written mostly in Greek for a Jewish audience. The literature ranges in date from about 100 BCE to 200 CE. The translator of "Joseph and Asenath," C. Burchard, speculates the tale was written to encourage conversions to Judaism.[10] The story is remarkable in its description of the struggle in Asenath's soul between her ego and Joseph's God.

The story begins in Heliopolis in the first of the seven years of plenty. Pharaoh had listened to Joseph's prediction of the coming famine, and Joseph was supervising bringing in the bountiful harvest so it could be stored. The high priest Pentephres heard Joseph was in the area and invited him to dine. But the invitation was more than hospitality: the priest thought very highly of Joseph and hoped to marry his daughter Asenath to him. Asenath, however, was proud and haughty and, of course, exquisitely beautiful. She lived in a tower with seven virgins to protect her, and no man had ever seen her. Within her splendid chambers were many idols of silver and gold, and she wore jewelry with the names of the gods engraved on them. She turned up her nose at the idea of marrying a man who not only had been a slave, but also had been accused of rape and thrown into prison. There was only one man in Egypt good enough for her, she declared, and that was Pharaoh's son.

At that moment Joseph arrived at the front gate. Curious, Asenath ran upstairs to the window to see him unobserved. Joseph arrived in a chariot dressed magnificently in a purple robe and a crown of gold with twelve golden rays. He carried a royal staff in his left hand and in his right hand was an olive branch. Pentephres and his wife bowed down before him. For Asenath, it was love at first sight: "And Asenath saw Joseph on his chariot and was strongly cut [to the heart] and her soul was crushed, and her knees were paralyzed, and her entire body trembled, and she was filled with great fear." She thought the sun from heaven had descended upon her house, and she could not hide the shameful remarks she had made about Joseph. All she wanted now was to be his maidservant.

After seating Joseph on a throne and washing his feet, the family served him dinner separately from the others because he never ate with the Egyptians. Finally, Joseph looked up and saw Asenath on the upper floor. Now he was afraid because every woman in Egypt wanted to sleep with him, and he remembered the words of his father, Jacob, to his sons: "My children, guard strongly against associating with a strange woman, for associating with her is destruction and corruption." Joseph demanded that she leave, but Pentephres explained to him that the woman was his virgin daughter who not only hates every man but also had never seen one until this day, and she would be like a sister to him. Joseph, relieved, asked to meet her.

Asenath was brought before Joseph and told to greet her brother with a kiss. But when she got close, Joseph stopped her. He declared he could not kiss her, "a strange woman who will bless with her mouth dead and dumb idols and eat from their table bread of strangulation and drink from their libation cup of insidiousness and anoint herself with the ointment of destruction." He explained that a man who worships God could kiss only a female relative or his wife. Further, a woman who worships God could never kiss a strange man. Hearing this, Asenath's eyes filled with tears. Joseph took pity on her and was himself "cut to the heart." He placed his right hand on her head and blessed her, saying:

Lord God of my father Israel,
the Most High, the Powerful One of Jacob,
who gave life to all things, and called them from the darkness to the
  light,
and from the error to the truth,
and from the death to the life,
you, Lord, bless this virgin,
and renew her by your spirit,
and form her anew by your hidden hand,
and make her alive again by your life,
and let her eat your bread of life,
and drink your cup of blessing,
and number her among your people,
that you have chosen before all things came into being,
and let her enter into your rest
which you have prepared for your chosen ones,
and live in your eternal life forever and ever.[11]

Joseph's powerful blessing caused Asenath to rejoice and flee to her room, where she fell on her bed in exhaustion and confusion. Joseph, meanwhile, finished his dinner and announced that he had to continue his journey gathering the harvest, but he would return in eight days.

Thus began Asenath's teshuvah. She cast aside her idols and her rich attire and sat in sackcloth and ashes, repenting for her sins. She neither ate nor drank for seven days and turned away the seven virgins who had been her constant companions. She was sure that everyone hated her now that she had abandoned her idols, and the Lord God must hate her too because she had worshipped many gods before. Slowly, finally, she realized that the God of the Hebrews is merciful and compassionate, who "does not count the sin of a humble person ... Therefore I will take courage and turn to him, and take refuge with him, and confess all my sins to him ... Who knows, maybe he will have mercy on me."[12]

Asenath begins a series of prayers and supplications asking for mercy for her sinful behavior. She ends with a prayer for Joseph, whom she loves deeply. She asks God to preserve him and to make her his maidservant, to make his bed and wash his feet and wait on him. At that moment, she rejoiced to see a star rise in the east. It was a sign! The heavens split open and her room was flooded with heavenly light, and the stunned Asenath fell on her face onto the ashes. A man's voice called, "Asenath, Asenath!"

"Who is he that calls me?" she replied. Her tower room was inaccessible; who could have entered? He called her again. "Behold, here I am, Lord," she said humbly. "Who you are, tell me."

"I am the chief of the house of the Lord and commander of the whole host of the most high. Rise and stand on your feet."

Asenath raised her head and beheld a man who looked like Joseph with crown and staff, but who also blazed like fire. (Although the text does not give his name, the editor assumes from his title and appearance it is the Archangel Michael.) The angel commanded Asenath to rise from the ashes, to wash, and to put on a new robe. She soon reappeared before him in new attire and veiled. "Remove the veil from your head," he said, ". . . for you are a chaste virgin today, and your head is like that of a young man." She removed the veil and heard his stunning pronouncement: the angel had heard her confession and prayer and witnessed the affliction of her seven days of fasting in ashes. "Courage, Asenath, chaste virgin. For behold, your name was written in the book of the living in heaven . . . from today, you will be renewed and formed anew and made alive again, and you will eat blessed bread of life, and drink a blessed cup of immortality, and anoint yourself with blessed ointment of incorruptibility . . . Behold, I have given you today to Joseph for a bride, and he himself will be your bridegroom forever and ever." The angel told her also that she had a new name: "City of Refuge, because in you many nations will take refuge with the Lord God, the Most High, and under your wings many peoples trusting in the Lord God will be sheltered, and behind your walls will be guarded those who attach themselves to the Most High God in the name of Repentance."

The angel went on to explain that the Angel of Repentance had entreated to God for Asenath and all who repented, and she was a guardian of all virgins. The other angels were in awe of her, he said, and he himself loved her very much like a sister. Finally, he announced that it was time for her to put on her wedding attire, for Joseph was going to marry her today.

Asenath fell at his feet in great joy. "Blessed be the Lord your God the Most High who sent you out to rescue me from the darkness and to bring me up from the foundations of the abyss, and blessed be your name forever. What is your name, Lord, tell me that I might praise and glorify you forever and ever." But the angel refused. God had inscribed his name in the book before all others because he was chief of the house of the Most High, and those names were unspeakable by man. (The story follows Jewish tradition of not pronouncing out loud the names of the four archangels, other than in prayer.)

Asenath asked the angel to partake of bread and wine. He said yes, but then demanded a honeycomb. She, of course, did not have one, but it suddenly appeared, big and white as snow. He asked her to eat of it, saying that all who attach themselves to God in repentance eat of it along with the angels, for those who eat of it have everlasting life. The angel and Asenath ate of the honeycomb, and he announced: "Behold, you have eaten bread of life, and drunk a cup of immortality, and been anointed with the ointment of incorruptibility." He repeated his promise that she would live forever and be "a walled mother-city of all who take refuge with the name of the Lord God, the king of the ages."

And so Asenath married Joseph and became the mother of Ephraim and Manassah. Torah relates how Joseph later was reunited with, and forgave, the brothers who sold him into slavery. Eventually the entire family was gathered in Egypt, where Grandfather Jacob gave his dying blessing to the two sons of the Egyptian woman.

Like Asenath, many women come to Judaism through marriage; but for many of them, the search began long before they met their husbands.

SHOSHANA

Like so many converts, Shoshana began her journey as a child. She grew up in a Catholic family in New York and went to parochial school. Her father was a convert to Catholicism, and he said that he loved the Church because it answered all his questions. However, the Church didn't answer Shoshana's. "It was in my late twenties that I realized that I had more questions than the Church could answer for me. Why did I feel so unsettled, so bored during services? I admired Christ, but the rituals around him were so boring. There was a slow process of drifting away, but I felt a real spiritual need."

At the age of thirty-one she moved from New York to Los Angeles to pursue her career as an actress. The need deepened, and she went into therapy. Her therapist recommended that she try meditation. She met a woman who introduced her to Siddaha Yoga, and she found it an amazing experience. She was involved in it for five years. Instead of praying to Christ, "a man of one spiritual entity," she prayed to a number of different parts of the Divine. "God dwells within all of us," she said.

Along the way she married a Jewish man, and they had an interfaith wedding with both a priest and a rabbi. (Fortunately, her Catholic family approved.) The relationship lasted four years. She started taking classes at a Reform congregation and attended Friday night services and Passover. "I felt so comfortable. I especially liked being able to have services at home. Judaism is very family oriented and grounding. And I really liked that everything is questioned. I love challenging authority!" Above all, she said, to participate in a religion she needs the mystical as well as the ritual. She was surprised and very pleased to find that the same four archangels that she had loved as a child were in the bedtime prayers.

A few years after her divorce, Shoshana met and married Joshua, also Jewish. This time, the ceremony was performed by only a rabbi. Shoshana continued her practice and studies of Judaism, becoming even more deeply involved. "It's hard to explain the process," she said. "There are so many facets." When she got pregnant, she found it imperative to convert for the sake of the family unit, if not for herself. "I needed the solidity of making that decision," Shoshana said. Her conversion ceremony took place just before her daughter's birth.

Some years later, Shoshana was stunned to learn the synchronicity of her actions: "I was about thirty-six when I found out. My father's oldest brother had died, and my aunt contacted my dad to let him know. That re-connected my dad with my aunt (his sister-in-law) and his younger brother after fifty-two years. I then met my first cousin (son to my dad's younger brother and my aunt), and in comparing our childhood histories, I found out that dad had been brought up as a Jew!"

Her father, the convert to Catholicism, had been born Jewish, and his family was from Czechoslovakia. Her first husband had been Jewish, and her current husband, also Jewish, was, like her father, of Czech descent. She had unknowingly married men very much like her father and was herself of Jewish ancestry on her father's side. For years many people she met had assumed she was Jewish, and now she knew why.

Today the one-time Christian who had meditated on Hindu gods is a Jewish wife and mother. "I do yoga when I go to a spa or can find a good class," she said. "I do not meditate, but I pray a lot. If I take up meditation again, I could easily incorporate it into my Jewish practice. I believe that all of my spiritual life can be integrated." And her daughter has grown into a teenager, had her Bat Mitzvah, and sounds the *shofar* (ram's horn) for the congregation on High Holy Days.

RUTH THE MOABITE

The story of Ruth, Judaism's most famous convert, begins several generations before her birth with yet another example of women defying conventional morality in order to have children, and therefore to have a place in the world. Chapter 19 of Genesis describes the result of God's curse of Sodom. Two angels visited Lot in that city to test his worthiness. Lot welcomed them to his house to eat. Soon, however, the men of Sodom banged on his door, demanding to rape the visitors. Standing in the doorway, Lot tried to appease them by offering up instead his two virgin daughters for them to do with as they pleased. The men of Sodom became even more enraged and tried to storm the door, but the angels pulled Lot back inside to safety and blinded the populace with a burst of intense light. The angels then told Lot and his family to flee Sodom at once, since it was about to be destroyed.

And so it was that Lot and his family fled Sodom. Lot's wife disobeyed the angels' warning to not look back and was turned into a pillar of salt. Eventually all that was left of the little band was Lot and the two daughters he had almost sacrificed to the rapacious crowd. They took refuge in a cave, and since fire and brimstone had consumed the entire country killing thousands, they assumed that they were the only people on earth left alive. The older sister said to the younger, "Our father is old, and there is not a man on earth to consort with us in the way of all the world. Come, let us make our father drink wine, and let us lie with him, that we may maintain life through our father" (Gen. 19:31–32). The plan worked, and both girls conceived. The older sister named her son Moab, the ancestor of the Moabites; and the younger, Ben-Ammi, the father of the Ammonites.

Many generations later, as Moses led the Israelites through the wilderness, they encountered both those nations. (Moab lies just east of the Dead Sea, with Ammon farther to the northeast.) Moses was commanded by God not to fight with them and to take food and water only after paying for it (Deut. 2:9). However, according to Deuteronomy 23:4–5, no Moabite or Ammonite or their descendants shall be admitted as members of the congregation of the Lord because when the Israelites passed through their land, they failed to offer them food and water. Worse, those nations had hired Balaam the Sorcerer to put a curse on the Israelites.

That proscription was ignored by Elimelech's sons. In the days of the Judges, Elimelech and his wife, Naomi, and their two sons left their home in Bethlehem to travel to Moab to escape the famine in Judah. Elimelech later died, and Naomi was left with her sons, Mahlon and Chilion, who married Moabite woman, Ruth and Orpah. After ten years, the sons also died. Naomi heard in the fields of Moab that God had remembered her people back home by giving them food, so she set out for Judah, with her daughters-in-law following her.

But Naomi urged them both to stay in Moab, secure in their late husbands' homes. She reminded these childless widows that she was too old to give them husbands, a thought that made her bitter. Orpah was persuaded and kissed Naomi goodbye, but Ruth refused to leave. Naomi urged her to do as her sister-in-law had, return to her people and her gods. But Ruth refused, saying: "Do not urge me to leave you, to turn back from following you. For where you go, I will go; where you lodge, I will lodge; your people are my people, and your God my God; where you die, I will die, and there will I be buried. Thus may Hashem do to me, and may he do more, if anything but death separates me from you" (Ruth 1:15–18).

And so the women traveled on to Bethlehem, where they were greeted warmly. However, as childless widows they had little status and no resources. It was the beginning of the barley harvest, so they were invited to glean in the fields. (Charitable custom required that the poor and the widowed be allowed to follow the harvesters and take what was left.) Ruth wound up in the field of Boaz, who was of the family of Elimelech. He had heard about her and was impressed with her loyalty to Naomi. He spoke with her kindly and invited her not only to glean as much as she wished from his field but also to eat with him and the harvesters at mealtime.

That evening Ruth related this to Naomi, who was very pleased, since Boaz was a kinsman who could redeem her. Also at stake for Ruth was the fact her husband Mahlon had died childless. As in the case of Tamar, it was the responsibility of a kinsman to marry her and bring forth an heir.

Ruth continued to glean in Boaz's fields until the end of the harvest. Meanwhile, Naomi must have been considering what to do. The harvest was over. What now? So one afternoon she said, "My daughter, I must seek security for you, that it will go well with you" (Ruth 3:1). She announced that Boaz would be at the harvest shed winnowing barley, and after that he and his harvesters would eat and drink and spend the night there. She told Ruth to bathe and anoint herself and dress in her best, then join him, but not to make herself known until it was dark and he was lying down. Then she should uncover his feet and lie next to him. (In the Bible, uncovering a man's feet is equivalent to revealing his nakedness.) "He will tell you what to do," she said (Ruth 3:1–5). Ruth agreed with the plan.

And so, in the middle of the night, Boaz was startled to find a woman lying at his feet. "Who are you?" he asked. She replied, "I am your handmaid, Ruth. Spread your robe over your handmaid, for you are a redeemer." Boaz blessed her for her act of kindness and reassured her that he would do as she asked. He said all the men of the town knew that she was a good woman. However, he added that there was another closer relative who also could redeem her. He asked her to spend the night with him, and on the morrow he would approach the other relative and ask if he would redeem her. If the answer was no, Boaz would redeem her himself. They spent the night together, and she left while it was still dark bearing food for herself and Naomi.

The next morning, Boaz went to the city gate (where all public business was transacted) and waited. Soon the other kinsman appeared, the late Elimelech's brother. Boaz called ten witnesses, and the negotiations began. Boaz told him that Naomi's property was for sale, and by rights it should be redeemed by him. If he refused, Boaz was next in line. Then he made it clear that the property was also Ruth's, and it needed to be redeemed to perpetuate the name of Ruth's deceased husband. (Boaz thereby brought in the law of the levirate.) The kinsman balked at this, claiming it would imperil his own inheritance.

Boaz then announced to the witnesses that he now had bought all that had belonged to Elimelech and his sons from Naomi; furthermore, he was taking Ruth as his wife to perpetuate the name of Mahlon. The people rejoiced, asking the Lord to make Ruth like Rachel and Leah, who had built up the house of Israel. And, they declared, "may your house be like the house of Perez whom Tamar bore to Judah," through their offspring. Ruth indeed bore a son, a child who would secure the future not just for her and Boaz but also for her mother-in-law, Naomi. The women declared to Naomi that Ruth, who loved her, was better to her than seven sons. Ruth gave the boy to Naomi to nurse. They called him Obed; he became the father of Jesse, who was the father of David. Thus it was that Tamar the Canaanite and Ruth the Moabite became the progenitors of the house of David.

Ruth has left a complex legacy. Her declaration of loyalty and faith to Naomi is an inspiration to all, not just converts. In her chapter on Ruth in *Praise Her Works,* Haviva Ner-David points out the similarity between Ruth and Abraham.[13] Both left their native land to go to the unknown; both were known for *chesed,* or "mercy and loving kindness." Abraham left the sides of his tent open for strangers, and Ruth devotedly cared for Naomi. Those virtues eclipse the ambiguities in Ruth's story. First, how could a Moabite marry into a Jewish family? The Gemara states that the prohibition applies to Moabite men, not women.[14] But Ner-David says that with Ruth, it became a matter of character, not ancestry. The sin of the Moabites was their refusal to offer sustenance to the wandering Israel-ites; but Ruth's loving kindness demonstrates that she could be accepted into the Jewish nation.

But what was Ruth's process of becoming a Jew? Was she inspired by her husband and mother-in-law? Why did she make that decision? Torah is silent on this. However, no person comes to faith entirely by association with others; there must also be an internal process. This last story of a modern convert demonstrates an awakening to God that began in Japan and came to fruition in New Mexico.

RO'A ANAVA

"Somehow I always knew I was Jewish." The journey of Ro'a Anava (Humble Seer) began with her family's move to postwar Japan. There, as a little girl she soon found that Japanese children were not much different from her, even though their families had once been the enemy and were now defeated. Ro'a was an adventurous child who at the age of four sneaked into her uncle's classroom to hear him teach history, her favorite subject. She was fascinated by Japanese culture, but she was not allowed to mingle with the local children. Meanwhile, her family insisted that she go to the Episcopal Church, but she pestered them and the priest with questions that they could never answer to her satisfaction.

Her epiphany came at the age of six when she went to a Shinto shrine. The appropriate ritual at this sacred site was to ring a gong, and the deity would appear. She rang the gong and waited. The priest had said that Jesus was a real man and God too; if that was so, surely at least one of the Japanese gods would reveal himself! A breeze rustled the maple leaves at her feet—but no god magically appeared. "That's when I knew," she said. "At six years old, I knew that God is beyond human form, that He is an indwelling spirit that's not material and not human."

When the family returned home to Kansas, others were suspicious of their contact with the "enemy," for the despised "Japs." Now she found herself different for two reasons: Ro'a the seasoned traveler had little in common with average American children, and she couldn't believe Christian doctrine. The world was much larger than this Kansas town. "I don't know exactly when I knew what I was," she said, "but what else could I be?" The process started when she became close friends with a Jewish boy, a relationship that lasted twelve years. She laughed. "When we got serious, suddenly I became the *shiksa* (non-Jewish woman) to his family, and that was the end of that! I thought then that I wanted to be Jewish, but I figured that they were never going to let me in."

Ro'a said that she tried to be a Christian, and she eventually married. When her sons were born, she made sure that the doctors circumcised them. Even though they weren't Jewish, it just seemed right. Along the way she started keeping kosher the best she could, avoiding pork and shellfish and not mixing meat and milk. Her husband, fortunately, didn't care.

Years went by, Ro'a's sons grew up, and Ro'a got divorced and moved to Santa Fe. "I couldn't wait any longer," she said. "It was a Thursday afternoon, and I sat staring at the phone. I told myself, it has to be now." She opened the phone book and found a synagogue. The rabbi himself answered the phone, and he didn't hesitate to invite her over. After a long talk, he said that she should attend Friday night services. She did, and Saturday morning as well.

That was the beginning of a year-long, painful process of questions, religious instruction, and learning Hebrew. Ro'a learned that the important question was "Who are you? What is your center?" The rabbi followed the tradition of turning her down three times, and it was very frustrating. "I spent most of the year crying! But I had no doubts."

Did the conversion ceremony itself make her feel any different? Does she feel more Jewish now than before? "No," she said. "It was a process … like a partial circle that came complete when I converted. I am now legitimate in other people's eyes." And, she explained, it was her participation in the *minhag* that really helped her understand Jews and Judaism. The fervent prayers, the give and take, even the occasional friction, firmed her identity.

"But who else could I be?" Ro'a recalled that day in the shrine waiting for a god to appear. To be a Jew, she said, "was intuitively obvious."

And so the process of teshuvah, of turning toward God, can be a journey winding through a labyrinth of years of doubts and searching. Tamar, Rahab, Asenath, and Ruth remind us that we don't have to be perfect to be loved by God or accepted as Jews:

"Remember the long way that the Lord your God has made you travel in the wilderness these past forty years, that He might test you by hardships to learn what was in your hearts: whether you would keep his commandments or not" (Deut. 8:2).

NOTES

1. Frank Anthony Spina, "Reversal of Fortune," in *Bible Review* 17, no. 4, Aug. 2001; Gary A. Rendsburg, "Unlikely Heroes: Women as Israel," in *Bible Review* 19, no. 1, Feb. 2003; and Jane Schaberg, "Before Mary: The Ancestresses of Jesus," in *Bible Review* 20, no. 6, Dec. 2004.

2. Penina Adelman, ed., *Praise Her Works: Conversations with Biblical Women* (Philadelphia: Jewish Publication Society, 2005).

3. Schaberg, 23.

4. Ibid., 15.

5. Spina, 26.

6. *Etz Hayim: Torah and Commentary* (New York: Jewish Publication Society, 2001), 858.

7. Stephanie Newman Samuels, "Rachav," in Adelman, *Praise Her Works.*

8. Ibid.

9. Ibid, 102.

10. C. Burchard, "Joseph and Aseneth," in *The Old Testament Pseudepigrapha: Expansions of the "Old Testament" and Legends, Wisdom, and Philosophical Literature, Prayers, Psalms, and Odes, Fragments of Lost Judeo-Hellenistic Works,* ed. James H. Charlesworth (Garden City, NY: Doubleday & Co., 1985), vol. 2.

11. Ibid.

12. Ibid.

13. Haviva Ner-David, "Ruth," in Adelman, *Praise Her Works.*

14. Ibid.

PART V

Worldview and Religious Practice

CHAPTER 12

Miriam's Well: Unearthing the Sacred in Jewish Women's Groups

Shelly Fredman

Mitzrayim/A Narrow Place

We were gathered in Julie Anne's[1] kitchen, the air rich with the smells of cumin and sesame—Emily's Chicken Marbella and Jane's Soba Noodle Salad. The nine women gathered around me had those contented looks on their faces, all of us filled with food, conversation, laughter that started deep in the belly and worked its way to your synapses. Now Liz, just hitting the second year of separation from her husband of two children and twenty-three years, unwrapped the blow torch.

It wasn't a blow torch, really; they call it something else in those fancy kitchen gadget stores where Liz likes to shop. But she had finally managed to light it and was aiming the blue flame at the top of a three-layer cake she had painstakingly constructed. Like her marriage.

There was the smell of burning sugar, and vengeance in Liz's eyes. We watched. I waited for the cake to burst into flames.

The mystics speak of a Primordial Torah, the original one, the one that has never quite made it to the page. The rabbis say it was written with black fire on white fire. Watching Liz, I wondered what kind of Torah was being written here. One we would all carry, in one way or another, into

our futures. And here, too, amid the destruction, the fire, were the sparks
of creation.

We didn't know it at the time, but five years hence, we women would
stand again together, this time in a garden in the lush green of late spring.
Pink peonies and larkspur nudged our shoulders as we crowded the *chuppah,* the bridal canopy, witnesses yet again, as Liz married for a second
time. Second chances. Second Eden.

But that night in Julie Anne's kitchen, we watched the sugar crackle
and burn. I remember falling into hysterical laughter once it was over, and
the cake remained, a tawny brown glaze crowning its top. Those first
moments had been tense, though. I was thinking, this too, should be a ritual. We'd created a half dozen over the years we'd been together, and this
one had all the loaded power I'd come to feel in ritual moments. Like all
good rituals, this one held the possibility of transformation. If we did this
right, Liz might actually begin to move from one state of being to the next.

The rabbis, you see, hadn't thought like women. They hadn't thought
to make ritual of the many seemingly small, important moments in a woman's life, like the losses of husbands and best friends. Of course, they'd
missed bigger ones too—giving birth, weaning a child.

So we didn't mark Liz's threshold—it came on us unawares, too
quickly. But it is part of our story. It is just one of the *mitzrayim*, the narrow places we had to walk through. What I've learned is that this path,
this Exodus, this journey, is meant to be walked—with women.

We called ourselves, eventually, the Seder Sisters. That, too, was
unplanned. It evolved. What started as a joke, a shortcut, a label, became
an imprimatur and a truth. We were ten. An *anti-minyan*, because we were
everything the men could never do or be. Where they gathered at *shul*
(school) at their pre-set times, three times a day to say the prescribed things,
we invented ourselves into being. We did this and we tried that. And when
that didn't work, we tried something else. It was evolutionary, creative, chaotic at times. Our process reflected the dynamism and diversity of the ten
individuals who made up the group. We were, when we began: a therapist,
a life coach, a filmmaker and writer, a wedding consultant and singer, a
community activist, a hospital chaplain, a dancer and teacher, an advertis-
ing agency owner and manager, an authentic movement teacher, and a professor and writer. Who we have become is a part of our story.

We began with a seder. A women's seder, held at Laura's house, in
the city of St. Louis. Laura had attended a women's seder I had coordi-
nated the year before, which had been inspired, in turn, by the first wom-
en's seder Esther Broner created in New York City and writes of in *The
Telling*. We were part of an unbroken chain, even at our birth. A
matriarchy.

Laura had gathered women she mostly didn't know well, but wanted to know better. She, like I, harbored dreams of community that we had not yet managed to build into our lives. We began with the emptiness, the not yet full, the desire. In *The Book of Ruth and Naomi*, Marge Piercy writes:

> *Show me a woman who does not dream*
> *a double, heart's twin, a sister*
> *of the mind in whose ear she can whisper,*
> *whose hair she can braid as her life*
> *twists its pleasure and pain and shame.*
> *Show me a woman who does not hide*
> *in the locket of bone that deep*
> *eye beam of fiercely gentle love*
> *she had once from mother, daughter,*
> *sister; once like a warm moon*
> *that radiance aligned the tides*
> *of her blood into potent order.*

I think, in the end, that's the one thing we all had in common. The yearning. In known and unknown ways, we were all searching for that "alignment of tides" that Piercy writes about. In our first seder, we began by talking about the desert.

MIDBAR/DESERT

Avivah Zornberg, in *The Particulars of Rapture*, characterizes the desert as the "endless emptiness" the Israelites walked through on their journey toward redemption. She says that here, God "teaches the profound goodness of the vacant time," how it "offers an opportunity for them to find their own desire." We women, too, began in the *midbar*, in the arid place, cut off from the noise and clamor of home, ties, children, civilization. If women are to re-create themselves, if they are bent on no less than transformation, a separation of this kind is essential. It is the first step.

At Laura's seder, we were each to reflect upon the deserts in our lives. Rachel, whose soft brown hair fell gently across her face, whose body moved through air effortlessly, making us all wish we'd been born dancers, spoke of the desert time at her son Adam's Bar Mitzvah, and of her inability to find her voice. Her husband, who later entered training at Elat Chayim to become a rabbi, had word after word to say to his son, but Rachel, strangely, had none. We wondered at this, because here Rachel was, cogently articulating a threshold moment when there should have been so much to say, and yet there was only silence.

Emily, whose endless energy echoes that of my mother, except that Emily's is tethered to a remarkable and hard-won faith in God, spoke of the desert time when she watched her sister-in-law die of lung cancer, at fifty, and how she tried to coax her brother and his children into having the conversations they weren't having as they watched their wife and mother die.

Jane, our golden-voiced soprano, lived in a house filled with wounded animals—a cat, a turtle, a parakeet. She was bent on rescuing them in ways she couldn't quite rescue herself. She told us about growing up with a mother who was devoted to Jewish causes but couldn't recognize Jane's spirit or understand it. Much later, at one of our weekend retreats, I would teach Jane to wash her hands the traditional way on Friday night, accompanied by blessings, and she would adapt it and use it religiously as a morning ritual.

Julie Anne, our sprite, spoke last. Hesitating, stopping now and then as if to be sure we were paying attention, Julie Anne told of being sent as a child to live with her aunt in Tennessee when her parents died in an air accident in Atlanta in 1962. "My Aunt Julie became my mother. I don't really remember my mother. My aunt suggested it was confusing to have a Julie and a Julie Anne in one house, so I quickly became Anne. I was Anne from age eight until I turned forty.

"We left our house—our dog, a brother, and all our friends. I came with a bike, a teddy bear. That's all. And I lost my name, too. I was in the desert the whole time I raised my children."

As each woman spoke, as different as their stories were, each struck a responding chord in me. There was a songline here, and I wanted to follow it. That first night, when we barely knew each other at all, there was a charge in that room, a spark. I told of my sojourn into the Orthodox world. I didn't know, then, that in speaking to this group of women I had taken my first steps out of it.

I told them of how, at twenty, I'd fallen in love with the traditions of Judaism, the cycles and seasons of the Jewish year, the gift of the Sabbath, the scholarship and study of text that allowed me to bring an English literature major's passion to the Torah, which made it possible for me to link the meandering moments of my life with the epic journey of the Jewish people.

The Orthodox Jews who taught me this beauty, though, were often a disappointment. Their tie to ritual often struck me as inert and pointless, disconnected at important times from a larger reality. I remembered a Shabbat, sitting in *shul*, when the areas all around us were in the midst of a devastating flood. Why were we sitting here, when holiness on that day, I believed, was happening on the levees where strangers were helping strangers sandbag?

There was a hunger in me, a desert. And I just knew I couldn't go on ignoring it. The depth of scholarship I'd discovered in this world—writings of Soloveitchik, Nahama Leibowitz, Rav Cook—were like fuel to a fire within. But I didn't just want to study Judaism. I wanted to live it. And if the command was to turn and turn the Torah, the teachings, the stories, again and again, if the chorus of voices and multiple views sitting along-side each other, evolving, was what had made the Jewish system so gor-geous and wise in the first place, then I needed a living laboratory to test out my ideas, to create rituals not yet uncovered, to add my voice to a thirty-five-hundred-year-old song.

Gazing around the circle that night, I had a hunch that this, poten-tially, was a group of women I could do that with. I'd been involved in a few other women's groups before. One, a study group of five women, had gathered weekly over the course of a year to read through the entire cycle of the Torah. Then, at our old shul, Young Israel, I'd been involved with a group of women who had met with various leaders and the rabbi in a move to make the *mechitza* (a screen that separates men and women) in the new shul we were building "more egalitarian" and to secure a Torah to dance with on the women's side on Simchat Torah. We failed on both counts. I'll never forget the look on the rabbi's face as he told us, "It is not halachically possible to have a Torah on the women's side." This, though we knew of shuls on the East Coast where they were doing just that. The rabbi's look was so distant, so cold. He just didn't know what it was like to sit on the other side of that wall, passive, motionless, watching the men. His was an inability to imagine, a failure of empathy that I later came to see as a component of evil. His patronizing tone sent me running, exploring.

I became involved at a more open Orthodox shul two miles west (and a long walk on Shabbat) that was launching a women's *tefillah* (prayer) group, with the blessing of its more liberal rabbi. But again, their commit-ment to *halacha* (law) was one I did not share.

As Rotem Wagner puts it in *Eretz Acheret*, "The tension, or more pre-cisely the contradiction, between the Torah as a real, historical book, whose text is fixed, and the idea of Torah as a multifaceted, atemporal book open to infinite readings, leads to the most original Jewish invention ever was created: the Midrash. That is to say, what allowed the living exis-tence of Torah as the first and last object of memory was the unique prac-tice invented by the Sages in which the practice of memory contains its opposite, forgetfulness, interwoven as warp and weft."

Judaism has survived, not because of our ability to remember, Wagner posits, but, rather, because we are open to infinite readings, which entail a foray into forgetfulness. The Orthodox Jews I lived among, who introduced me to the wisdom of the ancient texts, wanted their Judaism as written. But as I gazed around me at the seder table, at this new circle of women I had just met, I felt a possibility stirring. The other women at the seder felt it, too.

"We can't let this be over after tonight," Emily said. Emily, our gratitude viceroy, queen of the e-mails, would continue to rally us over the course of the next ten years—when energies waned, when we unearthed the deeper, more difficult meanings of calling each other "sister." A few months later we met again, not knowing why or how. Just that we couldn't let this slip away. We needed the intimacy, the communion, the power of women.

HAGGADAH/TELLING

The circle is an ancient, kabbalistic symbol of equality: all the points on the circumference are equidistant from the center, and hierarchies of male/female, teacher/student, high/low are obliterated. At the beginning of their Exodus journey, Miriam, the prophetess, Moses' sister, leads the Israelite women in a circle dance at the far shores of the sea, a recognition that the previous hierarchies that ruled in Egypt can be obliterated here, among women. Zornberg speaks of Miriam's "more sublime consciousness," how her song encompasses the other great polarities of birth and death. "Unlike the men, the women already know God," Zornberg says. The revelation at the sea is, in fact, a confirmation—they have known this God before, in the first life and death struggles they endured when they gave birth in the fields of Egypt.

This more subtle consciousness of women, then and now, remains hidden, subversive. It has yet to traverse the public sphere in any transformational way. But it was there in our small circle of women, as we began to tell each other our stories, and thereby, unbeknown to even ourselves at the time, to construct new realities. Power, silence, death and dying, mother and daughter, the body, God, parenting and prayer, these were our themes; at moments it felt as if we were, like the Israelite women, singing each other into being.

At the beginning, there was never a leader, only a theme. Sometimes one of us would facilitate the discussion. Often, we used a Jewish text as our springboard—a teaching on *lashon hara*, for example, on the dangers of speaking of another person, of gossip. We all came away from that discussion with an extra layer of consciousness around our speech, the power it has to cause embarrassment and pain. But we didn't simply read the rabbi's teachings against lashon hara as prescription. We questioned the wisdom, always, wondering aloud about times we'd spoken of someone else in pursuit of a fuller understanding of that person, or trying to gain insights into behavior by hearing another's point of view. Jewish wisdom wouldn't always work for us, but we uncovered deeper reads of our most pivotal experiences by exploring them out loud, in this roomful of women.

We hadn't intended to start a women's group, and from the beginning, I think, that lack of intention gave us permission to soar, to stretch the boundaries of what we could do and be for each other.

We found ourselves writing new *tkhines*—supplicatory prayers written in Yiddish in the 1700s—when Beth moved into a new home, finding a new way to bless the doorways before placing the mezuzah. We stood in Beth's living room again in the heart of winter, a tight circle now, locked in prayers of healing the night before Laura was to be operated on for cancer. We breathed in dried sage, a smudge stick, and we sang hopeful, lullaby-like songs to prepare Laura for surgery. The doctors would provide the anesthetic, but this was our part. Essential.

As Beth remembers, "We were all so scared for Laura and no one knew what to do with their feelings or prayers. And so we gathered and gave her tokens of ourselves—stones and old pieces of jewelry that she could bring with her to the hospital. We sang healing prayers and asked that God watch over her. And somehow it helped us all. It bound us up together just a little bit tighter."

Throughout the dark and light times of our lives, we held each other. We accused each other of being *liebesbedurftigkeit*, a German word Ruth taught us to signify one who is "needful of love." Ruth, our eldest at sixty, had lived through Kristallnacht as an eight-year-old child.

We went on weekend retreats, where we created Shabbat dinners together. We taught each other the blessings and prayers. We conducted study and prayer services on these retreats, and because we were not at our temple, Central Reform Congregation (CRC), we had time to slow the service down, to ask questions as they arose, to analyze or meditate upon a prayer before we said it. We studied Zornberg's books together on a series of Saturday afternoons. We met on Saturdays for services at CRC, the traditional but Reform temple I eventually joined. We became the group of women filling the front rows on the righthand side, an impromptu chorus the musicians counted on to back them up in song. Bar and Bat Mitzvah families, often a new one each week, didn't know the words and melodies, but we could rock the house. Besides, one of the musicians, Jane of the golden voice, was one of us.

Susan Talve, our rabbi and inspiration in terms of creating a healing community, was a sister in absentia. A good friend of some of us, she didn't have time for our monthly gatherings, but when she turned fifty we were there, in force, to celebrate her in poetry and to henna her hands.

In our eighth year, we sat on Rachel's couch and listened to her tell stories of her mother, who had died three days before. Since she had died in Chicago and Rachel had gone through her mother's last days without us, we heard about her mother's final moments. This wasn't sitting shiva as I'd known it, with friends and acquaintances dropping by. This was a circle of ten, who by that time knew the rhythms of Rachel's sadness, how it had been born of parents who'd come through Europe's fires, but not completely. This was a distillation of shiva, a telling of the truest kind.

Barbara Kane, who now leads the women's seder that Esther Broner originally created in New York, with the likes of Bella Abzug, Gloria Steinem, Letty Pogrebin, Grace Paley, and Marilyn French at the table, says that she is always surprised by how deeply touching and meaningful their once-a-year gathering of women continues to be. "Something emerges that is not speakable," Kane, a psychoanalyst, says. "But once we've shared it, it is almost like an extended prayer. We've heard something in each other."

In *The Feminine Face of God*, Sherry Ruth Anderson and Patricia Hopkins write of the "container of emergence" that women need to create in order for the spiritual moment to happen. Kane sees the roots of the women's seder experience in the profound listening experience, the listening to the words of women, which, ironically, Freud may have been the first to systematically attempt. Freud, however, was going after the curative, whereas the women's seder in New York City and our group in St. Louis and many of the thousands of women's groups throughout the country are aiming at transformation. The Exodus paradigm looms large behind us.

"At the Women's Seder, something gets concentrated," Kane says. "What is spoken is distilled, as a poem gets distilled. That's the first thing Esther Broner modeled. For the ritual to succeed, you must create a space and a time. In therapy, there's a frame: a set time. You leave one world and go into another. There's a container and a facilitator. Not just a cup of coffee without the cup."

Kane is quick to point out that Exodus itself is not just about liberation, it is also about separation. "At our Seders, we are enjoined to cross a liminal threshold in order to enter into a sacred time and space, a dimension resonant both with safety and danger. Some of us are afraid, nervous about speaking, so there's a tension in the room. There's something so ineffably private about the experience of speaking deeply of our own exoduses and separations. Being supported, we discover once again a depth and complexity of meaning that communally emerges."

In our tellings, among our ten, there have been both wondrous nights and abysmal ones. Sometimes we attacked our facilitator, as if the slightest nudges toward control were cause for outrage. Emily discovered a book she loved about Jewish mysticism and had us all read it. Ruth, our rationalist, couldn't stand reading about an ineffable God. She didn't get God. Another night, I attempted to share my love of Jewish short stories. Many of the women didn't like the ones I chose. I left that meeting feeling a great distance from these "sisters" I'd grown so close to. Or we experienced evenings where one or another of us went on too long in our circle time, using up everyone's "minutes." We resented it when Gail, who had enrolled in rabbinic training, lectured at us. Though we were sometimes delighted to hear about her teachings, when she tried to instruct us we rebelled. And then there were the nights we broke through. We spoke about our mothers. Beth told about coming home from school, at thirteen, distraught. "I told my mom I was unhappy about how unattractive I was, and she said, 'You are funny-looking. There are other important things in life.'" Liz talked about being a teenager, and her mom telling her, "You can't go out like that!" because she wasn't wearing any makeup. "One day I came to understand it was about her. Her insecurity. Prior to that, I thought it was about me." I told them about those endless, panicked moments in the car with my mother, just after my father left us.

When the Seder Sisters left each other on those nights, it was never just after the tellings; it was later, after apple pie, after laughter, after some of us lingered to do the dishes and see the kitchen restored to its former self. I moved into the night, lighter, stronger, closer to what I wanted to be, and always, ever, grateful to have found these women who complete my life.

If I happened to tell my husband, the next day, the subject of our discussion, I inevitably got "the look." It is not quite judgment, just a silent curiosity, something akin to wonder. He believes he doesn't share the need. All these forays into the personal, the emotional, the past. He has let the world convince him that our deep need for the feminine doesn't exist.

Kane, too, wonders about the need to tell, still. "Why? After thirty years? Why do we still need the Haggadah after all these years? The answer is lest we forget we were strangers in the land of the patriarchs. The story isn't told all at once. Dreams, too, have layers of meaning. And the layers only emerge when safety is established."

When I ask Kane why she thinks these kinds of conversations don't happen as readily in the company of men, she says, "It's very difficult for men to not be challenging. Also, they try to make it better, to protect us, to fix. And too many of us still seek to protect men, hoping they will 'have a good experience,' and not feel offended by our challenges. *Rechem*, the root of the word *rachamim*, means womb. Deep listening requires what might be called a vaginal capacity. Being receptive. It's not empathy. It's receptiveness."

Receptivity is key, because the search for elusive truths that testimony uncovers is a poetic, accidental process. As Zornberg explains in discussing the importance of narrative, of telling, "The mode of access is language, which is always 'in trial'; not a simple medium of historical transmission, but a testimony to unconscious, unpredictable and potentially liberating meanings. Something new is born in the unsettling play of language."

FINDING *SHECHINAH*

When I went to meet Barbara Kane, new mother of the New York seder that had inspired my own nearly ten years before, I was hoping to unearth Miriam's Well—to plumb the depths and the richness of women's spiritual experiences. I had dozens of questions for her: Why was the women's seder still important? Why had Broner's description of those original women reflected so much the experience of my own group—down to the fights, the glories, the anger, the jealousy, the struggle? What is it about the subversive but difficult to articulate power in their seder evenings, and in our study, celebrations, and rituals, that invites transformation? After all, since Broner invented the women's seder, there had been an explosion of interest in feminine spirituality. Broner says that, across the country, there's barely a college that doesn't have a women's seder today. Synagogues and Jewish community centers sponsor a women's seder, expecting thirty, and three hundred show up. "And everyone is writing their own Haggadah," Broner has said, "the need for it remains strong."

Kane wanted me to experience the site of the seder itself. In a recreation of the experience, she led me up to her fifteenth-floor Upper West Side apartment in the elevator and paused outside her expansive living room, just as she had done last year, in April, with all the women around her. It was January, though, and as we walked into the room, I stared ahead, mesmerized, not so much by the room itself, but by the large picture window and its stirring view of Central Park in winter.

We settled on a perch in her window seat, and as I gazed out, Barbara nudged the window open. "You must see the full view," she said.

It's two degrees out, I wanted to yelp. Instead, I told her I have a fear of heights. She didn't hesitate. She leaned out the window, telling me that in forty years of this, no one had fallen. She gently held me, a stranger, and urged me to her side.

And there was the glory on the other side of my fear. Central Park, in panorama, its huge reservoir of water flanked by spindly trees, the city etched in the distance, and the warmth of Barbara's arm around me. Safe. Another mother, I thought.

One of the important discoveries about being in our own group had been just this—our amazing ability to nurture and care for each other. No matter how well we had been raised, loved, and nourished, or not, each one of us, in her own way, was an unfinished piece. Jane had to learn that her voice, which I always saw, especially when she sang "Avinu Malkenu" on Yom Kippur, as a conduit linking heaven and earth, was, in fact, an instrument of God. Ruth had to learn it was possible to be loved completely, in all your harsh, critical, hyper-rational glory; that this miracle could occur even though the only God she had ever known had stood aside in Germany. And Rachel had to learn her inner darkness, her mother's darkness, which one day would burst to the surface in a diagnosis of breast cancer, was a darkness she could find in others and could, as a spiritual guide, help them to walk through.

She recently trained as a spiritual guide at Eilat Chayim and says she would never have embarked on that path without the seder sisters' voices and strength behind her. Rachel, who at that first seder couldn't find her voice.

My transformation would eventually make possible an autumn-of-life Exodus from my birthplace of St. Louis to New York City and the accompanying exile from the very women who had made that journey possible. For me, though, the initial move toward transformation began early in the life of the group. It was just before my fortieth birthday.

After a botched medical procedure, I began experiencing panic attacks, sleeplessness, and eventually a thick depression that lasted for weeks. In the grip of an overwhelming fear, I phoned Laura, an old pro at anxiety, who came over and sat up all night in bed with me, trying to calm me down enough so I could rest. The next morning, Laura called in the troops—two more sisters and Rabbi Susan. Rabbi Susan offered to accompany me to the emergency room—it turned out I'd become dehydrated and was barely eating. Only with Rabbi Susan at my side did I agree to go to the hospital. There, in the ER, she sat up with me into the cold hours of the night, talking, listening, patiently accompanying me into my fear and pain. Present in a way I'd never experienced anyone being present for me before.

My mother was famous in family lore for telling my sister and me to put on a heavier layer of makeup when any mishaps or sadness crept into our lives. Ignoring pain was a prescription for living. Now, Rabbi Susan sat in the pain with me, and as we spoke and I told her of the terror, we both began to realize this wasn't just a psychological problem, or a body problem. It was a God problem, too. I'd become increasingly drawn to the life of the spirit, and the world of tradition, but I'd also spent my entire life praying to a Father God, a Ruler, a King.

In *Reclaiming the Covenant: A Jewish Feminist's Search for Meaning*, Ellen M. Umansky writes:

> How meaningful today are images of God as King, Lord, and Shepherd? And why, if both men and women have been created in God's image, Should we not address the Divine as Father *and* Mother, Master and Mistress of Heaven?

I had read Umansky years ago, and I'd thought I had transformed my original notions of God, but in that midnight conversation with Rabbi Susan, I realized the old fossilized God had hung on somewhere deep within me—angry, judgmental, and male. He was there greeting me in the liturgy every year, as I stood in trial on Yom Kippur year after year, wondering if I was "good enough."

Rabbi Susan introduced me to the concept of *Shechinah*, the loving feminine presence, She Who Dwells Within. When she told me I might imagine laying my head down on my pillow, in the arms of this feminine Presence, this Shechinah, I didn't have to reach far to locate an idea of what that might be like. I knew a version of that Power, that Mystery, that She. That gentle and loving Presence. I'd felt her there when the Seder Sisters sang.

It was our closing song, the "Shechianu," and though it blessed the new, we sang it as ritual to end almost every gathering. This ceremonial moment, too, had developed. We sang it one time—Debbie Friedman's tune to the ancient blessing—led by Jane and two other members of the CRC choir: Beth, whose deep, true, I-will-hold-you-forever voice hints at the stability and sense of order she brings to the group—it was Beth who flew off to Florida to be with Laura in the last days of her mother's life—and Emily, who still can't believe that she, of all people, has ended up divorced, without a life partner; Emily, for whom E. M. Forster's "only connect" is one of the Ten Commandments.

We sang it once. Our voices locked and soared. When the spell was over and we'd finished, we remained in the circle. It became something we waited for—the *Shechianu*—a seal, a stamp on our spirit life. The harmony hinted at the idea of Rabbi Jim Goodman, who tells us that the separateness is an Illusion.

That evening in the hospital, after Rabbi Susan told me about Shechinah, I lay my head down on the pillow, and with the help of Xanex, had my first night's sleep.

I still love "Avinu Malkenu," especially when Jane is singing it. I still love the places I can get to, inspired by Father-Love. But my Judaism, my prayer, my world, is incomplete without Shechinah. And since Judaism is a patriarchal system, written and created by men, there is a great deal of work to do. In *Encountering the Divine Presence*, Rabbi Laura Geller speaks of a rabbi teacher at HUC telling her that there is a blessing for everything, and her wondering then, about all the life moments, as in when she got her period for the first time, and why there was no blessing for that.

When my daughter, Anielle, began her period, though being fifteen she refused to stand physically at the center of our women's circle, still she consented to participate from afar. So we stood one flight below her room and sang up the stairwell to her. I think of that moment as carving a place for Shechinah. Perhaps Anielle will journey forth with a different notion of God to accompany her because of the sacred space we created.

The feminine face of God can be seen only when we invite her in and acknowledge her power. Our group has created a place for her in our seders, in healing rituals, in movement exercises and experiences, in song, in the *sukkah*, or "harvest festival hut," each year, and beneath a chuppah. We have also made our way to her in less blatantly sacred places—a late-night session at Steak 'n' Shake, the smells of hamburgers and greasy fries, and Liz in a flood of post-divorce tears. We did not try to fix or quell, but simply held the tears, held her pain as Rabbi Susan had once held mine. I can still see Rabbi Susan in that hospital ER, her mass of black curls an angel's veil, her head almost nodding off because it was two A.M., and she'd been holding the world and its pain, unsteady, all day long.

When God divided the world, the story goes, She created the upper waters, the Sky, and the lower ones, the Ocean. Men are of the upper waters, energy poured in rain and thunder. But women are of the ocean. Receptive, vibrant, full. We hold the world in place.

WANDERINGS

The Israelites are led toward the promise of freedom by a zigzagged, crooked route. Their journeying is marked by fear and complaint, as Zornberg names it, "a radical doubt," that accompanies them through the wilderness. We women, too, journeyed through fear, jealousy, and anger, often revisiting questions of purpose and aim.

There were times in which our original lack of intention in forming the group undid us. Sometimes we couldn't decide whether we were a study group or a spiritual group or an activist group. When Laura, whose passion for service only grew stronger after her cancer, wanted us to get involved politically, she recruited us all to work on the Kerry campaign. I spent a series of Saturdays ringing doorbells in Rock Hill, getting to know and admire the black people who lived fifteen minutes and a world away from my door. But once the campaign ended, and Kerry lost, we had to find a new focus, and some of us, having tasted the physical world, were no longer content with study. Liz joined the board of Cultural Leadership, a black and Jewish dialogue group for high school students aimed at obliterating racism. The meetings began to intrude on Seder Sisters nights. Jane was angry because we'd stopped going to CRC—the services had grown enormous—and some of us missed the intimacy of the early days.

We went through another trial when Gail, hovering at the edge of the group and exhausted by her chaplaincy-training schedule at the hospital, seemed to be working to thrust herself into the center. She took up way more than her share of time in group dialogue, and though we glanced nervously around the table and harangued behind her back, not one of us was willing to confront her face to face. But she felt our resentment, and one evening, her anger, justified, blasted across that dining room table.

Scott Peck, in *The Different Drum: Community Making and Peace*, claims that building community really starts "when we are willing to deal with pain. Becoming vulnerable is what leads to greater intimacy." I myself have left a number of spiritual settings, not realizing that the pain that comes of being a part of a community is necessary. Somehow we feel that our spiritual settings should be free of conflict. This is wrong. Far into the life of this group of women, I finally began to see that the conflict is not only inevitable, it is essential for growth.

Letty Cottin Pogrebin puts it this way: "The fighting is a part of being human. Group process *is* difficult. There are shifting power alliances and the group divides along those lines. Students of the early feminist groups noted our expectations of sisterhood, how unrealistic they were. We create such deep attachments based on the idea that we're *finally* telling the truth about our lives. So it's natural for conflict to arise. It's especially disappointing, though, among women."

In our group, the conflict often coalesces around group identity. As Beth says, "I originally wanted us to be a spiritual study group. A place to explore our souls and our ideas about God and our heritage as Jews. And while our Jewishness is a glue and we have spent time talking about this—we can often be a truly terrible study group. We can't seem to agree on what to study or how to study. And when we do, half of us rebel and don't come to the meetings having prepared to discuss the topic at hand. I don't really want to be just a social group that comes together and eats and talks about our lives. But at this point I'm not willing to give it up, no matter what we are or become."

When I asked Liz about her struggles with the group, she said that she can't examine what the group means to her "without simultaneously looking at the struggle involved in being part of it. In every theme I could identify as a challenge, there is also a process of growth that has enriched me deeply. I have matured. I have learned to be more patient, more compassionate, more intuitive. These women have given me language, ways to name my experiences, my feelings. Perhaps the most important thing that I have gained is a sense of the sacred, the holy. I can honestly say that I have come to know G-d in a deeper way, because of this group. I walk in the world differently—with my head higher, my heart more available, my search for meaning more open and accessible—because of these nine women."

The writers of *Sacred Circles,* Robin Carnes and Sally Craig, claim that groups themselves tend to surface things that have shadowed our relationships in the past. In my experience, the first years were a kind of honeymoon existence. We granted each other a slack that waned as we came to know each other well. In the beginning, if one of us paired with another outside of group time, I tried to see these pairings or threesomes more philosophically, as an extension of the life force of the group. Eventually, though, my jealousy surfaced. It was often aimed at Laura and Beth, who enjoy a particularly deep and loving friendship, hearkening to the one I yearn for, Marge Piercy's eyebeam of sister love. And in all of this, a shadow of my mother's original favoritism toward my younger sister. In turn, Laura had introduced me to this group of women. I was a writer, like her, and she came to see me as usurping her power. Strife ensued between us, and there were times in which it was hard to be in the same room together. We tried talking it through, but the feelings ran so deep, we were never quite able to heal the rift.

Honestly, Laura and I are still at odds, but the battles have softened. We always seem to return to the sheltering *sukkat shalom* (tent of peace), the larger context of love and care that the sisters are in each of our lives.

Barbara Kane reminds us that the competition and conflict were there in the first women's stories, too. "Think of Rachel and Leah," Kane says. Broner believes that the brokenness is a reflection of our current political reality. She remembers a dramatic moment from a recent seder, when Rabbi Ellen Lippman was given the assignment of reinterpreting the seder plate. Lippman briefly explained the *matzoh* and *maror* (bitter herbs), and then she wrapped the plate in a pillow case, took a hammer in hand, and smashed the plate into bits. "The plate is broken," she said. "The world is smashed. We must reconstitute it." Every woman at that seder left with a shard. Instead of the broken *afikomen* (dessert matzah) eaten at seder's end to symbolize both the taste of slavery and the hope of redemption, thirty women headed home with a piece of brittle-edged porcelain in their palms, a living reminder that *tikkun olam* (repair of the world) has an everyday urgency.

MISHKAN/BUILDING THE TABERNACLE

"Build me a sanctuary that I may dwell among you." The intricacy and detail of this *mishkan,* this sanctuary, is always a surprise when I come upon it in the text, but it reminds me that building a dwelling for the sacred is delicate work.

We women, too, worked in objects—candles, herbs, fabric, totems, stones. One evening we created our own Stone of Losses. The original existed in Jerusalem, and I've always believed we should revive the concept. In the Temple courtyard, there was a huge slab of rock. People would bring things they'd found and place them there. Others would go, looking for objects they'd lost. A communal, public place to wear your grief and joy.

We sisters each brought a stone to our gathering and spoke of the things we wanted to unburden ourselves of. Beth wanted to let go of the pain of her son, Nathan's, dying, but hold onto his memory. Emily, the frantic rush to find a life partner. Ruth, the memory of roaming the streets on Kristallnacht and, I think, the concurrent death of hope. I can't remember whether it was Liz or Rachel or Ruth, but someone, when we had asked for stones, had brought a boulder.

The idea was that we'd carry each other's pebbles away, then place or bury them in a sacred spot near our houses. But no one wanted that rock! Gail reluctantly carried it home that night. As she says, "I worried about the karma it might be carrying, so I planted it in a large communal park."

In *Deborah, Golda and Me,* Pogrebin describes how the original seder women group, in 1986, created a stone ritual of a different kind. It had been a difficult year, Pogrebin writes, marked by misunderstandings and betrayals. They wondered if the seder itself would survive, if they could "rise above the hurt feelings." They would and did, creating a conflict resolution theme and passing a stone round the table, touching it, "hard and cold like an angry heart."

At another seder, in 1989, they declared their *chametz* (leavening) of shyness and loneliness. In St. Louis, we have written down our chametz on small sheets of paper and watched them burn. For women in a world largely configured by men, a marketplace world that devalues feminine wisdom, emotion, and intelligence, the power in these ritual moments, the drive to name our experience, creates an expansion we can then bring to bear on our communities.

That original building of a mishkan continues in various settings today. Broner recently attended a conference at the University of Southern California, "Unrolling the Unwritten Scroll," in which hundreds of women gathered and created a ritual wherein they named the women prophets in their lives, wrote down their stories, rolled them into scrolls, and danced.

Creating a sanctuary, a deeper level of affirmation and self-acceptance, where we can drop the roles, facades, and masks, requires intention and an eye for mythic truth. "Spiritual groups, while intensely personal, don't dwell on personalities," say the authors of *Sacred Circles*, "but instead explore the archetypal, even heroic patterns and journeys of people's lives."

Our group utilized the seasons and cycles of the Jewish year to guide us. Autumn was for awe, a yearly encounter with our most naked truths, and a turning toward *teshuvah,* "repentance." That we might enter Yom Kippur, the stripping of externals the day requires, more willingly. Sukkot found us in our sukkah, a temporary shelter of canvas and wood on our deck outside. I have always loved the idea that as our neighbors pack up lawn furniture and roll garden hoses, we Jews head outdoors. To taste the last plum, find the last star through the overhanging shelter of pine.

We created a centerpiece of a feather, a marble heart, a mirror, and a fish carved out of wood, symbols of that which lay at the center of our being, reminders that we were each created in the image of God. We had just come through a difficult time in the group, and we needed the physical reminder that it was all about listening.

During Hannukah, winter's darkness, we gathered with our families and before lighting ten menorahs, eyed them, magnificent, unlit, in their diversity—a moose menorah, a tarnished green metal one, probably someone's grandfather's, a menorah of dancing children, and a heavy silver one that rose above all the rest. After we sang the blessings, we stood in this feast of light and named, together, the moments of radiance we'd experienced in the past year. Some of the men attached to us hung back in belligerence, especially our fourteen-year-old sons, but others surprised us. One time Ruth's husband, Ben, seventy-six, drifting through the party chaos with his hearing aid, spoke, full-voiced, about his love for this group of women and the change they had manifest in Ruth's life.

In spring, we often had our version of a seder, skipping the matzoh and maror that we'd be eating one week hence, but identifying the current mitzrayims we were feeling narrowed by, and naming the Miriams in our lives.

Always, ritualistically, each gathering began with cocktails, catching-up time, and then we moved into our study or ritual and feast.

Did I mention that miraculously, I'd finally landed in a group where every woman at the table was passionate about food? It was as if in some former life, we may or may not have stood at Sinai together, but we definitely lived in the same kitchen. I often created summer pies of apple or peach, and where coring apples is often the dreaded, most tedious part of the pie process, I found that in feeding this group of women, there was a particular joy. The kitchen itself, home of the burned-out, overworked, exhausted pre-*Pesach* (Passover) mother, became a place I wanted to live in.

Always, we sealed the night with Shechianu.

In *Sacred Circles*, Robin Carnes and Sally Craig offer a wealth of guidelines we Seder Sisters didn't always remember to follow. Confidentiality is essential, for example. Being willing to say something critical to a fellow member's face is imperative. It is the other side of lashon hara. We erred here many, many times. It took us a long time to learn that we each must take responsibility for our own needs in the group. Just as in a marriage, you cannot expect the group to intuit your wants. This issue remains challenging for most of us.

Carnes and Craig recommend that one meeting a year be self-reflective—asking each other if there is growth, if the group is meeting its original intentions. Identifying our focus continues to trip us up. Some of us want to be more activist; others want more study, less unnecessary chatter. Rumi, the Sufi Persian poet, talks of creating a community of spirit, but that involves commitment. Just "showing up" when uncomfortable dynamics surface, when the temptation, for me, always, is to run away. Some of us have too many other commitments, or a passion for an organization or cause that flares. The group has to be a priority.

The power of storytelling is essential, as is ritual. Walter Benjamin believes we have lost the ancient art of sharing our stories, and that this storytelling impulse is an essential part of what it means to be human. In our group, we have tried to correct these imbalances in our culture, and we've tried doing it both playfully and creatively. We've had Rachel and Julie Anne, our dancers, lead us in authentic movement experiences, even those of us who are "movement-challenged." We've giggled in studies in silence. We've made mistakes. But we keep on searching, inventing, seeking to uncover Miriam's Well.

In our best moments, we know these rituals have the potential to connect us to sacred sources, the unconscious, an individual and collective past. We're trying to pry open "gates of awareness" so that we can access a healing presence, a Shechinah, that often feels as if it is in exile from a terrorized world.

What have I learned? I've discovered that the rough times, the brokenness, often provide an opportunity for spiritual growth. I've seen this both in the life of the group and in each individual woman's life. I've witnessed the stumble, followed by flight, a pattern, again and again. Liz—from destruction to Eden. Jane, learning that the blessings she didn't receive from her mother could still be unearthed—by herself.

After I turned forty, after the panic and depression, there was a day when Rabbi Susan told me that, like the Israelites, I could choose to live in the blessings or the curses, the two futures, the two realms of existence Moses offers as his closing benediction before he dies. In some prophetic way, Rabbi Susan offered up my life, and where before I saw everything my life was not, I've been living (mostly) on the blessing side ever since.

I've learned you have to be willing to move beyond what Scott Peck calls "pseudo-community," a place of surface niceties, where you each underplay differences and avoid conflict. Entering the chaos is a step forward; the conflict is not only healthy, it is necessary. We're often tempted to reign chaos in with rules, structures, policy. I've come to know that's a mistake. Instead, awareness and a willingness to stay in the turmoil are essential. Someone has to be courageous, open, and conscious enough to reflect the group's dynamics back onto itself. "We're attacking the discussion leader" is an apparently simple but revolutionary phrase we might have tried.

And power jousting is inevitable. Again, a willing voice, saying the "hard stuff" out loud, provides a corrective. If people take responsibility for their own needs, if they know the onus is on oneself, it becomes easier to create and maintain balance.

Emptiness is yet another stage of community that Peck describes. The Jewish equivalent is *Ein Sof*. The mystics begin with *ayin*, meaning "empty, nothingness," a metaphor for that which cannot be expressed. The mystics recognize that God is ineffable. Therefore, by moving into emptiness, we move further into the Mystery. This is an essential method of knowing.

To empty, within the group, is to let go of preconceived ideas of how things should be, to part with beliefs, assumptions, attitudes. Zornberg might call this opening to desire, with an emphasis on the opening part. Receiving. A woman's task and mystery. This is asking yourself, What stands in the way of my communicating with the people in this group? Can I let that go? If we are to create "containers of emergence," we have to relinquish our convictions that there's one way to do this. One way to see reality, to know God. This is the cultivating of the poet John Keats's negative capability, "when a man is capable of being in uncertainties, Mysteries, doubts, without any irritable reaching after fact and reason."

For Keats, his poetic heart renders that groping after facts and reason "irritable"; we have to work a lot harder to live in the place beyond reason, or perhaps, before it. Then we can begin to weigh in on the other side of a world tilted too much in the direction of fundamental truths. Truths held too dearly. Then we can return to our holy places, our synagogues, and our larger communities, as I've seen these women do, inspiring others with the larger truth that beyond all our preciously held prisms there is the richness of a kaleidoscopic reality and a fundamental base of faith and care that runs beneath us.

PROMISE/EXODUS, AGAIN

It was a bountiful spring day at Concordia Seminary Park; dogs and children spilled from the coffee shop across the street. We were seated in the grass beneath a shaded elm. It was the fortieth anniversary of the day that Julie Anne's parents were killed in an airline catastrophe. She wanted to move at the exact moment when, forty years earlier, her parents had died. As she danced before us, layers of narrative unfolded, silently. She hunkered into a ball, limbs folded over onto themselves, or leaped unencumbered, approaching delight. We watched and witnessed, all ten, and Rabbi Susan, too, who several years ago had given Julie Anne back her name. There was so much that can't be spoken in that dance, years of craving a mother's touch, a father's spotlight wonder. The spires of Concordia Seminary rose in the distance, and I wondered what the passing theologians thought of this sprite, this forty-five-year-old girl-woman leaping toward her future on their hill. When she finished, we didn't clap. This went beyond performance. Silent awe. What the body can hold and convey—layers of experience that exceed the realm of language.

"It was a pivotal time," Julie Anne says now. "It made me move into healing. I knew I was ready. I'd had two parents who weren't my parents. As a kid growing up in the South, three of us sat in the hall during Bible class. I always felt outside." And she continues, "In retrospect, I always wanted this group of women. The key was the asking and the knowing what I wanted. And this group gave it to me."

She says there "was something about it that was Jewish, family, women, that made it safe for me to ask." And so we showed up, sat in the grass, tracing Julie Anne's silent songline. Zornberg says that "the groping for a true narrative is the very purpose of Exodus." Sefat Emet sees the redemption from Egypt (mitzrayim) as a "freeing from the 'narrow places,' the meitzarim, the straits of the soul, into an expansiveness in which all potential is realized."

We were after transformation. And over the course of ten years of wandering, I watched each one of us attain that. Rachel, who couldn't locate her voice, became a spiritual guide. Laura, whose wounded parents were unable to break the cycle of neglect, founded College Bound St. Louis to nurture a new generation of young men and women. Emily left an unfulfilling job and became a career coach. Gail became a rabbi. And I left St. Louis, my hometown of forty-five years, and moved with my family to begin a life in New York. I am in the midst of transforming nearly every aspect of my existence. I have left the group that nurtured and completed me, but each and every day, I am buoyed by their strength and love. And e-mails and phone calls have become a lifeline, connecting me, still, to my source.

These women, and their chorus of hope and faith, are with me as I walk through a new mitzrayim. As Beth says, "When I think of the gifts I've received from being a part of this *chevra*, Seder Sisters, I have to say that I feel like I'm a part of a family. A family with a lot less downside than 'real' families—one that really thrives on love and laughter and friendship."

The gifts, as Beth calls them, are bounteous and full. They live with us, now, in our lives as rabbis, teachers, students, friends, and community builders. The power of women: singular, purposeful, receptive. We have journeyed from mitzrayim to Promise together, and the lessons of the journey lie within us, accompany us, still.

I will close with a prayer. May each of you who are reading this account, now, find your circle of women, find those coordinates of faith and spirit, hope, healing and renewal—a group of women willing to dance you into being on the shores of yet another Sea.

Notes

1. The names of the women involved in my group have been changed in order to protect their privacy.

CHAPTER 13

The Transformative Nature of the Rosh Hodesh Experience

Rabbi Jo David

The new moon, the new moon,
Slim, bright, pregnant with possibilities.
Our lives are like the new moon.
How great are our talents, which God has given us.
How little of them we reveal.
              —*Rabbi Jo David* from "Covenant of the Heart," WRJ Press

A number of years ago, preparing to lead my first Rosh Hodesh group, I came across a ritual in which women tied ribbons around their wrists and then tied themselves to one another. Initially, this appealed to me. I considered using ribbons of various colors to express a range of emotions. The participants would be directed to tie themselves with one or more ribbons to indicate their most significant feelings. Happily, before I could inflict this ceremony on anyone, sanity reasserted itself. I visualized the reactions of my "seventy-something" ladies (my new Rosh Hodesh group) being instructed to tie themselves to one another, and I was reduced to laughter-filled tears.

This was my "aha" moment, in which I came to understand that ritual can be effective only if the symbols and words chosen resonate for the specific group for which they are intended. I realized that rather than rely on a Rosh Hodesh manual, I would have to develop rituals and liturgy that suited the specific needs and sensitivities of the people with whom I was working.

Rosh Hodesh, literally "head of a month," is the term used for the beginning of each new month in the Jewish lunar calendar. It has traditionally been considered a woman's holiday. As such, it is pregnant with opportunities for spiritual growth for women. I think that it may even have possibilities for men, but that's another story.

In my congregational work, I have led many different Rosh Hodesh groups. Almost without exception, the outstanding feature of all these groups is that all the participants respond well to the spiritual challenges that Rosh Hodesh presents. However, a cookie-cutter approach to Rosh Hodesh programming is rarely effective.

Nonetheless, there are a few things that make group Rosh Hodesh rituals successful. While a leader can be important, sharing the work of planning and implementing a program will keep participants interested and involved. The presence of food is always a warm and welcoming touch. (I once led a group that brought their favorite holiday foods of the month, and copies of the recipes, to each meeting. By the end of the year, we had a wonderful cookbook.) It's also extremely important that the level of prayer, ritual, and study be suitable for the majority of the members of the group. It may take some time to discover the general comfort level, so having a feedback mechanism can be helpful.

This chapter explores the symbols and ideas associated with each of the months of the Jewish calendar. This material may serve as a resource for women who would like to explore the spiritual opportunities that Rosh Hodesh has traditionally afforded Jewish women.

ROSH HODESH IN TRADITIONAL JEWISH SOURCES

One might assume that Rosh Hodesh is one of the festival days mentioned in the Torah. In the Torah, we are told what offerings are to be made on the first of the month, and the term *Rosh Hodesh* is applied to the beginning of the new month. However, a ritualized Rosh Hodesh festival is not described, although it is alluded to in a variety of ways.

In Numbers 10:10 we read, "On the day of your rejoicing, and on your festive days, and at the beginnings of your months, you shall blow the trumpets over your burnt offerings and over the sacrifices of your peace offerings." The sacrifices to be offered at the time of the new moon are described in Numbers 28:10, 11–15.

From the Nevi'im, (the Prophets) we get more details about the observance of Rosh Hodesh, including the fact that it was a day on which special offerings were made in the sanctuary. Workday occupations were suspended (I Sam. 20:18–34; II Kings 4:23; Amos 8:5). In Isaiah 1:13–4, the new moon observance is listed as part of the larger festival calendar.

It is interesting to note that during the Syrian-Greek persecution of the Israelites in the latter part of the first millennium BCE, the observance of Rosh Hodesh was one of three prohibited *mitzvoth* (commandments). (The others were the observance of *Shabbat*, or the Sabbath, and the performance of circumcision.) Rosh Hodesh was targeted because in the time before a set calendar was produced, the declaration of Rosh Hodesh each month by the *beit din* (court) in Jerusalem enabled the Jewish people to observe their festivals and sacrifices at the proper time. Without the certainty of the beginning of the month, the accuracy of the Jewish calendar would be destroyed, and the observance of the festivals would be undermined.

TRADITIONAL PRACTICES RELATED TO ROSH HODESH

We have virtually no information about the actual observance of Rosh Hodesh. Prior to the destruction of the Temple in Jerusalem in 70 CE, one may reasonably assume that the Torah-mandated sacrifices were offered. After the destruction of the Temple in Jerusalem by the Romans in 70 CE, the rabbis attempted to create an alternative to the Temple-based monthly offerings by making Rosh Hodesh a women's holiday. Unfortunately, we have no written record of the reasons the rabbis chose to do this. However, since the cycle of the moon and a woman's monthly cycle are approximately the same length (twenty-eight to thirty days), one might speculate that this was a contributing factor in their decision making.

The post–Temple Rosh Hodesh rituals appear in a variety of rabbinic texts. In addition to declaring that Rosh Hodesh was a festival for women, the rabbis created a variety of additions to the daily worship liturgy and the *birkat hamazon* (blessing after a meal).

Most of the post-Temple rituals and liturgy for Rosh Hodesh are found in the Talmud and in other rabbinic writings. In Tractate Megillah 22b, we learn that on Rosh Hodesh, women are exempt from work. In a comment on this passage, Rashi specifies that women may not engage in spinning, weaving, and sewing. The reason given is that these are the skills that women used to contribute to the building of the Tabernacle. The Talmud Yerushalmi (Pesachim 4:1; 4:6; Taanit 1:6) mentions that it is the custom for women to abstain from work on Rosh Hodesh. The Shulchan Aruch also recognizes this as a valid religious practice (Orach Chayim 417).

According to the Pirke De-Rabbi Eliezer, a ninth-century CE *midrashic* work (scholarly exposition of the Talmud), the Israelite women refused to contribute their earrings for the construction of the Golden Calf. As a reward, God gave Jewish women a special holy day each month on which they are to be free from work. According to this source, it is customary to wear new clothing on Rosh Hodesh.

The synagogue service is rich in Rosh Hodesh traditions. On Rosh Hodesh, there is a full Torah service featuring special Torah and Haftarah readings as well as other specific prayers for the festival. If Rosh Hodesh falls on Shabbat or on another festival, special liturgical additions are included. In addition to the monthly celebration of Rosh Hodesh, two other ritual practices are observed in many communities.

On the Shabbat prior to Rosh Hodesh, we observe the *birkat ha Hodesh* (the blessing of the month). This takes place after the Torah service. The congregation stands while an announcement is made detailing the day of the week the new month will begin. In some communities a Torah [KB1] scroll is held during the announcement. The liturgy is taken from the Talmud (Berakot 16b), which states that this prayer was the daily prayer of Rav, the founder of the Babylonian Academy in Sura in the third century CE. This prayer was adopted as the liturgy for the birkat ha Hodesh in the eighteenth century.

The prayer asks that we be granted "life and peace, joy and gladness, salvation and comfort." It also asks for the ingathering of the Jewish people. The themes of revival and renewal are relevant to the cycle of the moon, which, though it fades, renews itself each month.

The ritual of announcing the coming of the new month in the synagogue is a rabbinic nod to the ancient ceremony that took place in Israel each month at the time of the new moon. The new month was officially proclaimed by an authorized rabbinic court. During this ceremony the exact time of the new moon's appearance was stated. Those participating stood as this was done (Mishna Berurah 117:1; Iggrot Moseh, Orach Chaim 1:142). For this reason, it is the custom today to stand while the new month is announced.

The other ritual associated with the new month is *birkat halevanah*, "the blessing of the new moon." Another name for this is *kiddush halevanah*, "the sanctification of the new moon." This ceremony takes place on a Saturday night after *havdalah* between the fourth and the sixteenth of the month. The moon must be visible. This ritual is discussed in the Talmud (Sanhedrin 42a; Sofrim 20:1–2).

The material in Tractate Sofrim suggests that the blessing of the moon must take place after Shabbat, when people are happy and dressed in nice clothing. One looks up at the moon and with feet together recites the prescribed benediction. Then one says, *"simman tov"* (a good sign) three times and executes three dancing gestures in the direction of the moon. Some sofrim (scribes) say that one should jump toward the moon. Following this, one says three times, "Just as I cannot touch you, may my foes never be able to harm me." After this, one should wish one's neighbor *shalom* (peace) three times, and then return home.

The Talmud associates Rosh Hodesh observance with the appearance of the *Shechinah,* who for the rabbis of the Talmud was a nominally feminine manifestation of the Divine. According to Sanhedrin 42a, Rabbi Aha ben Hanina said in the name of Rabbi Assi in Rabbi Yohanan's name, "Whoever pronounces the benendiction over the new moon in its due time welcomes, as it were, the presence of the Shechinah." The Shechinah later became incorporated into Jewish mystical traditions related to the Sabbath by the kabbalists of Safed. Although the feminine nature of the Shechinah was implicit in the name itself (a female-gender Hebrew noun), neither the Talmud nor the mystics did very much to develop the potential of the female nature of this aspect of the Divine. Rather, the Shechinah was usually explained as the "indwelling presence" of the Divine.

ROSH HODESH IN MODERN TIMES

As the Jewish feminist movement began to develop in the 1970s, its leaders searched for authentic Jewish traditions and rituals that could be used to connect Jewish women to their religious and spiritual roots. Very early on, the women's festival of Rosh Hodesh was adopted as an opportunity to develop women's study, prayer, consciousness-raising, and support groups. The development of Rosh Hodesh groups also owes a great deal to the ideas of egalitarian participation in the havurah movement and the emerging *tefillah*, or prayer, groups found in some traditional Jewish communities.

The fact that Rosh Hodesh was an authentic women's holiday gave it special power. Its place within the Jewish calendrical cycle is firmly rooted in Judaism's most sacred texts. Because of this, Jewish men (and Jewish women) could not dismiss Rosh Hodesh as a "women's lib" attempt to challenge the Jewish male hierarchical structure in the synagogue and in other ritual settings. At a time when the larger women's movement in America was struggling to find or create points of unique connection with which to "liberate" women, Jewish women had a ready-made and traditionally authentic focal point for the development of new women's rituals and roles within the Jewish community.

Another important element in the development of Jewish feminism was the existing connection of the Shechinah to Rosh Hodesh. It was inevitable that, over time, the concept of the Shechinah as an expression of Jewish female spirituality would develop in important and exciting new ways.

As the Jewish feminist movement evolved, it became clear that one of the advantages of a Rosh Hodesh group was that it did not have to be attached to a synagogue in order to be effective. This liberated women and made it possible for them to step away from male rabbinic concepts of spirituality and ritual leadership, and to develop their own religious and spiritual models. It also provided opportunities for women to assume spiritual leadership roles that had previously been closed to them.

While many synagogue-affiliated sisterhood organizations eventually experimented with or adopted some sort of Rosh Hodesh programming, Rosh Hodesh groups were also formed at Young Men's Christian Associations (Ys) and Jewish Community Centers (JCCs). Some groups were also created by groups of women acting independently.

Certain themes quickly became associated with Rosh Hodesh groups. Popular themes included the study of the spiritual nature of each month, an exploration of the holiday of the month, the study of the month's Torah portions, and an examination of biblical texts in which women were prominent players. Themes that have special resonance for women—the monthly cycle, the life cycle, women's roles in the Jewish community-also became popular, as were the ideas of rebirth and renewal.

Some of these groups were fiercely feminist and dealt with issues like gender-neutral language in Jewish worship, inclusive language, and the creation of Hebrew prayers that were gender neutral or written in a feminine idiom. Other groups focused on recasting Jewish rituals and holidays to express women's concerns and issues, women's participation in synagogue leadership—both on the *bimah* (dais within the synagogue) and within the lay leadership structure—and the feminine aspect of the Divine.

In some groups, this resulted in the incorporation of Goddess imagery in rituals and prayers. In other groups, especially those in traditional communities, the development of a Rosh Hodesh group within the synagogue led to more general women's tefillah groups. Other groups were run on more traditional Jewish female models, as an outgrowth of a congregation's sisterhood programming, for example. These groups tended to be study oriented rather than ritual oriented.

As Rosh Hodesh groups began to establish themselves, certain "female" ritual elements and foods began to emerge as normative. The use of water and water imagery, often referred to as *mayim chayim* (living waters), was one of the early ritual elements.

Many Jewish feminist water rituals are associated with Miriam. In Numbers 20:1–2, we read that Miriam has died, and the Israelites no longer have water to drink. The Talmud (Taanit 9a) explains, in the name of Rabbi Yossi, the son of Rabbi Yehuda, "The well was provided [to the Israelites during Miriam's lifetime] because of Miriam's merit." "Miriam's

Well" entered the realm of midrash as testimony to the greatness of this unique leader. The inclusion of a cup of water on the Passover seder table (Miriam's cup) and the creation of special "Miriam's Cup" vessels for this use are an outgrowth of the desire of many women to include women's stories and female-oriented rituals into traditional Jewish ceremonies.

Candles were another ritual element that became popular with Rosh Hodesh groups early on. This was a natural extension of the traditional link between Jewish women and Shabbat candle lighting.

Food was and continues to be an important part of many Rosh Hodesh programs. Food ranged from that which might be considered to have a "feminine" connection, like fruits with seeds, egg dishes, round berries, and crescent-shaped rolls, to family recipes for Jewish life-cycle events and holidays. Some groups preferred to use Jewish ritual foods that were familiar to them (like *challah*, an unleavened bread, and wine) and cake and tea and coffee.

Rosh Hodesh groups developed their own programs based on the needs and interests of their members. Some groups were very experimental, whereas others focused on mainstream ritual forms and liturgy.

As large segments of the Jewish community became more accepting of sexual orientation that went beyond the parameters of heterosexuality, some Rosh Hodesh groups created a safe Jewish haven for members of the lesbian, bisexual, and transgender communities. Some younger Jewish women found Rosh Hodesh groups to be a focus for the development of new forms of spirituality and rituals.

The development of "women's seders" may be traced to the ritual creativity fostered in Rosh Hodesh groups. In addition, the placement of an orange on the seder plate to represent gay and lesbian Jews may have been suggested by the emergence of Jewish lesbians as important players in the emerging Jewish feminist movement.

THE JEWISH CALENDAR

One of the most common Rosh Hodesh themes, especially for beginning groups, has been and continues to be an exploration of the inherent meaning of each month that is celebrated. While there are many midrashic and mystical sources for this information, one that is often presented relates to the zodiac.

THE ZODIAC AND JEWISH TRADITION

The zodiac, which was developed in Babylonia in the sixth century BCE, was certainly known to the Jewish refugees and deportees who settled in

Babylonia after the destruction of the First Temple in 586 BCE. Many discussions about the "truth" inherent in astrology can be found in the Talmud and in a wide variety of ancient and modern rabbinic texts.

One of the earliest rabbinic works to deal with astrology is the Sefer Yetzirah. Written between the third and sixth centuries CE, this is primarily a mystical work. It translates the Latin names of the twelve signs of the zodiac into Hebrew and explains the ways in which these signs are relevant to Jewish life and Jewish spirituality.

Depictions of the signs of the zodiac, as well as depictions of concepts related to the cycles of the year, have been found in seven early synagogues in Israel. One of the most famous is the mosaic floor discovered in Beth Alpha, in the Beit Sh'an Valley in northeastern Israel. Believed to date back to the fifth century CE, the Beth Alpha synagogue floor incorporates the twelve signs of the zodiac and has inscriptions in Hebrew and Greek.

THE DEVELOPMENT OF THE JEWISH CALENDAR

Some of the months of the Jewish calendar and their order in the calendar have their source in the Tanach (Hebrew Bible), although their names are actually Babylonian.

The first month of the Jewish calendar is the month of Nissan, the month in which Passover begins. In Exodus 12:2 we read, "This month shall mark the beginning of your months; it will be the first of the months of the year." However, the month is not given its Torah name Aviv until Deuteronomy 16:1: "Observe the month of Aviv, and offer a Passover sacrifice to the Lord your God, for it was in the month of Aviv, at night, that the Lord your God freed you from Egypt." Later in the Tanach, we find that this name has been changed to Nissan (Neh. 2:1; Esther 3:7).

In the Megillat Esther, we learn that the third month of the Jewish calendar is called Sivan (Esther 8:9), that the tenth month is called Tevet (Esther 1:16), and that the twelfth month is Adar (Esther 3:7).

From Nehemia we learn the name of the sixth month, Elul (Neh. 6:15). Kislev is mentioned as the ninth month in Zechariah 7:1, and the eleventh month, Shevat, is mentioned in Zechariah 1:7.

First Kings 6:1 and First Kings 6:37 list the second month of the year as Ziv. The seventh month was called Ethanim (I Kings 8:2). The eighth month was called Bul (I Kings 6:38).

When the Jews returned from their first exile in Babylonia in the early sixth century BCE, they brought with them new names for these months and for Aviv. Therefore, Aviv became Nissan, Ziv became Iyar, Bul became Mar Cheshvan, and Ethanim became Tishrei. In addition, they brought with them the names of Tamuz (the fourth month), Av (the fifth month), Tevet (the tenth month), Shevat (the eleventh month), and Va-Adar or Adar Sheni (the thirteenth month), which is added seven times in a nineteen-year cycle to keep the agricultural festivals Passover, Shavuot, and Sukkot in their proper seasons. Rosh Hashanah is made "early" or "late" by the insertion of Adar Sheni.

SPIRITUAL CONCEPTS RELATED TO THE MONTHS OF THE JEWISH CALENDAR

There are many different ways to interact with each of the months of the Jewish calendar. A great deal of material is available on the meaning of each month. However, for completeness and complexity, nothing comes close to the Sefer Yetzirah.

The Sefer Yetzirah is one of the earliest kabbalistic works. The first commentaries to the Sefer Yetzirah were written around the tenth century CE, but parts of the text can be traced to the sixth century or possibly earlier. This book presents a fusion of "magical" and "meditative" kabbalistic ideas and practices. It contains much material about the letters of the Hebrew alphabet and their spiritual powers.

The Sefer Yetzirah is an extremely complicated work. Numerous commentaries have been written over the centuries in an effort to clarify and organize the material for the reader. At times, the commentaries are as difficult to unravel as the original text. The most accessible material in the Sefer Yetzirah is a series of verses that attach to each month a Hebrew letter, a symbol of the zodiac, and a part of the body. Other material links a tribe of Israel, a "sense" (or human attribute), and, in some cases, an angel or a color to a specific month as well.

At the beginning of the following discussions of each month are noted the astrological sign, the letter of the alphabet, the tribe, the part of the body, and the "sense" (human attribute) that is presented in the Sefer Yetzirah. As will be seen, each of these topics can be interpreted in many different ways. Not all of these topics are discussed in every month.

THE MONTH OF NISSAN

Astrological sign: Aries, Taleh, Lamb; Letter of the alphabet: Hey;
Tribe: Judah; Part of the body: right foot; Sense: speech

Nissan is the first of the twelve months of the Jewish calendar. The first day of Nissan is the first of the four "new years" of the Hebrew calendar. Rosh Hodesh Nissan is the new year for kings (Mishnah Rosh HaShana 1:1).

The first commandment given to Israel before the Exodus from Egypt states, "This month [the month of Nissan] shall be for you the first of the months" (Exod. 12:2). Nissan begins the spring. The three months of the spring period—Nissan, Iyar, and Sivan—correspond to the tribes of Judah, Issachar, and Zebulun. In the Torah, Nissan is referred to as the month of the spring (Hodesh Ha'Aviv).

In the Talmud (Tractate Rosh HaShana 11a), Nissan is referred to as the month of the redemption: "In Nissan our forefathers were redeemed from Egypt and in Nissan we will be redeemed."

The sign of the zodiac for Nissan is the lamb, which is also the traditional Passover sacrifice. There is a tradition that the lamb possesses the ability to arouse mercy by using its voice. For this reason, the human "sense" related to Nissan is that of speech.

Speech, in its many varieties (verbal, non-verbal, sign language, and other modalities) gives one the ability to express feelings and insights and to share these with others. God created the world with speech: "And God said, 'Let there be light'" (Gen. 1:3). Just as the world began with speech, so too does the year, beginning with Nissan and the sense of speech which is associated with it.

The spiritual focus of the month of Nissan is the festival of *Pesach,* or Passover, during which we tell the story of the Exodus from Egypt. The Haggadah tells us, "The more one tells of the Exodus from Egypt, the more is one to be praised," which is one reason why a seder can get a little long. Embellishing the story of the Exodus is a very significant spiritual aspect of the seder.

THE MONTH OF IYAR

Astrological sign: Taurus, Shor, the Ox; Letter of the alphabet: Vav;
Tribe: Issachar; Part of the body: right kidney; Sense: thought

Iyar is the second of the twelve months of the Jewish calendar. In the Bible, the month of Iyar is called the month of Ziv (radiance), thus the month of Iyar is associated with light. It is also referred to as the month of (natural) healing, for its name is an acronym for "I am G-d your Healer" (Exod. 15:26).

Iyar is a link between the months of Nissan and Sivan. On the second night of the seder, in Nissan, we begin the 49-day counting of the *omer,* or *sefirat haomer* (sheaf of grain). This continues through Iyar, and concludes in Sivan with the celebration of Shavuot, the commemoration of the giving of the Torah to the Jewish people. Shavuot is also a celebration of the wheat harvest.

The symbol of the zodiac, *shor*, the ox, represents the origin of the "animal soul" of humankind. During Iyar we strive to purify our soul through the counting of the omer in preparation for receiving the Torah during Sivan. In Hebrew, the root of the word *shor* also means "to look" or "to observe." Iyar is a month during which we seek self-improvement through introspection and examination of those things that make us not animal but human.

Isaachar, the tribe associated with Iyar, was considered to be a tribe of scholars. There is a midrashic tradition that members of the Sanhedren (the Jewish court system in Israel during Second Temple times) were mostly drawn from the tribe of Isaachar. There is also a teaching that the members of the tribe of Isaachar were masters of the "secret" of the Jewish calendar.

The "sense" of thought is associated with Iyar. There is a connection between introspective thought and numerical calculation, like the calculation of the Jewish calendar. Psalm 90 says, "Teach us to number our days, that we may obtain a wise heart" (Ps. 90:12). As we count the omer, we reflect on our thoughts and feelings, with the intention of calculating what we must do to lead a better life.

The Sefer Yetzirah links the right kidney to the month of Iyar. There is a tradition that "the kidneys give advice." In particular, the right kidney is thought to relate to spiritual advice and introspection, acting in a way similar to that of the conscience.

THE MONTH OF SIVAN

Astrological sign: Gemini, the Twins; Letter of the alphabet: Zayin;
Tribe: Zebulun; Part of the body: left foot; Sense: action

Sivan is the third month of the Jewish year. According to tradition, it is also the month in which the Torah was given to the Children of Israel. This event is celebrated during the festival of Shavuot. As the third of the first three months, we are reminded of other important "threes" in Jewish tradition: the three segments of the Tanach: Torah, Nevi'im (Prophets), and Ketuvim (Writings); the three divisions of the Jewish people: Kohanim, Levi'im, and Israelim; and the three people most responsible for our journey to the Promised Land: Moses, Aaron, and Miriam.

The shape of the letter *zayin* is a *vav* with a crown on its head. Thus, this letter reminds us of the tradition that every Jewish soul received a crown when the Torah was given to the people Israel.

We are also reminded of the tradition that all Jewish souls were assembled at Mount Sinai when the Torah was given. At the end of

Deuteronomy, God makes a covenant with the Israelites who are about to cross over into the Promised Land and says, "Not with you alone do I seal this covenant, but with whoever is here, standing with us today before the Almighty our God, and with whoever is not here with us today" (Deut. 29:13). The Talmud explains this passage by saying that this applies not only to people who are born into the Jewish community but also to converts (Shavuot 39a). The biblical Book of Ruth, which deals with the issue of conversion, is the section of the Tanach that is traditionally read during Shavuot.

The sign of the zodiac associated with Sivan, Gemini (the twins, or *teomati*), can be compared to the two identical tablets of the covenant given to Moses. The giving of the Torah to Israel is referred to as a wedding between God and Israel. In the Song of Solomon (5:2), the highest level of marriage is referred to as bride and groom being identical twins: *tamati*. Some rabbinic commentators read this as "teomati," suggesting the twins of the zodiac.

THE MONTH OF TAMUZ

Astrological sign: Cancer, Sartan, the Crab; Letter of the alphabet: Chet; Tribe: Reuben; Part of the body: right hand; Sense: sight

Tamuz, the fourth month of the Jewish calendar, begins the summer season. The three months of this season, Tamuz, Av, and Elul, correspond to the tribes of Reuben, Simeon, and Gad.

According to tradition, the seventeenth of Tamuz is the day during which the Israelites committed the sin of the Golden Calf, which resulted in the destruction of the first set of the tablets of the Ten Commandments. In memory of this serious transgression, the seventeenth of Tamuz initiates a three-week period of mourning that ends on the ninth of Av, the commemoration day of the destruction of the Temple in Jerusalem. Midrashic tradition also teaches that it was in the month of Tamuz that Moses sent the spies into the Promised Land, and that they returned on the ninth of Av. The result of the report of the spies was another thirty-eight years of wandering in the desert.

The sign of the zodiac related to Tamuz is *sartan,* or Cancer, the crab. One of the meanings of the root of sartan, *seret,* is a visual "strip," or a strip of film. This relates to the sense associated with Tamuz, that of sight.

Just as we can see through a strip of film, in a spiritual sense we long to see through physical reality in order to perceive God. The sense of sight associated with Tamuz helps us to pierce the veil of the physical world in order to experience that which lies beyond our physical senses.

A kabbalistic teaching suggests that we must "remove the body" (the "outer shell") by focusing our sight with *kavanah* (spiritual intention) in order to reveal that which is hidden from us.

The index finger on the right hand, the body part for this month, helps us to direct our sight. When we read from the Torah scroll, we use a *yad*, or "hand," to assist in our reading. A yad is formed in the shape of a closed hand with the index finger extended.

Another use of the forefinger occurs during a Jewish wedding. The ring is always put on the bride's right forefinger. This custom, which is believed to be over a thousand years old, is performed because of the ancient tradition that a special blood vessel ran from the right forefinger directly to the heart. Thus, when the ring is placed on the forefinger, we are reminded of the beautiful verse from "The Song of Songs": "Set me as a seal upon your heart, like the seal upon your hand" (Song of Sol. 8:6).

THE MONTH OF AV

Astrological sign: Leo, Aryeh, the Lion; Letter of the alphabet: Tet;
Tribe: Simeon; Part of the Body: left kidney; Sense: hearing

The month of Av (or Menachem-Av, the consoler of Av) is the fifth month in the Jewish calendar. The Hebrew word *Av* means "father." Av is a name often used to refer to God, especially to God's aspects of mercy and goodness, as in the phrase "Av HaRachamim" (father of mercy).

Av contains within it the "low point" of the Jewish calendar: Tisha B'Av (the ninth of Av). Tradition teaches that this day, which is marked by fasting and by the reading of the Book of Lamentations, is the day when all the worst things in Jewish history occurred. Among these is the sin of the spies who were sent to assess the Promised Land and the destruction of the First and Second Temples. The three weeks that connect the seventeenth day of Tamuz to the ninth day of Av are days of repentance and mourning. These weeks of mourning the tragedies that afflicted our people in ancient times also serve to help us begin to orient ourselves to the introspection necessary for the personal repentance that is the focus of the High Holy Days.

There is a traditional teaching that the Messiah was born on Tisha B'Av. The Messiah is likened to a groom, and the people of Israel are his bride. The Messiah comes to redeem Israel from her state of physical and spiritual exile. On the fifteenth of Av (Tu B'Av), the Messiah reveals himself and betroths Israel to him. This is related to the custom that Tu B'Av and Yom Kippur were historically days on which one would meet one's *beshert* (one's soul mate). In commenting on this tradition, the Mishna

Ta'anit 26 says, "There are no happier days for Israel than the fifteenth of Av and Yom HaKippurim."

Aryeh (the lion, Leo), Av's zodiacal sign, presents a wide variety of possible interpretations. Many different traditional texts use the symbol of the lion for a multiplicity of purposes. In Jeremiah 4:7 we read, "The lion has come up from his thicket: the destroyer of nations has set out." This reference is generally understood to be related to Nebuchadnezzar, who was responsible for the destruction of the First Temple. In Amos 3:8, however, we see the word *aryeh* in relation to God: "A lion has roared, who can but fear? My Lord God has spoken, who can but prophesy?"

The tribe associated with the month of Av is Shimon. The name *Shimon* comes from the Hebrew root "to hear." The sin of the spies on the ninth of Av entailed their speaking evil of the land of Israel and the people's accepting ("hearing") the evil speech.

According to Rabbi Shimeon Bar Yochai, "hearing" is "receiving." Thus, hearing is an active rather than a passive experience. When we truly listen to others, we are better able to understand them and to reach out to them with caring.

There is a tradition that the kidneys, which are understood to be male and female, (one male, one female in each person) help us to achieve balance in our lives. In the kabbalistic tradition, anything on the right is more "spiritual" than that which is on the left. The right kidney, associated with the month of Iyar and the "sense" of thought, helps us seek right actions through introspection. The left kidney, associated with Av, helps us to bring a consciousness of the world into our lives through positive action.

THE MONTH OF ELUL

Astrological sign: Virgo, Betulah, the Virgin; Letter of the alphabet: Yud; Tribe: Gad; Part of the body: left hand; Sense: action

Elul is the sixth month in the Jewish calendar. It has three different names: the month of repentance, the month of mercy, and the month of forgiveness. After two months during which we mourn many different disasters in Jewish history, Elul is a month that is set aside for us so that we can prepare ourselves for our confrontation with God and for our judgment during the High Holy Days in Tishrei.

It is also one of the months in which a "new year" falls. Rosh Hodesh Elul is the new year for cattle. All cattle, no matter when they were born, become one year older on that day. The purpose of this new year was to ensure that cattle offerings brought to the Temple would be the right age for the particular offering. For example, in Leviticus 22:27, we read that cattle must be at least eight days old before they can be offered for sacrifice.

An important tradition in Elul is the blowing of the *shofar,* or ram's horn, during the morning service, except on Shabbat, when, traditionally, no instruments may be played. We blow the shofar to remind people that the day of reckoning is coming (the High Holy Days), and that they should prepare themselves for this encounter with the Divine.

Yud, the letter associated with the month of Elul, is the smallest letter of the Hebrew alphabet, and the letter that occurs most frequently in the Torah. It is used as both a consonant and a vowel. There is a common phrase that is used to indicate that the smallest detail has received attention. We refer to the "jot and tittle." The jot comes into English through the Greek word *iota,* which is based on the Hebrew word *yud.* A tittle is a small dot or a serif.

In the month of Elul, as we begin to reflect on the deeds we have performed during the year, the yud reminds us that the smallest detail—whether of language, thought, or deed—is significant. It's easy to remember the very good things we've done, and the very bad things, but these are the exceptions. Our lives are largely composed of the jots and tittles, and it is to the reflection on these minutiae that the month of Elul is dedicated.

The zodiac sign of the month of Elul is *betulah* (Virgo, the virgin). In the Torah, the status of virginity was related to financial rather than moral considerations. A woman's virginity, or lack thereof, affected financial issues related to betrothal, marriage, and divorce. The word *betulah* in relation to a woman appears only once in the Torah in relationship to Rebecca (Gen. 24:16). Even today, in a traditional *ketubah* (a Jewish wedding contract), the status of the bride's virginity is noted, and this affects the amount of money that is "paid" for her.

There is an interesting kabbalistic teaching about Rebecca and Isaac. In *gematria* (Jewish numerology), the union of Rebecca and Isaac is equal to the word *tefillah,* "prayer": 208 (Issac) + 307 (Rebecca) = 515 (tefillah).

In the Torah, we read that when Rebecca was unable to conceive, Isaac prayed on her behalf (Gen. 25:21). Why doesn't the Torah mention Rebecca's prayer?

Rabbinic literature has much to say about this question. Some of the commentaries suggest that Rebecca's prayers weren't good enough for one reason or another. However, another understanding of this text might be that Rebecca actually did pray on her own behalf. However, without her husband's cooperation and support, it wasn't possible for her to become pregnant. Thus, when Isaac joins Rebecca in prayer, they are rewarded, not with one child, but with two, illustrating the efficacy of prayer.

The tribe of Gad has a numerical equivalent of 7: *gimmel* (3) + *daled* (4). Gad was Jacob's seventh son, brought into life by Zilpah, Leah's slave. Gad participated in the plot to send Joseph into slavery. He later moved to Egypt with his seven sons. In blessing him in Genesis 49:19, Jacob indicates that Gad is a warrior who, though embattled, will emerge victoriously. Why does the Sefer Yetzirah select Gad as the poster child for Elul? Perhaps there is a connection between Gad and the "sense" related to the month of Elul, the sense of action. Gad, the warrior, is a man of action. As such, he is an example of how we should pursue the personal spiritual review necessary to be performed in Elul. Some people may think of introspection as a passive act. The selection of Gad suggests the opposite: that we should be like vigilant soldiers in our quest to scrutinize our lives, that we should approach this task as one might approach a military campaign, leaving nothing to chance and applying an active rather than a passive strategy.

THE MONTH OF TISHREI

Astrological sign: Libra, Moznayim, the Scales; Letter of the alphabet: lamed;
Tribe: Ephraim; Part of the body: gall bladder; Sense: physical love

Tishrei is the seventh month in the Jewish calendar. It is the month in which we celebrate the creation of the world and the new year for people. It also begins the three-month period of autumn consisting of Tishrei, Chesvan, (sometimes called Mar Chesvan), and Kislev.

There is a tradition of not announcing the coming of Rosh Hodesh Tishrei and not blowing the shofar on the last day of Elul. These traditions are based on the belief that Satan, God's "prosecuting attorney," is especially vigilant before the High Holy Days with regard to the misdeeds of human beings. Not announcing Rosh Hodesh Tishrei and not blowing the shofar are both efforts to fool Satan about when Rosh Hashanah will actually take place. In other words, these omissions are intended to catch him unaware so that he cannot bring bad reports about us to God.

The extremely high level of anthropomorphism with respect to God during the High Holy Days is unique in the Jewish liturgical calendar. During the rest of the year, God is presented as a savior, a king, a source of mercy. During the High Holy Days, God is presented as a judge, a witness, a prosecutor, a lawyer for the defense, a king, a shepherd, and a father, just to mention a few of God's High Holy Days personae. The liturgy is insistent on presenting God in these guises throughout the holidays.

The most common overarching metaphor for the High Holy Days is that of God sitting with an open book in which the deeds of each individual are written. After reading the page for an individual, that person is judged, his or her fate for the next year is determined, and that fate is inscribed and "sealed" in the Book of Judgment. Our work during the High Holy Days is to add to our good deeds through acts of repentance, restitution, and charity in order to encourage God to be lenient with us.

Lamed, the letter associated with Tishrei, is the only letter in the Hebrew alphabet with an ascender that goes above the line. There are many different ways to understand this from a spiritual perspective. One possibility is that the upward reaching top of the lamed reminds us of the spiritual work required during Tishrei—to rise above our earth-bound considerations in an effort to understand God's special teaching for us. Another idea is that the uplifting lamed reminds us of the words of Psalm 121: "I lift up my eyes to the mountains, where is the source of my help? My help comes from the Lord, the maker of Heaven and Earth" (Ps. 121:1–2).

Libra's set of scales is a symbol that reminds us that during the High Holy Days our deeds are weighed. It is our hope that the good deeds will outweigh the bad deeds, and that we will be blessed with a good year.

The Hebrew word *moznayim* (scales) is derived from the word *oznayim* (ears). The inner ears give us our equilibrium and balance. If something happens to disturb that balance, we feel off-kilter, and navigating the world becomes a difficult and upsetting experience.

This idea of balance, or the lack of balance, is fundamental to our understanding of the High Holy Days. We strive to put into balance those things in our lives that have gone out of kilter. When we repent our bad behaviors and make a commitment to change, when we make restitution for things that need to be fixed, when we make charitable donations to help others, not only are we acting to bring balance and control back into our own lives, but we are also working as God's partner to help heal the world by right actions.

The tribe of Efraim is associated with the month of Tishrei. Efraim was one of the sons of Joseph. When we use the traditional blessing to bless our children, we say (to a boy), "May you be as Efraim and Menassah" (Joseph's other son).

The name *Efraim* means "that which is fruitful." The relationship between Tishrei and Efraim can be inferred from Efraim's name. Rosh Hashanah is the celebration of the creation of the world. The first commandment in the Torah is "Be fruitful and multiply" (Gen. 1:28). Merely to create something is not enough. In order for that something to endure, it must increase and adapt to change. One of the messages of Tishrei is that we must constantly consider our behavior and change, as necessary, so that we can add to the growing goodness in the world. We must be "fruitful" in the use of our lives. On Rosh Hashanah, we re-dedicate ourselves to this task.

The sense related to Tishrei is that of physical intimacy. This is also related to the creative aspect of Rosh Hashanah. There is a rabbinic concept: "On earth as it is in Heaven." In other words, it is our responsibility to emulate God's actions. God's creation of us is mirrored in our creation of our children. At Rosh Hashanah, as we begin a new year, we recommit ourselves to a full range of creative efforts.

The part of the body related to Tishrei is the gallbladder. The gallbladder is a sac-like organ located near the liver. It stores the bile produced in the liver, which aids in the digestion of fats. When a person eats, bile is released from the gallbladder to the intestine to aid in the breakdown of fats. Conditions that slow or obstruct the flow of bile from the gallbladder can result in gallbladder disease.

In our daily prayers, we give thanks to God for making sure that our bodies work properly. This prayer is also said by traditional people when going to the bathroom. After thanking God for fashioning the human body, "creating openings, arteries, glands, and organs," the prayer continues, "Should any of them by being blocked or opened, fail to function, it would be impossible to exist." Although very small, the gallbladder plays an extremely important function in the body. Anyone who has ever suffered from gallstones will attest to the pain that can be caused by a malfunction of the gallbladder.

What does this have to do with Tishrei? The new year is often portrayed as "religion on a grand scale." But it is actually the smallest acts that are most important—introspection, *teshuva* (repentance), deeds of loving kindness, *tzedaka* (the giving of charity), our private prayers and discussions with God—which help us move from a state of yearning for forgiveness to the promise of a new beginning. Without the small actions, the grand liturgy of the High Holy Days has little impact on us. The image of the small gallbladder reminds us that it is often the smallest things in life that are the most important.

THE MONTH OF CHESHVAN, OR MAR-CHESHVAN (BITTER CHESHVAN)

Astrological sign: Scorpio, Akrav, the Scorpion; Letter of the alphabet: nun;
Tribe: Manasseh; Part of the body: intestine; Sense: smell

Cheshvan, sometimes called Mar-Cheshvan, is the eighth month of the Jewish calendar. In the Tanach, it is called Bul (I Kings 6:38). The term *Bul* suggests various agricultural ideas. According to Rashi, Bul is related to the Hebrew word *baleh,* which means "that which withers" (for example, grass), and the word *bolelin,* the "mixing of feed for the animals."

Another idea is that this comes from the word *Yevul* (produce) because during Cheshvan, plowing and planting begins in Israel.

According to a midrash, more rain falls in this month in Israel than in any other month. Therefore a connection is made between bul and *mabul* (flood), suggesting that Noah's flood began in this month.

The term *Mar* (bitter) *Cheshvan* is sometimes used because this is the only month in which there are no holidays. According to tradition, the reason there are no holidays in Cheshvan is that the Messiah's inauguration of the Third Temple will take place during Cheshvan. Therefore, the month is reserved for the future celebration of this event.

Nun, the letter associated with Cheshvan, has the numerical equivalent of 50. It has a "final" form (used only at the end of a word), which is basically a straight line that descends below the normal line on which Hebrew letters end.

The original pictograph from which nun is derived is believed to be that of a snake or an eel. In Aramaic, a sister language to Hebrew, *nun* is the word for "snake or eel." Nun is one of seven letters that, in some scribal traditions, get a special crown, a *tahg,* when written in the Torah.

During Hannukah, when the dreidel falls on the letter *nun,* one does nothing. However, the letters of the dreidel are an acronym to remind us of the importance of the holiday: *"Nes Gadol Haya Sham"*: "A great miracle happened there." (In Israel, *nun, gimmel, hey, pey*: A great miracle happened here.)

The nun, for which we do nothing (much like the month of Cheshvan), stands for the word *nes* (miracle). This suggests that in the quietness of rest, relaxation, and reflection great miracles may be born.

The tribe of Menasheh is named after the elder of Joseph's two sons. His name means "causing to forget." The choice of this tribe may be a warning to us not to quickly forget the vows that we made during Tishrei. The letters of the name Menasheh can be rearranged to spell *neshama* (soul). This is a hint to us that in the quiet of Cheshvan, we should continue to listen to the prompting of our soul, which we heard so clearly during the High Holy Days. The respite given to us by a month with no holidays or special religious observances is an opportunity to continue the holy work of repairing our own lives and working together as God's partner in repairing the world.

The sense of smell is associated with Cheshvan. At the beginning of Leviticus we read about the sin offering. The person making this offering puts his hand on the head of the animal, in this case a cow or bull, so that the person's sins may be transferred to the animal. The animal's death and incineration are a substitute for the life of the person who brought the offering. When the animal is being consumed by fire on the altar, the Torah says that this is a *rayach nikoach* (a pleasing scent) for God (Lev. 1:1–9).

The sense of smell is one of the most powerful of our senses, with the power to evoke strong emotions. The smell of cookies fresh from the oven, bread baking, apple pie rich with cinnamon—all are scents that make many of us feel warm and safe. In *Remembrance of Things Past,* Marcel Proust tells a story of how the taste and smell of a piece of a madeline (a scallop-shaped cookie) dipped in tea vividly brought back forgotten memories of childhood.

The sense of smell is very fragile. Anyone who has ever tested several different perfumes knows that after three or four it is hard to tell one from the other. When our sense of smell gets overloaded, we need to take a break, or smell something, like coffee beans, whose smell has the power to refresh our senses. In some ways Cheshvan is a time during which we can "rest" our spiritual sense of smell after the many "assaults" on this sense during the holidays in Tishrei. This rest helps us prepare for the next four months, which feature holidays that require intense focus and spiritual intention as we move from the plenty of the harvest to the difficult time of winter.

THE MONTH OF KISLEV

Astrological sign: Sagittarius, Keshet, the Bow or the Archer; Letter of the alphabet: samech;
Tribe: Benjamin; Part of the body: kivah; Sense: sleep

Kislev is the ninth month in the Jewish calendar. It is the last of the months of the fall period. Hannukah begins on the twenty-fifth day of Kislev and continues into Tevet, the first month of winter. Hannukah is the only holiday that spans two months, although one might also think of Pesach and Shavuot as being connected by the counting of the omer.

During Kislev, we read about a number of dreams in the weekly Torah portions. The subject of dreams in this part of Genesis is extremely rich and varied. Some of the dreams, like Jacob's dream of the stairway and the angels, reveal God's presence in a specific place and in relation to a specific person. Other dreams, like Joseph's dream about the sheaves in the field bending down to him, are prophetic. The third dream-related segment of Genesis deals with Joseph's powers as an interpreter of dreams for Pharaoh's cupbearer and baker.

The holiday of Hannukah can be understood as being about the dreams of an oppressed people fighting for religious freedom. (There are, of course, many other ways to discuss this holiday.) This suggests to us that perhaps Kislev is an appropriate time of the year for us to explore both our sleeping and waking dreams.

The Hebrew letter related to Kislev is *samech*. The letter name is from the same Hebrew root that means "to support, to lean, and to lay one's hands on another [to ordain]." The ceremony of ordination of Jewish clergy, from earliest times, depended upon a teacher physically laying his hands on a student in a ritual that implied the physical transfer of knowledge and power from teacher to student. This ritual is derived from the last section of Deuteronomy. Moses has died, and Joshua becomes the new leader. The Torah comments: "Now Joshua son of Nun was filled with the spirit of wisdom because Moses had laid his hands upon him" (Deut. 34:9).

The sign of the zodiac related to Kislev is *keshet* (the bow; Sagittarius, the archer). During the High Holy Days we confess our sins by saying *"al chet"* for the sins. The rabbis teach that al chet is not only a formula for the confession of a sin, but a confession of having "missed" the spiritual bull's eye, as an archer might miss a target. The Maccabees had a clear objective: the expulsion of the Seleucid Greeks from the Temple in Jerusalem and the re-establishment of traditional Jewish practices throughout the land of Israel.

Although the Maccabees achieved these goals, their descendents, the Hasmoneans, seemed to have lost their moral compass. The Hasmonean Empire, founded in 141 BCE, was marked by murder, fratricide, matricide, and political intrigue. The Maccabees' one-hundred-year decline into moral decay was capped by the act of combining the monarchy and priesthood, a shocking violation of Jewish law by Mattathias in 40 BCE. Just a few years later, the Hasmoneans were deposed by Herod, a non-Jew selected by the Romans as "King of the Jews."

The sign of Sagittarius shows the archer with bow in position to shoot, but we cannot see the target at which he is aiming. The story of the Maccabees and the Hasmonean dynasty reminds us that it is not enough to "aim" for a goal. Rather, it is extremely important that we be able to visualize the goal before we let go of the arrow.

The tribe related to Kislev is that of Benjamin. There are different traditions about Benjamin. In Genesis 42, Jacob sends ten of his sons to Egypt to get food because there is a famine in Israel. He keeps Benjamin, the only remaining son of his beloved Rachel, from going. In explaining this, the Torah comments, "For Jacob did not send Joseph's brother Benjamin with his brothers, since he feared that he [Benjamin] might meet with disaster" (Gen. 42:4).

When Jacob is dying, however, and is blessing his sons, he says of Benjamin, "Benjamin is a ravenous wolf; in the morning he consumes the foe, and in the evening he divides the spoil" (Gen. 49:27). Hardly loving words. Then again, in Deuteronomy when Moses blesses the tribes, he says of Benjamin, "Beloved of the Lord, he rests securely beside Him; ever does He protect him, as he rests between his shoulders" (Deut. 33:12).

The different views of this tribe are resonant with the many different themes related to Kislev. While Hannukah is a festival related to the recapture and re-dedication of the Temple in Jerusalem, it is also the story of a Jewish civil war fought between traditionalists and those who would incorporate Greek ideals into their lives. It is a story of the victory of the weak over the mighty. We can speak of Hannukah in historical terms, thanks to the two books of Maccabees, as well as to the account of the Jewish historian Flavius Josephus, who connects the struggle for the Temple with a festival of lights. Clearly, the tribe of Benjamin was rich in history, as is the festival of Hannukah, the religious focal point of the Kislev.

The word *Kivah,* which describes the part of the body related to this month, has no authoritative translation. Some commentators of the Sefer Yitzirah suggest the term *gall*. Others suggest that this term refers to the right hand.

THE MONTH OF TEVET

Astrological sign: Capricorn, Gedi, the goat; Letter of the alphabet: Ayin;
Tribe: Dan; Part of the body: liver; Sense: anger

Tevet is the tenth month of the Jewish calendar. It begins with the final days of Hannukah. The sign of the zodiac associated with Tevet is *Gedi* (Capricorn, the goat). The name *Tevet* has a Babylonian source. In the Scroll of Esther (chapter 2) the month is referred to as "the tenth month, which is the month of Tevet."

The sign of Capricorn is related to the personal qualities of confidence, calm, perseverance, and reliability. Coming as it does at the time of year that foreshadows spring, the fact that Capricorn is an earth sign is very significant. It absorbs the fire of Sagittarius and channels it into the air of Aquarius, which combines with the elements to bring forth the water of Pisces.

Although Tevet begins with the final days of Hannukah, there are no other holidays or festivals in this month. In fact, the overall mood of the month is one of sadness. There are a number of sad days of note attributed to this month. These include the siege of Jerusalem by Nebuchadnezzer;

the exile of Yechoniah, King of Israel, the sages, and the Jewish noble families; the deaths of Ezra the Scribe and Nechemia, both great leaders of the Jewish people after the destruction of the First Temple; and the translation of the Torah into Greek. (Whether this last is actually a great tragedy depends very much on one's religious and theological orientation.) In Israel today, the tenth of Tevet has been designated as *Yom Hakaddish Haklali*—a public day of mourning for those whose date or place of death is unknown.

In some communities, three fast days are observed. The eighth and the tenth day of Tevet are known as "fast days for the righteous" and are optional. The tenth of Tevet is a public fast for the entire Jewish community during which we mourn those whose date or place of death is unknown.

The sense associated with Tevet is anger. There are many types of anger. Anger can be a destructive emotion when it is expressed in destructive ways. However, it can also be a constructive emotion. One of the most useful expressions of anger is that generated by witnessing wrong acts committed against human beings, against the earth, and against other living things. When our righteous anger is stimulated, we can be led to engage in acts of healing, compassion, and love.

THE MONTH OF SHEVAT

Astrological sign: Aquarius, Deli, the Pail, the water carrier;
Letter of the alphabet: Tzadee;
Tribe: Asher; Part of the body: possibly right foot; Sense: taste

Shevat is the eleventh month of the Jewish calendar. The fifteenth day of Shevat is the new year of trees (*Tu B'Shevat*). The purpose of this holiday is much like that of Rosh Hodesh Elul. One of the most important of the Temple offerings was that of the *bikurim* (the first fruits). All trees become one year older on Tu B'Shevat. The name of the holiday comes from the combination of two Hebrew letters that spell out the number 15, the date on which the holiday is celebrated: *Tet* (9) + *Vav* (6) = 15. The letters together can be pronounced "tu."

The holiday of Tu B'Shevat is not mentioned in the Torah, but it is discussed in the Mishna (Tractate Rosh Hashana 1:1). The school of Hillel set the date at the fifteenth of the month of Shevat. The school of Shammai set it at the first of Shevat, Rosh Hodesh Shevat. Over time, the view of Hillel was the one that became the traditional date for observing this holiday.

Because this holiday was also called a Rosh Hashanah (New Year), the idea developed that it should be celebrated in some way. During the seventeenth century in Israel, Rabbi Isaac Luria, the great kabbalistic leader, created a Tu B'Shevat seder during which various fruits were eaten, including the seven native fruits of Israel: pomegranates, grapes, figs, dates, wheat, barley, and olives. The idea of a Tu B'Shevat seder has gained popularity through the years. There are now many Tu B'Shevat *Haggadot* for home and community use.

The tradition of planting trees on Tu B'Shevat began in the late nineteenth century and was quickly adopted by the Jewish National Fund, which today sponsors many projects in Israel related to land use, water, reforestation, and ecological education.

Eating and the sense of taste are related to Shevat. During the Tu B'Shevat seder we eat many different types of foods, especially those from trees. In the kabbalistic seder, there is an idea that each food that we eat has a spiritual aspect that becomes incorporated into our body when we ingest it. In this way, the spiritual content of each food becomes part of us.

There are three different categories of foods in the seder: fruit with a hard shell, fruit with a pit and a soft shell, and food that can be completely eaten. These three types of foods can be interpreted in many ways. For example, the fruit with an inedible shell can describe a person who keeps others out of his or her life. The fruit with a pit can be understood as symbolizing one who seeks union with the Holy One but who maintains a hard "inner core" that does not permit the person to give himself or herself completely to this union. The fruit that can be completely eaten might be seen as representing a person for whom there are no defensive barriers in a relationship.

THE MONTH OF ADAR

Astrological sign: Pisces, Dagim, the fish; Letter of the alphabet: koof; Tribe: Naftali; Part of the body: spleen; Sense: laughter

The month of Adar is the twelfth month of the Jewish calendar. In a leap year, when an additional month of Adar is added, both Adar I and Adar II are considered to be the twelfth month. Adar II is the month that is added in the leap year.

Adar is considered to be a month filled with happiness and laughter. As a famous saying goes, "When Adar comes, joy is increased." The joyous holiday of Purim, which is based on the biblical Book of Esther, commemorates the salvation of the Jews of Persia from extermination by evil forces led by Haman, a descendent of our ancient enemy Amelek.

The astrological symbol of two fish swimming in opposite directions has many different meanings. One of the fish is swimming toward the "future" while the other is swimming into the "past." Adar, the last month of the Hebrew calendar, is linked to the first of the month, Nissan, by the fish that, swimming in opposite directions, will eventually meet.

Adar and Nissan are also linked by parallel stories of redemption. In Adar, the Jewish people are saved from extinction through human intervention (as told in the Book of Esther). In Nissan, the Jewish people are saved by intervention of the Holy One, as told in the story of the Exodus.

Fish have a special aura of holiness. There is a tradition that during the famous flood, fish were not destroyed because they did not participate in the evil behaviors of land animals. It is for this reason that we entrust our sins to fish on Rosh Hashanah during the ritual of *tashlich*. We throw our sins into the water and the fish "eat" them so that fewer transgressions will appear on our page of "bad deeds," thus moderating the severity of God's judgment.

The sense of laughter associated with Purim derives from the tradition of merrymaking that is such an important part of the holiday celebration. The drinking of wine and other intoxicants is a ritualized part of the holiday, which often leads to laughter. The Talmud teaches: "On Purim, one has an obligation to become intoxicated to the point that he does not know the difference between 'Blessed is Mordechai and Cursed is Haman'" (Megillah 7b).

Our heightened awareness of substance abuse in the Jewish community today makes this commandment very problematic. It is important to note that this is a rabbinic ruling that is not based in the Torah. Therefore, it may be set aside, if necessary, for the greater good of individuals and the community. While many people will quote the Talmud's so-called commandment to get drunk on Purim, very few take note of the related story. A rabbi became so drunk on Purim that he killed his best friend. Horrified at what he had done, he prayed until his friend was brought back to life. The next year, he asked his friend to join him at a Purim party. His friend declined by noting, "Miracles do not happen all the time" (Megilla 7b). There are many ways to have fun on Purim. Getting drunk does not need to be one of them.

REFLECTIONS FOR THE MONTHS OF THE YEAR

As we've seen, each month has a wealth of possibilities for spiritual growth, reflection, study, and personal and group action. As part of a personal or group ritual, a prayer relating to an aspect of the month may be offered. What follow are thematic ideas for a prayer for each month, as well as a sample prayer for the month of Nissan.

NISSAN—PRAYER FOR SPIRITUAL AND EMOTIONAL FREEDOM

Concepts: slavery and redemption for oneself, for the community, for the world; strength and healing.

Sample Prayer for a Group Rosh Hodesh Ritual for Nissan   We give
thanks to the One who led us out of slavery in Egypt and guided our steps
toward redemption. May it be the will of our Redeemer to help us sense
the possibilities for healing and redemption in our daily lives. May we be
given the strength to work for our personal salvation and for the healing of
the world. Reveal to us the path of our lives, the path that will lead us to
sweetness, healing, and joy. Amen.

IYAR—A PRAYER ABOUT COUNTING

Concepts: What do numbers mean to us? How do we "account" for our
lives, our actions? How do we understand our challenges and blessings?

SIVAN—A PRAYER FOR REVELATION

Concepts: Understanding the world and our place in it, understanding the
purpose of our lives, re-dedication to Torah and Jewish learning.

TAMUZ—A PRAYER ABOUT MEMORY

Concepts: Dealing with tragedy, memory, and healing; our birthright as Jews.

AV—A PRAYER ABOUT MOVING FROM SORROW TO JOY

Concepts: The meaning of Jewish community; the Holocaust; the importance of Israel for Jewish individuals, the Jewish community, and the non-
Jewish world; the healing power of love.

ELUL—A PRAYER ABOUT SPIRITUAL SEEKING

Concepts: the spiritual search, one's relationship to individuals and the
community, the power of forgiveness, forgiving others, forgiving ourselves.

TISHREI—PRAYER FOR HEALING AND HOPE IN THE NEW YEAR

Concepts: The nature of sin, creation and redemption, renewal, one's relationship with the Divine, our relationships with those close to us.

CHESHVAN—A PRAYER FOR BALANCE

Concepts: The importance of balance in our lives and in the world, creating a quiet space, retreat and relaxation.

KISLEV—A PRAYER ABOUT DARKNESS AND LIGHT

Concepts: Israel, the role of darkness and light in the world; building
hope, faith, and community.

TEVET—A PRAYER ABOUT STRUGGLING TOWARD NEW BEGINNINGS

Concepts: Liberating ourselves from darkness, death and rebirth, cycles.

SHEVAT—A PRAYER ABOUT SPIRITUAL SPRING CLEANING

Concepts: Renewal, nurturing hope, the "Promised Land," stewardship of the earth.

ADAR—A PRAYER ABOUT EMBRACING CONFUSION

Concepts: The world turned upside down, changing our parameters, sobriety, the nature of joy.

Sample Prayer for Adar   Hi, Blessed One! Are You still watching out for me? Lately the world has seemed to be a pretty crazy place! How about arranging a day when only nice things happen in the world? With all the silliness going on, it would help me to have a little clarity. Also, a winning lottery ticket would be nice. Good health for my loved ones and me would be very much appreciated. Are we okay with *our* relationship? Is there anything special I can do for you? I saw some early crocus blossoms today. Thank you. They were lovely. See Ya soon. Amen.

CHAPTER 14

A Renewed Mikvah

Leah Lax

Mikvah: An ancient ritual bath in which Jewish women traditionally immerse after their monthly cycle and before the resumption of sexual relations. It is also used for conversion.

Mikvah: Passed down from mother to daughter for over three thousand years as a private, often secret practice. Today, mikvah has expanded for non-orthodox Jews to include men and women immersing to mark life transition.

The small, tiled pool is filled with warm water to shoulder height. A woman stands alone, poised on the steps leading into this bath that Jewish women have been using for millennia. Under the six-foot-square pool hides one more container, a collection of "living water" from a natural source. Through a conduit, this water "kisses" the filtered, chlorinated water in the immersion pool.

The woman descends the steps and slowly sinks beneath the surface with knees pulled up and arms outward, submerged in the water, in herself, in God. Then she stands, covers her head with a cloth, crosses her arms over her bare chest, and recites the ancient, prescribed blessing. Again she slips beneath the water. For a moment, she is poised there as if the water can sustain her. And then she emerges, fresh and sensual and real.

THE MIKVAH IN HISTORY

The practice of mikvah immersion has been a strong, silent presence in the history of Jewish life. Since ancient times, married Jewish women who live according to the tenets of Jewish law have gone once each month, in private and at night, to immerse in a mikvah. They go seven days after the conclusion of their menses, following two weeks of physical separation from their spouses. So the mikvah immersion is often a joyous thing, marking as it does the transition point to the resumption of sexual relations.

In the Shulchan Aruch, the centuries-old sourcebook of Jewish law, it is stated that if a group of Jews wants to establish a new community and funds are limited, building a mikvah is to take priority over the purchase of a Torah scroll. To the modern, Jewish mind, this is an extraordinary statement.

Through most of the twentieth century, mikvah practice was upheld in the orthodox Jewish community but largely ignored or forgotten elsewhere in the Jewish world. For many, mikvah had become an embarrassing vestige of another era that was assumed to be one of ignorance, less bodily cleanliness, and misogyny, as if the Code of Jewish Law had once deemed it necessary to issue a ruling for women to bathe at least once a month, and as if, beneath the ruling requiring separation of husband and wife during her menses hid superstitious fear of women's blood. Mikvah seemed to stand against the new feminism. The more secular, modernized Jewish movements sought distance from mikvah and its attendant, myriad laws governing sexual relations and the timing of immersion. Reform and Conservative rabbinical seminaries did not include these laws in their curriculam. Knowledge of the intimate and powerful position mikvah once held throughout the Jewish world fell away.

But the Torah scroll, the second-place priority in Jewish law, of course retained its honored position as the primary source of Jewish wisdom. Historically, its teachings have clarified the boundaries and identity of the Jewish community in a larger and often hostile world, and that contribution continues. A Torah scroll is feted, dressed, and housed in beauty at the center point of a synagogue built to contain it, and it is read with fanfare at the center point of the Sabbath service. Thus, the injunction in Jewish law to finance a mikvah before a Torah scroll became a paradox, ignored. Forgotten was the once-fundamental connection of mikvah immersion to sexual relations and conception, which is why it was the mikvah that was deemed the guarantor of a future for any Jewish congregation, and why the injunction was made to make mikvah a communal priority.

But the position of honor for mikvah in Jewish law is rooted in that Torah scroll. In chapter 15 of Leviticus, there is a list of situations in which a person might suffer an "emission" that rendered one ineligible to enter the ancient Temple in Jerusalem. A woman who has her menses is included in that list. Everyone on the list, male or female, is enjoined in the text to immerse in a mikvah to attain sufficient spiritual cleanliness before entering the Temple or presenting a sacrifice.

Besides suffering an emission, there were other situations that, according to the Torah text, require immersion in a mikvah, such as someone who has had contact with the dead. A *cohen* priest (high priest), who had to enter the Temple each day, would immerse in a mikvah every morning. Archeologists have unearthed dozens of mikvahs in the vicinity around the Temple mount.

This requirement of mikvah immersion to guarantee purity for the Temple is part of the Purity Laws in Leviticus, expanded upon at length in the Mishnah. After the destruction of the Temple by the Romans in 70 CE, the Purity Laws became obsolete. Individuals no longer needed to prepare themselves to enter the Temple.

In chapter 18 of Leviticus, we find another grouping of laws: the Holiness Code. These laws legislate specific values and modes of conduct and dress that were to be unique to the Jewish nation. All are part of a general message: if Jews do not define themselves as different from surrounding cultures, they will be absorbed, assimilated, and the Jewish nation will be lost. After the destruction of the Second Temple and final disbursing of Jews into other countries, after the Purity Laws became obsolete, the Holiness Code remained as a means of preserving Jewish identity.

In this Holiness Code is a second injunction relating to a menstruating woman: if a man has sexual relations with a *niddah*, a menstruating woman who has not yet been to the mikvah, he will be spiritually cut off from the Jewish people, an appropriate warning for one who might drift away from Jewish identity. The relevance of the Holiness Code in Jewish law as a hedge against assimilation is one explanation as to why mikvah immersion for married women, which is part of that code, continued to be observed even after the Purity Laws fell away, that is, even after all the other reasons in the law that required ritual immersion were deemed no longer relevant.

It is true that, from the old root of the Purity Laws, there continued to be men who immersed in a mikvah to attain a higher spiritual plane, parallel to ancient "purity" or *taharah*. They used mikvah as a preparation for prayer, for Torah study, or for the Sabbath and Holy Days. But they did so on a voluntary basis, without any legal injunction. The rule of Jewish law gave more urgency and greater spiritual status to women's immersions.

Because of mikvah's connection to sexual relations, a body of detailed laws and guidelines governing sexual behavior grew around the laws of mikvah immersion. Many of the laws seek to protect the male from the possibility of contact with menstrual blood, and in them hide ancient fears of female bodies and their mysteries. The assertion in the Torah text that a man who lies with a menstruating woman will suffer spiritual death fed, and can continue to feed, those fears. But many other of the laws seek to elevate the sexual act, preserve its modesty, and protect the woman. Men are enjoined to give their wives pleasure, and never to attempt sex without their consent.

Over centuries, Jewish law related to mikvah contributed to the marginalizing of women in Jewish life. In classic Jewish law, all Jewish, married women, when they are out in public, officially carry the status of niddah, one who has not yet been to the mikvah; an untouchable. Therefore the law requires that women in public spaces keep their bodies covered, never touch a man, sing, or touch a Torah scroll. Jewish law requires married women to cover their hair and forbids any woman from being alone in a room with a man who is not her husband. These laws precluded women from participation in the synagogue, or from working closely with any man in a public setting. And the laws gave rise to negative superstitions about the niddah status. There are many comments in Jewish texts reinforcing such attitudes.

But orthodox communities also understood the powerful place of mikvah in Jewish law and have always upheld mikvah as the key to a Jewish future. Positive superstitions arose as well, attributing mikvah immersion with great spiritual strength, a source of blessings on a family, and insisting that mikvah immersion guarantees a pure soul for the child that is conceived afterward. The strictness and urgency in the law of immersion is why there is a long history of startling stories of Jewish women who risked their lives to immerse in a mikvah under dire conditions; these are women who felt they held within themselves, through their mikvah immersion, the future of the Jewish people.

From the beginning, alongside the written law, the realm of rabbis and male scholars, was the unwritten body of associations, values, and apocryphal stories that were attached to the actual observance of this rite, and this unwritten "law" was the realm of the women who kept it. Many prayers have been written by and for women to recite in the mikvah. The mikvah became a beloved, feminine space. Women came to see the mikvah as a private sanctum, a place of spiritual "cleansing," where God listens with special attention. Mikvah, in this context, was devoid of negative superstitions and became a source of great spiritual—and sexual—power.

A custom of immersion for orthodox men as a personal preparation for prayer has continued until today. Some families have a tradition of immersion before the Sabbath and holidays. Unlike the women, orthodox men will immerse in small groups of family or community members, and often value the sharing of this private ritual and the deep sense of group spirituality.

Along with a new sensitivity to feminist consciousness, orthodox presentation of mikvah has changed in recent years. Books from orthodox sources now emphasize traditional mikvah observance as respectful of women's boundaries, encouraging better communication between partners, and as an erotic enhancement to the married relationship. The period of separation is presented as one that fosters desire and leads to a monthly renewal in the marriage. Perhaps this change prepared the way for the more recent interest in mikvah immersion in the Jewish community at large.

Today, a rejuvenation of mikvah observance crosses all denominational lines and all genders in Judaism, and mikvah has firmly emerged beyond the exclusive realm of the orthodox. A new generation has chosen to dispose of ancient intimations of misogyny and fear of menstrual blood and focus on the raw power of this nude immersion in warm water. Community mikvahs have been built around the country to accommodate all types of Jewish congregations, and many old mikvahs have been renovated to meet the demand.

For Reform, Conservative, Reconstructionist, Renewal, and non-denominational Jews, immersion has expanded beyond the restrictions of Jewish law to apply to life situations, such as a marker of transition points or as a spiritual means of healing from trauma. Both women and men immerse, alone or sometimes in groups led by a spiritual leader. There has also been a resurgence of traditional mikvah immersion before marriage, before conversions, and as a monthly ritual related to a woman's cycle.

To immerse today is to continue a connection to generations past. Unlike the traditional body/spirit dichotomy, immersion is silent prayer deeply connected to the body and to sexuality. The act is primal and birth-like in its emersion from warm water into the world.

The ritual of immersion in its resurgence is a powerful tool in the modern search for spirituality and its meaning. Mikvah becomes in itself a meditation.

OUT OF THE SILENCE

I was raised in a secular, Jewish home, more imprinted with liberal politics and my mother's love of art and culture than I was by Judaism. At fifteen, on a fervent, adolescent spiritual quest, I discovered Orthodox Judaism and the vast body of Jewish law. It promised clarity, firm answers to unanswerable questions, a defined path just as I was setting out to adulthood. By seventeen, I had graduated, left home, and entered a Hasidic community. At eighteen, I accepted the ultimate fulfillment of a Hasidic girl—an arranged marriage, which took place one month after my nineteenth birthday. There I remained for twenty-seven years and raised seven children. My mother grieved.

My first mikvah immersion occurred just before my wedding. There was little room for visceral response to that first entry into the mikvah water. My mind was full of the detailed laws that I had studied in advance governing the act, how to prepare oneself beforehand, how to immerse, what to meditate on, what blessing to recite, and, my greatest fear, what might invalidate the immersion. All I wanted was to get it right. I was promised that this immersion would make of my body a holy gift to my new husband and bring blessings on our children that would come. I was awed into silence.

Through the years, mikvah changed for me. Housed in a small, back room in our synagogue with an outdoor entrance, our mikvah became a quiet, separate space from my busy life. The water seemed otherwordly, apart from time or space, where I was suspended, if just for a moment; it seemed appropriate to me, it seemed true, that the mikvah was deemed a place where one was closer to God.

In time, the mikvah lost its connection, for me, to my marriage or to our sexual relationship. Instead, it became a place of meditation and prayer. In the mikvah, I stood stripped of all the pretenses I was forced to build as I struggled to maintain outward loyalty to commitments I had come to doubt. There I was exposed; I found honesty before God. The more I engaged in the spiritual struggle that would result in my departure from the Hasidic community and re-evaluation of my entire life as a Jew, the longer I stood each month, alone, in that warm water.

In December 1999, before I departed my marriage and community, I gave my friend Janice Rubin a copy of "Munya's Story," my short story about a mikvah attendant who confronts a survivor of sexual abuse. In it, the survivor seeks to use mikvah as a way to heal. Janice read the story and was intrigued to discover that women were stretching the parameters of traditional mikvah for personal spiritual needs. She is a photographer; we began to brainstorm the possibilities of mikvah and photography.

I decided to help Janice, who wanted to simulate the ritual immersion with models so that she could photograph them in the mikvah. I watched from the rail, or sometimes waded in and held the light equipment, as Janice sat under the water at the bottom of the mikvah with a waterproof camera and wearing goggles and weights on her ankles and wrists. The models were clearly moved by this experience. As each woman went through the act of immersion over and over, in and out of the water, I saw before me a swirl of elements: the female body, ancient water, whispers of birth, death, rejuvenation, transcendence.

To me, the figures in her photographs, hovering beneath the water's surface, appear inner-focused in a new dimension, unconscious of their nudity, as if engaged in silent prayer. It was the power of those images that lured me into accepting her invitation to expand the project and conduct interviews of women around the country who had been to the mikvah.

After years of lecturing on the topic, years in which I accompanied hundreds of women to the mikvah as a personal attendant, I was moving away from my enthusiasm for orthodox mikvah usage. I had seen the demands that mikvah laws could make on a relationship; I had watched the way it was possible to drown oneself in the mikvah and in Jewish law. The silence and modesty that surrounded traditional mikvah observance now seemed to resonate with unspoken complexity. In the end, I decided that The Mikvah Project could be an exploration for both Janice and me. Perhaps I might give a voice to so many women who never had the courage to speak before.

So, we set out, interviewing women in New York, Chicago, Denver, Houston, and Los Angeles. About half of our subjects were orthodox women for whom mikvah was a monthly religious obligation, and the other half were Jewish women who had gone to the mikvah for other reasons. Some of the more secular group went each month, although they did not consider themselves "orthodox," or committed to broad adherence to Jewish law. Others had single experiences in a mikvah as part of a personal, creative ritual.

To me, at the time, the mikvah held a firm stamp as a woman's place. If I had it to do again today, I would also ask men to tell me their stories. The experience of the mikvah transcends gender; I know that today. But men have not been silenced and marginalized over generations by mikvah laws. Men have not felt the necessity of law, or risked their lives for mikvah, or ever been told that their bodies must be purified for birthing a new generation. At the time, I found it more compelling to focus on women. Besides, I was seeking to hear snatches of my own voice in those interviews; something else I only know now, looking back.

Just about every woman that I interviewed had never spoken about the mikvah to anyone before. The long history of silence has crept into the mikvah experience of the most secular women. Most had tears when they told their stories to me. Most eventually came, in the interview, to that awed moment when they said that, in the mikvah, "It's just me and God." There seemed to be a kind of raw confrontation that occurred there. "In the mikvah," one of the women told us, "you can't hide. Not from yourself, and not from God." Many felt that momentary sense of being in another dimension. The mikvah is so full of Jewish history and so private at the same time that it can seem to be a place that is clean of connection to the present world.

All the types of mikvah immersion in Jewish law signal a change of status, such as from non-Jew to Jew in the conversion ritual, from unmarried to married, from *tameh*, a status that forbids sexual relations, to *tahor*, when sexual relations are permitted. That function continued into all the personal and creative usages of mikvah that we found. Each woman sought out the water to mark a change in life. One woman who went to the mikvah after a divorce told us, "I needed something to divide that portion of my life from what was to come. From that point on, I could look forward instead of backward." Women compared the warm mikvah water to fetal waters and the emergence to birth. Many spoke of the sense of renewal, strengthening, and discovery of a spiritual core.

I dreamed I was walking through a contaminated mikvah, and all around me were members of my Hasidic community. The monthly obligation to go to mikvah, and the obsessive hours of attention to the details of preparation for it required in our Hasidic community—every dot of makeup or polish, every scab or bump on the skin or rough cuticle, had to be removed, smoothed, and inspected by an attendant—besides running there at night on a prescribed date regardless of fatigue, tedium, or health, made mikvah observance a challenge. The mikvah's spiritual core had receded. These interviews were bringing it back to me.

Mikvah seems old-fashioned, and the attendant laws governing sexual relationships, laws that define clear boundaries and insist on modesty and mutual respect, can seem old-fashioned as well. "Mikvah entails monogamy," one woman told me. "It says that sex is holy and private. As a teen growing up in the sixties, no one I knew believed that. I was going to move to New York, become a poet, and never let anybody hurt me."

This woman talked to me about how pressured she felt in her early years by the sexual permissiveness of the era. Sex seemed to have become a kind of currency. For her, the period of abstention during the menses that is required before traditional mikvah immersion became a declaration that no one has free license to her body. She spoke at length about the eroticized female forms that bombard our culture and the pain that media-generated female images have caused her. She felt the nude confrontation with God in the mikvah like a validation. I thought of those unself-conscious, ethereal images Janice took in the mikvah. The woman called immersion an embrace.

Very few of my subjects talked about the mikvah in the context of their marital relationship. Several spoke of the excited anticipation they had felt at the mikvah as a new bride, but I was not surprised that mikvah gradually became a solitary, feminine rite for so many. I see that, not as a waning, but as a gradual appropriation of mikvah for oneself, a move beyond awed purification of one's body like a sacrifice. I was not alone in finding the pool an ideal place of prayer. "As Jews," one woman told me, "we always put things on to pray—a *kippah*, a prayer shawl—but for me, my best place of prayer is in the mikvah, wearing nothing at all."

As a product of this society, I still retained that Westernized, Christian concept that all things physical and body-related are base, that to attain a life of the spirit is to seek moments of transcendence that constitute an escape from this physical world and from the body and its desires; the spiritual nobility in an ascetic life. It is not fair to call this idea specifically Christian; I had heard it often in the Hasidic world in stories of venerated holy men who lived a life apart, a life of letters, while maintaining just the barest obligatory connection to wife and world. But then I found an unmarried woman who went to the mikvah every month as a way of re-orienting herself with God. She performed the preparations for mikvah required in Jewish law—the careful manicure, pedicure, and thorough bathing—as part of the ritual itself; her *bathing*, and her body, was a form of prayer. As she removed her nail polish and filed her nails, she asked herself, "What did these hands do in the past month? What or whom did they fail to reach out to? What will I commit them to for the month to come?" Then she made a promise to herself and to God. *And these feet,* she thought. *Where did they run?* She continued in this vein in the bathtub as she scrubbed each part of her body. When she was finished, she was ready to meet God in the mikvah, nude, exposed, body and spirit as one. I began to feel that mikvah transcends the Western spirit/body dichotomy in a most feminine way. Her nude body became a source of prayer, her most essential tool to connect with the spiritual. I was finally moving toward healing the impetus to escape my physical reality in order to find God.

For the women I found who went to mikvah in this mode of body-as-prayer, who had that level of awareness, new discoveries had to be waiting. One Hasidic young woman, newly married, told me, "Before my marriage, when I faced going to mikvah, I thought I was going to have this amazing spiritual experience. Now I know that I don't even know what that means. When I went on the night before my wedding, I cried the whole time, and I didn't know why I was crying. Sexuality hadn't entered my life yet, but I was going to the mikvah in order that it would. I had this overwhelming sense that I was going into the water a girl, and coming out a woman."

Then I encountered another woman who also spoke of an awakening in the mikvah.

This ultra-orthodox woman, who lived in Jerusalem, had repressed her homosexuality in order to comply with Jewish law. She married and birthed five children. Every month when she went to the mikvah, she prayed that the water would transform her. "I begged God to let me go under the water and come up straight," she told me. Then one mikvah night, she raised her head from beneath the water, stood up, and ... "I cried and cried," she said. "I couldn't stop. I had come up straight, all right—straight in my mind with who and what I am. I knew then that this, too, is from God, and that I would be all right."

Only now, when I look back, do I understand that traveling the country and listening to women talk about mikvah helped me to clarify my own situation. The mikvah laws, for me, created a kind of sexuality in a box, pre-packaged, ready-defined. Sexuality can be celebrated, Jewish law had told me, but only on certain days of the month at certain times and in specific ways. At any other than the prescribed times, and in any other manner other than what is legislated, sexuality, in my Hasidic world, was suppressed. I was lulled into that, silenced by Jewish law. After hearing the stories of these two awakenings, I continued to go to the mikvah myself, but each time I came more to life.

Although they were in the minority, I found a number of women who disliked the mikvah laws. One women said that when she was ten years old, she found a book in their home that detailed the mikvah laws. "The part that shocked and disturbed me," she said, "was the discussion about the internal examinations you are supposed to make with a small cloth for seven days before immersing, to make sure you are not bleeding any more. I got really scared, and I didn't feel comfortable asking anyone about it. Instead, I said, 'I am not growing up.' I had a lot of negative feelings about my sexuality after that through much of my adolescence."

Some had a hard time with attendants. The lesbian woman who cried in a mikvah in Jerusalem was chastised by her mikvah attendant. Another woman said, "I came to mikvah before my wedding with a deep feeling that something was special here. But I was alone, without family. The mikvah attendant said, 'You're not such a young bride, are you?' This wasn't the celebration I wanted."

Another woman told me, "I felt exposed sitting in that waiting room with the other women. It reminded me too much of African menstrual huts."

There were women who felt intruded upon by the laws, and women who felt unfairly exposed before a stranger (the attendant), and women who felt lonely during the separation each month. But then I met a woman who was approaching menopause who had gone to the mikvah throughout her long marriage. After menopause, when she no longer would have a cycle, she would stop going to the mikvah, and they would no longer separate from one another beforehand. She acknowledged that the separation period was difficult, but said that she was going to miss it very much because it reminded her of her desire for her husband. "When else," she said, "except when he is out of town, do I have that reminder, that opportunity to long for him? I treasure that longing," she said. "It is frustrating, agonizing, wonderful." Overall, still, The Mikvah Project was reframing the issue for me. I saw then that only those who harbor desire for their husbands in the first place will feel the strain of separation, and find in it the joy of reunion.

I was particularly moved by those women who had gone to mikvah as a means of healing from or coping with past trauma. One spoke of dragging herself to mikvah each month while she was suffering abject pain. She asserted that the mikvah helped her through the ordeal. "During my illness," she said, "I was this howling, hurt, trapped animal—a completely physical creature. Then, for the moment when my head slipped under the surface of the mikvah water, I became a spiritual person. I had escaped." I took note of how the pain had made her suicidal. The immersion into a place devoid of air seemed like a death wish fulfilled, followed, each time, by rebirth. No wonder it had helped her through.

Then I met a woman in her seventies who went one time to the mikvah before her recent marriage. She spoke about how mikvah helped her to face the inevitability of death. "The way I felt when I went in the mikvah, I'm sure that in the womb that is how you feel, and we're going back there. It felt like home, like after you die, and we'll feel at peace, without worry or anything. That is where we are going back. I'm sure."

I had traversed every phase of life and all kinds of life passages with these women. The warm silence of mikvah immersion with its simple, whispered blessing allowed each to find in it what she needed. I began The Mikvah Project with Janice Rubin intent on breaking what I took to be an oppressive silence among Jewish women about mikvah, a silence that was a legacy of generations. It is true that we allowed many women to speak what had been unspeakable for them. But in the end, the only silence I truly broke was my own. In the end, I found the silence in a mikvah to be the silence of the womb, of the spirit, of a peaceful death, and I returned to that.

TODAY

The Mikvah Project featuring Janice Rubin's photography began to tour the United States in 2000 and is still ongoing. Today, it has shown in twenty-four cities. As the exhibit has traveled, we have often traveled with it, always discovering more stories. There was the retired military man who told me about how he assisted a general in the liberation of a concentration camp after World War II because he spoke Yiddish. The emaciated inmates approached him on the first day with a request: they wanted a mikvah. The U.S. Army built them one, right on the grounds of the concentration camp. There is the woman I met, who seemed quite rational, who hears thousands of ghosts each time she immerses, from all the generations of Jewish women who have come before her in the mikvah, all whispering to her.

Mikvah is an ongoing story.

I fantasize sometimes about returning to the mikvah. I said I would go after we completed the Jewish divorce ceremony. I did not. I said I would go several years later when my new partner and I exchanged rings and made a private commitment. That was a good time to go—when I had finally come to live the blessings in my body and found the depth of desire. I didn't. I said I would go when the day comes that we can attain a legally binding marriage, or when my cycle stopped with its monthly reminders about life and death. Now I don't know. When I go back to mikvah, I will find there a modest, Hasidic bride, and I will find a lonely, tired mother of a large brood that she loves to distraction. I will find a woman who stands each month in silence, unable, because of the mikvah, to ignore doubts and desires that may dismantle her life; she turns them, helpless, over to God. And all these women who were once me will recede into the crowd of generations of women, all whispering there. I don't know if I can do that.

Suggested Reading

Adelman, Penina V. *Miriam's Well: Rituals for Jewish Women around the Year*. New York: Biblio Press, 1986.

Anderson, Sherry Ruth, and Patricia Hopkins. *The Feminine Face of God: The Unfolding of the Sacred in Women*. New York: Bantam, 1991.

Antonelli, Judith. *In the Image of God: A Feminist Commentary on the Torah*. Lanham, MD: Jason Aronson Publishers, 1997.

Bartell, Mark. "What Is Spiritual Suffering?" *Journal of Pastoral Care & Counseling* 58, no. 3 (Fall 2004): 87–201.

Baskin, Judith, Shelly Tenenbaum, and Rela M. Geffen. *Gender and Jewish Studies: A Curriculum Guide*. Mt. Vernon, NY: Biblio Press, 1994.

Baskin, Judith, Shelly Tenenbaum, and Rela M. Geffen. *Jewish Women in Historical Perspective*. Wayne, IN: Wayne State University Press, 1998.

Baum, Charlotte, Paula Hyman, and Sonya Michel. *The Jewish Woman in America*. New York: New American Library, 1975.

Bednarowski, Mary Farrell. *The Religious Imagination of American Women*. Bloomington: Indiana University Press, 1999.

Bialik, Hayim. *The Book of Legends*. New York: Schocken Books, 1992.

Borowitz, Eugene. *The Jewish Moral Values*. Philadelphia: Jewish Publication Society, 1999.

Borowitz, Eugene. *Studies in the Meaning of Judaism*. Philadelphia: Jewish Publication Society, 2002.

Braude, Ann. *Women and American Religion*. New York: Oxford University Press, 2000.

British Broadcasting Corporation. *Religion & Ethics, Judaism, Jewish Faith and God*. London: BBC, 2006. http://www.bbc.co.uk/religion.

Brody, Jane. "Get a Grip: Set Your Sights above Adversity." *New York Times*. Tuesday, 1 March 2005. Science Section.

Broner, E. M. *Bringing Home the Light: A Jewish Woman's Handbook of Rituals.* Tulsa, OK: Council Oak Books, 1999.

Buber, Martin. *The Way of Man According to the Teaching of Hasidism.* New York: Citadel Press, Kinsington Publishing Corp., 1994.

Byrne, Patricia Huff. "'Give Sorrow Words': Lament—Contemporary Need for Job's Old Time Religion." *Journal of Pastoral Care & Counseling* 56, no. 3 (Fall 2002): 255–64.

Cantor, Aviva. *Jewish Women/Jewish Men: The Legacy of Patriarchy in Jewish Life.* New York: HarperOne, 1999.

Care Databases (1962–1999). "Implications for Health Care Ministry." *Journal of Pastoral Care & Counseling* 56, no. 3 (Fall 2002): 227–32.

Carnes, Robin Deen, and Sally Craig. *Sacred Circles: A Guide to Creating Your Own Women's Spirituality Group.* New York: HarperOne, 1998.

Christ, Carol P., and Judith Plaskow, eds. *Womanspirit Rising: A Feminist Reader in Religion.* New York: HarperCollins, 1992.

Curzon, David, ed. *Modern Poems on the Bible: An Anthology.* "The Book of Ruth and Naomi," Marge Piercy. Philadelphia: Jewish Publication Society, 1994.

Deutsch, Nathaniel. *The Maiden of Ludmir: A Jewish Holy Woman and Her World.* University of California Press, 2003.

Dittes, James E. *Pastoral Counseling: The Basics.* Louisville, KY: Westminster John Knox Press, 1999.

Firestone, Tirzah. *The Receiving: Reclaiming Jewish Women's Wisdom.* San Francisco: HarperCollins, 2003.

Fish, Harold, ed. *The Holy Scriptures.* Jerusalem: Koren Publishers, 1992.

Fishbane, Michael. "Prayer." *Contemporary Jewish Religious Thought,* ed. Arthur A. Cohen and Paul Mendes-Flohr. New York: Charles Scribner's Sons, 1987.

Fogg, Sarah, et al. "An Analysis of Referrals to Chaplains in a Community Hospital in New York over a Seven Year Period." *Journal of Pastoral Care & Counseling* 58, no. 3 (Fall 2004): 225–35.

Frymer-Kensky, Tikva. *Reading the Women of the Bible: A New Interpretation of Their Stories.* New York: Schocken Books, 2002.

Geller, Laura. "Encountering the Divine Presence." In *Four Centuries of Jewish Women's Spirituality,* edited by Ellen M. Unamsky and Dianne Ashton. Boston: Beason Press, 1992.

Gottlieb, Lynn. *She Who Dwells Within: A Feminist Vision of a Renewed Judaism.* San Francisco: HarperSanFrancisco, 1995.

Greenberg, Blu. *On Women and Judaism: A View from Tradition.* Philadelphia: Jewish Publication Society, 1981.

Greenstone, Julius H., Emil G. Hirsch, and Solomon Schechter. "Hospitality," The Jewish Encyclopedia, 2002, http://JewishEncyclopedia.com.

Grossman, Susan, and Rivka Haut, eds. *Daughters of the King: Women and the Synagogue.* Philadelphia: Jewish Publication Society, 1992.

Hamlen, Geraldine G. "Challenges to Preparing and Conducting Christian Worship in Nursing Homes." *Journal of Pastoral Care & Counseling* 58, no. 4 (Winter 2004): 325–34.

Hammer, Jill. *Sisters at Sinai: New Tales of Biblical Women*. Philadelphia: Jewish Publication Society, 2001.

Hauptman, Judith. *Rereading the Rabbis: A Woman's Voicemail*. Boulder, CO: Westview Press, 1998.

Hebrew-English Tanakh. Philadelphia: Jewish Publication Society, 1985.

Kates, Judith A., and Gail Twersky Reimer, eds. *Reading Ruth: Contemporary Women Reclaim a Sacred Story*. New York: Ballantine Books, 1994.

Kensky, Tikva Freymer. *Studies in Bible and Feminist Criticism*. Philadelphia: Jewish Publication Society, 2006.

Klapheck, Elisa. *Fraulein Rabbiner Jonas: The Story of the First Woman Rabbi*. Jersey City: John Wiley & Sons, 2004.

Landes, Daniel. "Prayer as Petition: The Philosophic Basis for Halakhic Prayer." In *The Amidah*. Vol 2 of *Traditional Prayers, Modern Commentaries*, edited by Lawrence A. Hoffman. Woodstock, VT: Jewish Lights Publishing, 1998.

Levin, Rabbi Dr. Myer. *Naomi and Ruth*. Baltimore, MD: Project Genesis, 2005. Available at http://www.torah.org.

Maimonides. *Guide to the Perplexed*. Trans. with introduction and notes by Shlomo Pines. Chicago: University of Chicago Press, 1963. Vol. 2.

Maimonides. *Mishneh Torah: Hilchot De'ot*. Trans. with commentary and notes by Za'ev Abramson and Eliyahu Touger. New York: Mozanim Publishing Corp., 1989.

Mazow, Julia Wolf, edited by *The Woman Who Lost Her Names: Selected Writings by American Jewish Women*. New York: Harper and Row, 1980.

Meyers, Carol, ed. *Women in Scripture*. Boston: Houghton Mifflin, 2000.

Midrash Rabbah. *Genesis*. Trans. H. Freedman. London: Soncino Press, 1983.

Nadell, Pamela S. *Women Who Would Be Rabbis: A History of Women's Ordination, 1889–1985*. Boston: Beacon Press, 1998.

Orenstein, Debra. *Lifecycles: Jewish Women on Life Passages and Personal Milestones*. Woodstock, VT: Jewish Lights Publishing, 1994.

Orenstein, Debra, and Jane Rachel Litman. *Lifecycles: Jewish Women on Biblical Themes in Contemporary Life*. Woodstock, VT: Jewish Lights Publishing, 1997.

Patai, Raphael. *The Hebrew Goddess*. Detroit: Wayne State University Press, 1978.

Peck, M. Scott. *The Different Drum: Community Making and Peace*. New York: Simon and Schuster, 1987.

Piercy, Marge. "The Book of Ruth and Naomi," *Mars and Her Children*. New York: Knopf, 1992.

Plaskow, Judith. *Standing Again at Sinai: Judaism from a Feminist Perspective*. San Francisco: Harper and Row, 1990.

Plaskow, Judith, and Carol Christ. *Womanspirit Rising.* San Francisco: Harper San Francisco, 1991.

Pogrebin, Letty Cottin. *Deborah, Golda, and Me: Being Female and Jewish in America.* New York: Crown Publishers, 1991.

Raver, Miki. *Listen to Her Voice: Women of the Hebrew Bible.* San Francisco: Chronicle Books, 1998.

Regina Jonas on the Web: Available at http://www.spiritus-temporis.com/regina-jonas/.

Rich, Tracey. *Judaism 101.* Berwyn, PA: Available at http://www.jewfaq.org, 1995–2008.

Robinson, B. A. *Same-Sex Relationships in the Bible.* Ontario. Available at http://www.religioustolerance.org, 2007.

Rosen, Norma. *Biblical Women Unbound.* Philadelphia: Jewish Publication Society, 1996.

Sarna, Jonathan D. *American Judaism: A History.* New Haven, CT: Yale University Press, 2004.

Schachter-Shalomi, Zalman, and Ronald S. Miller. *From Age-ing to Sage-ing.* New York: Warner Books, 1995.

Schneider, Susan Weidman. *Jewish and Female: Choices and Changes in Our Lives Today.* New York: Simon and Schuster, 1984.

Sharma, Arvind, ed. *Women in World Religions.* Albany: State University Press of New York, 1987.

Simon, Rita J., and Pamela S. Nadell. "Gender and the Clergy." *Sociology of Religion,* Spring 1995.

Spretnak, Charlene, ed. *The Politics of Women's Spirituality: Essays by Founding Mothers of the Movement.* Garden City, NY: Doubleday, 1982, 1994.

Taitz, Emily, Sondra Henry, and Cheryl Tallan. *JPS Guide to Jewish Women: 600 BCE–1900 CE.* Philadelphia: Jewish Publication Society of America, 2003.

Teubal, Savina J. *Sarah the Priestess: The First Matriarch of Genesis.* Athens, OH: Swallow Press, 1984.

Umansky, Ellen M. *Lily Montagu and the Advancement of Liberal Judaism: From Vision to Vocation.* Lewiston, NY: Edwin Mellen Press, 1983.

Umansky, Ellen M. *Reclaiming the Covenant: A Jewish Feminist's Search for Meaning.* Minneapolis, MN: Winston Press, 1985.

Umansky, Ellen M., and Dianne Ashton, eds. *Four Centuries of Jewish Women's Spirituality.* Boston: Beacon Press, 1992.

Walter, Benjamin. *Illuminations.* London: Fontana, 1973.

Yalom, Irvin. *The Theory and Practice of Group Psychotherapy.* New York: Basic Books, 1995.

Zolty, Shoshana Pantel. *And All Your Children Shall Be Learned: Women and the Study of Torah in Jewish Law and History.* Lanham, MD: Rowman & Littlefield, 1997.

Zornberg, Aviva. *The Particulars of Rapture: Reflections on Exodus.* Garden City, NY: Random House, 2001.

About the Editor and Contributors

Malka Drucker has written twenty-one books, including the Southwest PEN award winner *White Fire: A Portrait of Women Spiritual Leaders in America* and *Rescuers: Portraits of Moral Courage in the Holocaust* (both with Gay Block). She is also the author of *The Family Treasury of Jewish Holidays, Jacob's Rescue, Frida Kahlo*, and other award-winning books for young people. Her latest children's book, *Portraits of Jewish American Heroes*, was published in 2008. Ordained at the Academy for Jewish Religion, Rabbi Drucker is the founding spiritual leader of HaMakom: The Place for Passionate and Progressive Judaism, in Santa Fe, New Mexico. Her Web site is www.malkadrucker.com.

The Contributors

Debra Band, a Hebrew manuscript illuminator, is the artist and author of *The Song of Songs: The Honeybee in the Garden* (2005) and *I Will Wake the Dawn: Illuminated Psalms* (2007), the latter in collaboration with Arnold J. Band, of UCLA. She lives in Maryland with her husband and sons.

Ellen Bernstein is founder and former director of Shomrei Adamah—Keepers of the Earth, the first Jewish environmental organization. She is author of *The Splendor of Creation: A Biblical Ecology*, the editor of *Ecology and the Jewish Spirit: Where Nature and the Sacred Meet*, and the co-author of *Let the Earth Teach You Torah*. She holds degrees from University of California, Berkeley in Conservation of Natural Resources, from Hebrew College in Jewish Studies, and from Columbia University in Non-Profit Management. She currently works as a consultant and teacher.

Jo David is a published author of books, articles, and poetry on a wide variety of topics. *The Book of the Jewish Life* is the life-cycle textbook for Reform religious schools. Her poem about Rosh Hodesh appears in *Covenant of the Heart* and was reprinted in *The Reform Jewish Reader*. She has served congregations around the world and is the founder of the Jewish Appleseed Foundation, a not-for-profit organization that mentored small Jewish communities in the United States and abroad. Rabbi David has a private rabbinic practice in New York City that focuses on pastoral counseling, bereavement, family education, and outreach to interfaith couples and families.

Judith Edelstein received a BA in English from the City College of New York and an MA in Creative Writing from the City University of New York. She was ordained by the Academy for Jewish Religion, a pluralistic seminary, in 1997. In addition to applying for certification in Clinical Pastoral Education, she was awarded a Doctor of Ministry in Counseling from Hebrew Union College in 2005. Rabbi Edelstein is currently the Director of Religious Life at the Jewish Home and Hospital Lifecare System in Manhattan. Formerly, she served as the rabbi of Temple Hatikvah, in Flanders, New Jersey.

Shelly Fredman has taught writing at the honors college of the University of Missouri–St. Louis, Washington University, City University of New York, New York University, and the Skirball Center in New York. She earned an MFA from Washington University. Her essays and fiction have appeared in *Best Jewish Writing 2002*, *First Harvest*, the *Chicago Tribune Magazine*, *Hadassah*, *Lilith*, *Natural Bridge,* and the *Sagarin Review*. A St. Louis native, she now resides in New York City.

Lynn Gottlieb entered pulpit life in 1973 as rabbi to Temple Beth Or of the Deaf in New York City. In 1981 Lynn became the first woman ordained in the Jewish renewal movement after studying with Rabbis Wolf Kelman, Everett Gendler, Zalman Schacter, and Yitzhak Greenberg. Lynn's creativity, peace and justice activism, feminism, and focus on spiritual meaning helped shape the Jewish renewal movement. In 1974 Lynn founded a Jewish feminist theater troupe called Bat Kol, which brought feminist midrash, ceremony, and storytelling to hundreds of communities throughout the United States, Europe, and Canada, paving the way for the spread of Rosh Hodesh and experimental Jewish ceremony that responded to the needs of women's lives and the diversity of Jewish life. In 1983 Lynn moved to Albuquerque, New Mexico, co-founding Congregation Nahalat Shalom as a spiritual community that brought together vibrant streams of Jewish life, including Jewish feminism, peer-group education, the study of kabbalah, and a focus on Jewish-Palestinian reconciliation. She moved to Southern California to head Interfaith Inventions, which brings together local youth and faith-based communities to nurture interfaith and multicultural relations in summer camps, retreats, and workshops. It is an extension of her work as co-founder of the Muslim-Jewish PeaceWalk that brought pilgrimages between synagogues and mosques and other supporting faith communities throughout the United States and Canada in the past few years. As part of her interfaith community efforts, she is currently working on issues that relate to the way globalization is impacting the lives of young women around the world.

Leah Lax is a co-creator, with Janice Rubin, of *The Mikvah Project*, an intimate portrayal of mikvah usage today. *When Time Becomes a Woman*, a memoir, describes her many years among the Hasidim and is a meditation on fundamentalism. She is a graduate of the University of Houston Creative Writing Program and mother of seven.

Pamela Treiber Opper is a clinical social worker and poet who advocates for Holocaust survivors and counsels first- and second-generation survivors. Treiber has presented nationally on the groupwork she has done with Holocaust survivors, teaches Holocaust Studies at Oklahoma City University, and is the recipient of the Woman of Valor award. She is also the first-prize recipient of the Academy of American Poets. She presently lives in Oklahoma City with her husband and her daughter.

Hara Person is the editor-in-chief of the Union of Reform Judaism Press. She is a graduate of Amherst College, holds an MA in Fine Arts from New York University and received ordination from Hebrew Union College–Jewish Institute of Religion. She is co-editor of *That You May Live Long: Caring for Aging Parents, Caring for Ourselves* (2001), editor of the anthology *The Mitzvah of Healing* (2003), and co-author of *Stories of Heaven and Earth: Bible Heroes in Contemporary Children's Literature* (2005). In addition, she is the adjunct rabbi of the Brooklyn Heights Synagogue. Rabbi Person lives in Brooklyn, New York, with her husband and two children.

Sandy Eisenberg Sasso received her BA magna cum laude and MA from Temple University. She was ordained from the Reconstructionist Rabbinical College in 1974 and received her Doctor of Divinity after twenty-five years in the rabbinate. She is the recipient of a Doctorate of Ministry from Christian Theological Seminary, an Honorary Doctorate of Humanities from DePauw University, an Honorary Doctor of Humane Letters from Butler University, and an Honorary Doctorate of Divinity from Christian Theological Seminary. Rabbi Sasso is the author of the nationally acclaimed children's books *God's Paintbrush, In God's Name, But God Remembered: Stories of Women from Creation to the Promised Land and A Prayer for the Earth* (now titled *Noah's Wife: The Story of Naamah*), *God In Between, For Heaven's Sake, God Said Amen,* and *Cain and Abel: Finding the Fruits of Peace,* and *Adam and Eve's First Sunset*. She is the co-author of *God's Paintbrush Celebration Kit: A Spiritual Activity Kit for Teachers and Students*. *Abuelita's Secret Matzahs* was published in spring 2005 and is the winner of the Sugarman Family Children's Book Award. Her newest children's book, *Butterflies under Our Hats*, was published in April 2006. She writes a monthly column in the *Indianapolis Star* on religious and spirituality issues, and she is the 2004 recipient of the Helen Keating Ott Award for Outstanding Contribution to Children's Literature. Rabbi Sasso serves as the chairperson of Spirit and Place, an annual festival in Indiana celebrating the arts, religion, and humanities. Rabbi Sasso was the first woman ordained from the Reconstructionist Rabbinical College.

Alice Shalvi was born in Germany in 1926 and educated in England (1934–1949). Shalvi immigrated to Israel at the end of her studies in English Literature and Social Work and has lived in Jerusalem since then. She was on the faculty of the English Department at the Hebrew University from 1950 to 2000. She served as head of Pelech Religious Experimental High School for Girls from 1975 to 1990 and as founding chairwoman of the Israel Women's Network from 1984 to 2002. Most recently she has been connected with the Schechter Institute of Jewish Studies, where she has served successively as rector, president, and chair of the Executive Committee.

Joy Silver is President/CEO of RainbowVision Properties, Inc., in Santa Fe, New Mexico, and Board Member of the GLBT Historical Society in San Francisco, California, and the Lesbian-Gay Aging Issues Network (LGAIN) Leadership Council. She is also a member of the American Society on Aging (ASA), San Francisco. She was formerly a member of Mayan, New York City in the 1990s, the Moonfire Spirituality Network, 1984–1990, and a former member of Lilith, All Female Rock Band, 1974–1979.

Sheila Peltz Weinberg has served in multiple capacities in the Jewish community, including Hillel director, day-school teacher, and community relations professional. She is a 1986 graduate of the Reconstructionist Rabbinical College and has served as a congregational rabbi for seventeen years. She has introduced meditation into the Jewish world as a form that can enliven and illuminate Jewish practice, ideas, and community and teaches mindfulness meditation in a Jewish idiom to lay persons, rabbis, and cantors. She is also a senior teacher and director of community outreach of the Institute for Jewish Spirituality, a retreat-based program for Jewish leaders. Weinberg has written extensively on a variety of subjects, including Jewish spirituality, social justice, feminism, and parenting. She is a major contributor to the Kol Haneshamah prayer book series. Her recently released CD *Preparing the Heart: Meditation for Jewish Spiritual Practice* integrates Jewish sacred text and meditation.

Judith Willmore is a psychotherapist living in Albuquerque. Ten years ago she followed Joseph Campbell's advice and followed her bliss: she moved to New Mexico, got a master's degree in psychology, and now works with adolescents and their families. In New Mexico she also found the realization of another dream: she converted to Judaism.

Index